The Web
Resource Space Model

Web Information Systems Engineering

and Internet Technologies

Book Series

Series Editor: Yanchun Zhang, Victoria University, Australia

The Web
Resource Space Model

Hai Zhuge
Chinese Academy of Sciences

 Springer

Hai Zhuge
Key Lab of Intelligent Information Processing
Institute of Computing Technology
Chinese Academy of Sciences
P.O. Box 2704-28
No. 6 Science South Road
Zhong Guan Cun, Beijing, China 100080
zhuge@ict.ac.cn

ISBN-13: 978-1-4419-4446-7   e-ISBN-13: 978-0-387-72772-1

Printed on acid-free paper.

9 8 7 6 5 4 3 2 1

springer.com

Contents

Preface

Birds of a feather flock together. Web resources of a category work closely for efficiency.

Classification is a method of efficiently managing various resources. It is also a basic method for human beings to know the real world and synthesize experience.

A Web Resource Space Model (in simple RSM) is a semantic data model for specifying, storing, managing and locating Web resources by appropriately classifying the contents of resources. It enables users or applications to operate resources by the SQL-like query language.

A Web resource space is a multi-dimensional classification space where dimensions are discrete. Its intrinsic characteristics are worth studying as it is not an ordinary distance space. A resource space can be normalized to increase the correctness of resource management by setting constraints on dimensions.

Aiming at a Web semantic data model with characteristics of normalization and autonomy, this book develops the RSM systematically in methodology, model and theory. It concerns the following contents:

1. The general methodology of the RSM, which includes the origin, fundamental concepts, characteristics and the development method. It helps understand the RSM and design resource spaces for applications.
2. The relationship between the Resource Space Model and the Semantic Link Network. The integration of the two models forms a richer semantic data model to support advanced distributed applications.
3. The completeness and necessity theory for query operations of the Resource Space Model.
4. The algebra and calculus theory for query operations of the Resource Space Model. The query capability and expressive power of the Resource Space Model are studied from two perspectives: resource space algebra and resource space calculus.

5. The complexity of searching the resource space. We intend to unveil the relationship between the searching efficiency and the number of dimensions as well as the relationship between the searching efficiency and the distribution of coordinates.

6. The physical storage mechanism of the resource space. Its multi-dimensional and discrete characteristic is different from the relational database index (one dimensional) and previous multidimensional index (sequential numerical dimensions).

7. The P2P-based decentralized resource space. It is an approach to enabling the Resource Space Model to synergy normalization with autonomy. A structured P2P resource space solution and an unstructured P2P resource space solution are studied.

8. The probabilistic Resource Space Model, which enables users or applications to store and retrieve resources uncertainly. It is a more general Resource Space Model.

I would like to take this opportunity to thank my students Erlin Yao, Yunpeng Xing, Xiang Li, Chao He and Liang Feng who make important contribution to this work. Thanks also go to all team members of the China Knowledge Grid Research Group for their help and cooperation.

Research work was financially supported by the National Basic Research Program of China (2003CB317000), the EU 6th Framework Project GREDIA (IST-FP6-034363), and the International Cooperation Program of the Ministry of Science and Technology of China (2006DFA11970).

The Web resource space is a part of the resource space we live in. The RSM is a promising model for effective management of versatile resources. Integrating the RSM with the Semantic Link Network, the database models and the Web ontology mechanisms could form a powerful semantic platform for the future interconnection environment.

Hai Zhuge
August 9, 2007

Chapter 1 Resource Space Model Methodology

Classification is not only an approach to efficiently managing resources but also a basic method for human to know the real world.

The Web Resource Space Model realizes birds of a feather flock together in the digital interconnection environment. It specifies and manages various Web resources by normalizing classification on contents of resources.

1.1 Origin of the Resource Space Model

Files are expanding in our daily-use PCs or laptops due to easier download from websites and email attachments. Management of these accumulating files is troublesome if we arbitrarily save them. For example, saving files in the desktop of Windows seems convenient, but this will cause inefficient retrieval of files and slow down the speed of machine in the long run. Appropriately naming folders to contain various files is a way to efficient file management and retrieval. Inappropriately naming will cause trouble in retrieval of files due to synonym or poor meaning.

Goods in supermarkets are arranged by classification. Goods are placed and updated according to the commonsense of the classification shared between customers and sellers. Chain supermarkets often arrange goods in a uniform style and place good categories in the same order so that customers can quickly reach their targets. This order is an experience for customers to raise the efficiency in selecting goods by going directly to the interested category or region. We can also find that some closely relevant goods are arranged in neighborhood. This neighbor information also helps customers to select goods. These strategies bring efficiency and convenience for sellers to manage goods and for customers to select goods.
Biologists classify organisms into categories by judging degrees of apparent similarity and difference. On discovering an unknown organism, scientists begin their classification by looking for anatomical features that have the same function as those found on other species, and then determine

whether or not the similarities are due to an independent evolution or to descent from a common ancestor. If the latter is the case, then the two species could be classified into the same category.

Children start to learn concepts by classifying real-world objects into categories and by generalizing and specializing categories via instances. So classification is not only an approach to efficiently managing resources but also a basic method for human to know the real world.

A (Web) Resource Space Model (in simple RSM) is a semantic data model for specifying, storing, managing and locating contents of (Web) resources by appropriate classification on the contents of resources.

The notion of the Web resource space was initiated in 2002 as a multi-dimensional knowledge space (Zhuge, 2002). Its basic model was proposed in 2004 (Zhuge, 2004a-d).

A resource space is a multi-dimensional classification space where dimensions (axes) are discrete so it is different from ordinary distance space. Its intrinsic characteristics are worth studying.

A resource space can be normalized to ensure the correctness of managing resources by setting constraints on axes.

The Resource Space Model methodology is a study of the basic method for designing resource spaces and helping the development of its applications.

Data model and algorithm are the core of software systems.

File system is the first milestone towards effective computing resource management. It is a method for storing, managing and retrieving resources in form of files by establishing mapping between a directory indexing structure and a storage device. The directory indexing structure can keep track of the files and path syntax required to access them. It defines the way files are named as well as the maximum size of a file or volume. A file system is a component of most operating systems. IT professionals have used various indexing techniques to raise the efficiency of managing data in files.

The file system can be regarded as a 1-dimensional resource space.

Database is another milestone towards effective resource management. Most databases use file systems as the underlying mapping mechanism between the higher level indexes and the storage devices. Database theories and systems have influenced the world for forty years (Bachman, 1969). Especially, the Relational Database Model and systems have achieved a great success (Codd, 1970). The Relational Database Model uses relational tables to describe basic relations between data types. Its normal form theory ensures the correctness of data operations.

Both the file system and the database system are invented at the age of mainframe and centralized computing.

The World Wide Web is a huge decentralized file system. There is no central control for adding, updating and removing Web pages. The management of the Web resources challenges traditional data models.

Object-oriented databases and object-relational databases extend the application scope of the relational databases by borrowing the advantages of the object-oriented methodologies and programming languages like inheritance and encapsulation to model the real-world and they enable complex objects to be effectively managed (Kim, 1990; Rumbaugh et al., 1991; Mok, 2002). But, their limitations emerge in Web-based applications, which require resources to be managed in an open, decentralized, platform-irrelevant and content-based way.

In data warehousing and OLAP area, the multi-dimensional data model was used. It is suitable for storing large-scale historical data. To support decision-making based on large data sets, data mining techniques are needed to discover the rules in large data sets (Han and Kambr, 2000). But, the read-only model is limited in ability to meet the needs of resource management in the Internet environment where resources are complex and have to be frequently operated. Compared with the relational data model, it is weak in theory on data management.

Fig. 1.1 depicts a file system on disk. The file system realizes the mapping from the directories and files of various type onto the disk space by establishing the index on the linear disk space. Users or up-level applications can operate files according to their names and path regardless of their physical storage.

Fig. 1.2 shows the keyword index on the World Wide Web. The Web is actually a decentralized file system, which enables users to browse Web pages by their URLs. Search engines establish indeces on Web pages distributed on the Web by collecting and classifying Web pages according to keywords and then recommending Web pages sharing the same set of keywords according to the page rank (S.Brin and L.Page, www7.scu.edu.au,1998).

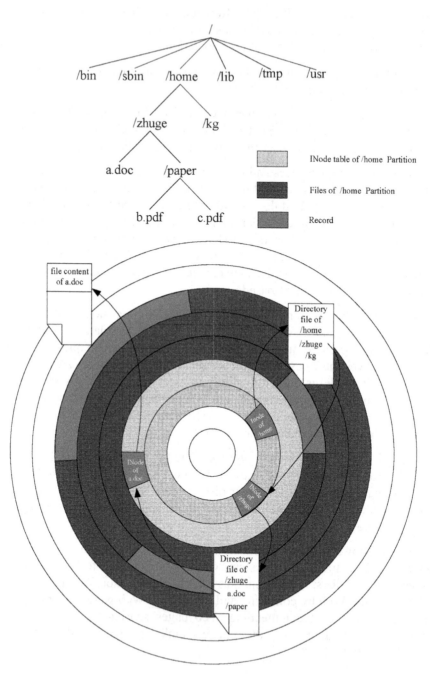

Fig.1.1. The EXT2/3 file system.

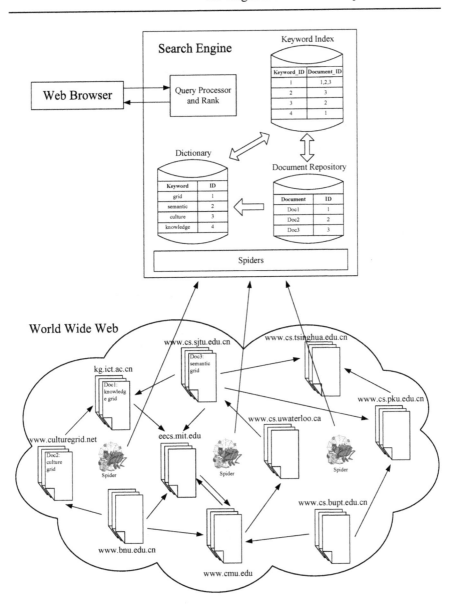

Fig.1.2. Index on the World Wide Web.

Comparison of the file system on disk and the file system on the World Wide Web implicates the evolution of file systems.

With the development of Web applications, effective management of the contents of various resources on the Web becomes a challenge. The new generation data model should be a semantic-rich model that is able to manage content rather than file name. But to precisely describe the content of an individual resource is difficult and a formal description is not easy for sharing among people of different communities. The Resource Space Model can reflect the content of resources by classification semantics.

People often use the classification method to manage various contents in daily life. For example, researchers are organized into research groups according to the research topics they are working on. Publishers classify their products (books, journals and conference proceedings) into different categories according to disciplines and contents.

A set of resources can be classified by different classification methods as shown in the left hand of Fig. 1.3. Multiple classification methods constitute a multi-dimensional semantic space over a set of resources as shown in the right hand of Fig. 1.3, where each axis represents a kind of classification method.

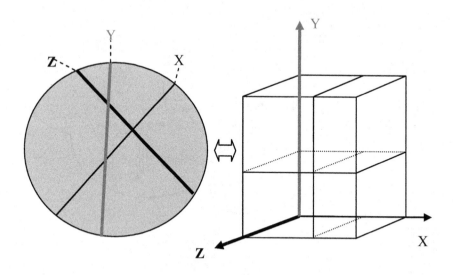

Fig. 1.3. Multiple classification methods over a set of resources constitute a multi-dimensional classification space.

The Resource Space Model is such a semantic space that manages information, knowledge and service resources. Information resources refer to various types of electronic files that can be transmitted through the Internet, and can be read or perceived directly or indirectly. Knowledge resources include metadata, relation and strucuture as well as the abstract concepts, axioms, rules and methods that can be represented in a certain machine-understandable form. Knowledge can be generated from understanding the information resources or generalizing human experience. Service resources refer to the reusable capability processes for performing tasks, solving problems, or processing information or knowledge resources.

A resource space can be presented in:

1. *conceptual* or *logical aspect*— the definition of an *n*-dimensional resource space;
2. *user view aspect*— a subspace of the whole resource space displayed in user-understandable form;
3. *representation aspect*— the cross-platform understandable definition based on standard description languages like XML, RDF and OWL; and,
4. *storage aspect*— the physical storage of the resource space including the storage of the space structure, relevant index and resource entities.

The characteristics of the Resource Space Model require a specific method to help design resource spaces. Before presenting the design method, we first introduce the basic notion and components of the Resource Space Model.

1.2 Basis of the Resource Space Model

1.2.1 Definitions and Characteristics

The semantic basis of the Resource Space Model is *name space, basic data type, set* and *partition*.

Concepts are labeled in the name space as consensus of a community, while their semantics are determined by classification and use-case in four worlds — the real world, the document world, the machine world and the mental world (Zhuge et al, 2006). Some basic concepts in the name space do not need to be explained. They can be used to define other concepts. A set of concepts can represent a certain semantics. Classifications on concepts form concept hierarchies.

The basic semantic elements of the Resource Space Model are *resource, resource space, axis* and *coordinate.*

A resource in the machine world has name, type and content. Concepts are basic elements of the composing content. For example, a Web page has a URL, and its content can be represented by a set of concepts.

A *Resource Space* is a multi-dimensional classification space. It consists of a name and a set of axes, denoted as $RS(X_1, X_2, ..., X_n)$. Each *axis* X_i represents a classification method. X_i is partitioned by a set of coordinates denoted as $X_i = <C_{i1}, C_{i2}, ..., C_{im}>$.

A point in the space, determined by one coordinate at every axis, represents a set of resources of the same category.

An axis can be regarded as a 1-dimensional resource space.

A *coordinate* C represents a set of resources, denoted as $R(C)$. Resources represented by axis X_i are the union of all the resources represented by its coordinate: $R(X_i) = R(C_{i1}) \cup R(C_{i2}) \cup ... \cup R(C_{in})$. The semantics of a coordinate is represented by name, basic datatype, a set of concepts, or a coordinate tree (low-level coordinates finely classify their common ancestor). The semantics of a coordinate is regulated by the semantics of its axis.

A coordinate C is called independent from another coordinate C' if there is no intersection between $R(C)$ and $R(C')$. Using existing taxonomy and commonsense as the classification method is a way to establish concensus between designers and users.

The resource space, axis, coordinate, and point are sets in nature.

A coordinate regulates a set of points. An axis regulates a set of coordinates. An axis name represents higher classification level than its coordinates. A resource space regulates a set of axes and the refined classification relationship. A resource is determined by locating the point it belongs to and by selecting from the resource set according to its name and content description.

Two axes can be regarded as equivalent if their names are the same in semantics and the names of all the corresponding coordinates are the same in semantics.

The following are two operations on axis:

1. If two axes $X_1 = <C_{11}, C_{12}, ..., C_{1n}>$ and $X_2 = <C_{21}, C_{22}, ..., C_{2m}>$ have the same axis name but have different coordinates, then they can be merged into one: $X = X_1 \cup X_2 = <C_{11}, C_{12}, ..., C_{1n}, C_{21}, C_{22}, ..., C_{2m}>$. In this case, the name of X represents X_1 and X_2.

2. An axis X can be split into two axes X' and X'' by dividing the coordinate set of X into two: the coordinate set of X' and the coordinate set of X'', such that $X = X' \cup X''$. If the two axes need to be merged for the future use, the names of X' and X'' should be the same in semantics.

The semantics of axis and coordinate can be formally defined or informally defined. For example, the semantics of a coordnate can be defined by a set of concepts, which regulate the semantics of the resources it may contain. The above definitions enable a resource space to represent any form of resources.

If we use a set of domain concepts K_C to describe a coordinate C, and the resources contained by C share common concept set K_R, then we could find a mapping between K_C and K_R such that corresponding concepts are the same or share a common ancestor. This mapping is useful in automatically classifying resources.

Let $X=(C_1, C_2, ..., C_n)$ be an axis and C_i' be a coordinate at another axis X', we say that X *finely classifies* C_i' (denoted as C_i'/X) if and only if:

1. $(R(C_k) \cap R(C_i')) \cap (R(C_p) \cap R(C_i')) = $ NULL $(k \neq p,$ and $k, p \in [1, n])$; and,
2. $R(C_1) \cap R(C_i') \cup R(C_2) \cap R(C_i') \cup ... \cup R(C_n) \cap R(C_i') = R(C_i')$ hold.

As the result of fine classification, $R(C')$ is partitioned into n categories: $R(C_i'/X) = \{R(C_1) \cap R(C_i'), R(C_2) \cap R(C_i'), ..., R(C_n) \cap R(C_i')\}$.

For two axes $X = (C_1, C_2, ..., C_n)$ and $X' = (C_1', C_2', ..., C_m')$, we say that X *finely classifies* X' (denoted as X'/X) if and only if X finely classifies C_1', C_2',..., and C_m' respectively.

Two axes X and X' are called *orthogonal* with each other (denoted as $X \perp X'$) if X finely classifies X' and vice versa, i.e., both X'/X and X/X' hold.

Establishing orthogonal relationship between relevant classifications deepens people's understanding on the real world.

The following three normal forms are for designing a good resource space.

1. A *first-normal-form* resource space is a resource space and there does not exist name duplication (semantic overlap) between coordinates at any axis.

2. A *second-normal-form* resource space is a first-normal-form, and for any axis, any two coordinates are independent from each other.

3. A *third-normal-form* resource space is a second-normal-form and any two axes of it are orthogonal with each other.

The following are four operations of the resource space:

1. **Join operation.** If two resource spaces RS_1 and RS_2 specify the same type of resources and they have n $(n \geq 1)$ common axes, then they can be *joined* into one resource space RS such that RS, RS_1 and RS_2 share these n common axes and $|RS| = |RS_1| + |RS_2| - n$, where $|RS|$ represents the number of dimensions of the RS. RS is called the *join* of RS_1 and RS_2, denoted as $RS_1 \cdot RS_2 \Rightarrow RS$.

2. **Disjoin operation.** A resource space RS can be *disjoined* into two resource spaces RS_1 and RS_2 (denoted as $RS \Rightarrow RS_1 \cdot RS_2$) that specify the same type of resources as that of RS such that they have n $(1 \leq n \leq min(|RS_1|, |RS_2|))$ common axes and $|RS| - n$ different axes, and $|RS| = |RS_1| + |RS_2| - n$.

3. **Merge operation.** If two resource spaces RS_1 and RS_2 specify the same type of resources and satisfy: (1) $|RS_1| = |RS_2| = n$; and, (2) they have $n-1$ common axes, and there exist two different axes X_1 and X_2 satisfying the merge condition, then the two spaces can be *merged* into one RS by retaining the $n-1$ common axes in the new space and including a new axis $X = X_1 \cup X_2$. RS is called the merge of RS_1 and RS_2, denoted as $RS_1 \cup RS_2 \Rightarrow RS$, and $|RS| = n$. The second condition can be extended as follows: they have $n-k$ common axes $(1 \leq k < n)$, and there exists one-one mapping between the rest k axes of the two spaces such that the merge condition can be satisfied, then the two spaces can be *merged* into one RS by retaining the $n-k$ common axes in the new space and including k new axes, each of which is the union of the corresponding axes.

4. **Split operation.** A resource space RS can be *split* into two resource spaces RS_1 and RS_2 that store the same type of resources as that of RS and have $|RS| - 1$ common axes by splitting an axis X into two: X' and X'', such that $X = X' \cup X''$. This split operation is denoted as

$RS \Rightarrow RS_1 \cup RS_2$. (In contrast to the merge operation, this split operation can be extended to the case that RS_1 and RS_2 have $|RS| - k$ common axes by splitting every of the k axes into two.)

Several strategies can be adopted to realize the join operation. One strategy is that only those resources specified in both original resource spaces are reserved in the new resource space. The join operation would result in many empty nodes. Therefore, the join and merge operations are usually used for generating views of existing resource spaces. If RS_1 and RS_2 are 3NF, then RS is a 3NF according to the normal form theory of the Resource Space Model.

The Resource Space Model is equipped with an SQL-like resource operation language to support operations on resource space. The basic operations are introduced in The Knowledge Grid (Zhuge, 2004d).

Efficient resource management depends on the human behavior mode of dealing with resources and the mode of storing resources in the resource space. The degree of matching between the two modes determines the efficiency.

Fig.1.4 depicts the interaction between the human behavior and the resource space.

Storing resources in the right category with high probability leads to better retrieval result. The query language bridges the mutual understanding between the behavior modes and the resource storage. The semantic mechanism like domain ontology helps explain the output resources and the input on storage and query.

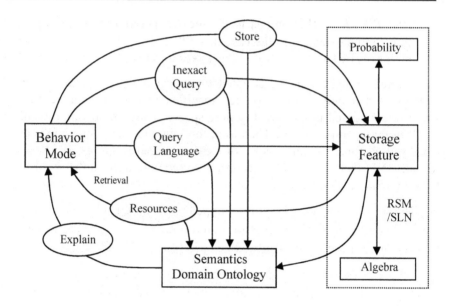

Fig. 1.4. Interaction between the human behavior mode and the resource storage mode.

1.2.2 Resource Space Definition Language

The Resource Space Definition Language RSDL defines the commands for specifying and modifying resource spaces, in particular, the schemas for resource spaces.

A resource space can be created by the following command, where *RS* is the name of the resource space, X_i is the name of its axis, C_{ij} is the coordinate of X_i, and the *URSL* is the location of the resource space. The integrity constraints set constraints on axes to ensure the correctness of operations.

CREATE SPACE *RS* $(X_1, X_2, ..., X_n)$ **[AT** *URSL*]
WHERE $X_1 = \{C_{11}, ..., C_{1u}\}, ..., X_n = \{C_{n1}, ..., C_{nv}\}$
    <integrity constraint₁>

......

  <integrity constraint$_m$>

The drop command is for deleting a resource space including all the indices and schemas.

DROP RSPACE *RS*

The modify command is used on an existing resource space to add or drop axes or coordinates. For example, an axis can be added to a resource space by using the following command, where *RS* is the name of an existing resource space, *axis$_i$* is the name of the axis to be added, and $<C_{i1}, ...,$ $C_{ij}>$ is its coordinate list.

MODIFY SPACE *RS*
ADD AXIS $X_i <C_{i1}, ..., C_{ij}>$

The axes of a resource space can be listed by using the following command, where *RS* is the name of an existing resource space.

USING *RS* **LIST AXES**

Similarly, the coordinates of a given axis in a resource space *RS* can be listed by using the following command:

USING *RS* **LIST COORD OF AXIS** *X*

1.2.3 Resource Space Manipulation Operations

The Merge operation makes resource spaces $RS_1, ...,$ and RS_n at $URSL_1, ...,$ and $URSL_n$ respectively into one resource space *RS* subject to any specified conditions and places the new resource space at *URSL*. It can be represented by the following command, where $|RS_i|$ is the number of axes of resource space RS_i and $X_{ik}(RS_j)$ represents that axis X_{ik} of resource space RS_j is to be merged ($i=1, ..., n$). The constraint clause specifies *common_axis_number* as the constraint name. The predicate of the check clause is the constraint of the merge operation.

MERGE $RS_1, ..., RS_n$ [**AT** $URSL_1, ..., URSL_n$]
INTO RS [**AT** $URSL$]
WHERE *new_axis* $(RS) = X_{1\mu}(RS_1) \cup ... \cup X_{nv}(RS_n)$
CONSTRAINT *axis_number*
    CHECK $|RS_1| = ... = |RS_n| = |RS|$
CONSTRAINT *common_axis_number*
    CHECK *number* (*common_axes*) = $|RS| - 1$.

The split operation separates a resource space *RS* at *URSL* into each RS_i at each $URSL_i$. The axis *X* of *RS* will be separated into X_{1i} (RS_1), ..., and $X_{nj}(RS_n)$. The Split command is represented as follows, where the check clause requires that no coordinate or axis be removed in the split operation.

SPLIT RS [**AT** $URSL$]
INTO $RS_1, ..., RS_n$ [**AT** $URSL_1, ..., URSL_n$]
WHERE X (RS) **JOIN-INTO** X_{1i} (RS_1) = <*coordinate_set$_1$*> & ...
    & X_{nj} (RS_n) = <*coordinate_set$_n$*>
CONSTRAINT *axis_split*
CHECK X (RS) = X_{1i} (RS_1) $\square ... \square X_{nj}$ (RS_n)

If resource spaces RS_1, ..., and RS_n store the same type of resources and they have k ($k \in [1, \text{minimum}(|RS_1|, |RS_2|)]$) common axes, then they can be joined into one resource space *RS* such that RS_1, ..., and RS_n share these k common axes and $|RS| = |RS_1| + |RS_2| - k$. The join operation can be represented as follows:

JOIN $RS_1, ..., RS_n$ [**AT** $URSL_1, ..., URSL_n$]
INTO RS [**AT** $URSL$]
WHERE COMMON AXES (*axis$_1$*, ..., *axis$_\mu$*)
CONSTRAINT *common_axis_number*
CHECK *number* (*common_axes*) $\leq |RS| - 1$

If two resource spaces RS_1 and RS_2 store the same type of resources and have n ($n = |RS_1| = |RS_2|$) common axes, they can be united into one resource space RS by eliminating duplicates. RS is called the union of RS_1 and RS_2, and $|RS| = n$. The union operation requires that the resource spaces to be united have the same number of axes and the same axis names. It can be represented as follows:

UNION $RS_1, ..., RS_n$ [**AT** $URSL_1, ..., URSL_n$] **INTO** RS
CONSTRAINT *axis_number*
    CHECK $|RS_1| = ... = |RS_n| = |RS|$
CONSTRAINT *common_axis_number*
    CHECK *number* (*common_axes*) = $|RS|$.

1.2.4 Resource Space Modification

A newly created resource space has no resources. The following command can insert resources into the resource space.

INSERT $R_1..., R_m$ **INTO** $RS_1..., RS_m$ [**AT** $URSL_1, ... , URSL_m$]
    [**WHERE** *<conditional expression>*]

Instead of specifying a resource set directly, we can use a select statement to extract a set of resources as follows.

INSERT INTO RS *<axis$_1$, axis$_2$, axis$_3$>*
COORD *<coord$_1$, coord$_2$, coord$_3$>*
BY SELECT $A_1, A_2, ..., A_n$
FROM $RS_1, RS_2, ... , RS_m$
[**WHERE** *<conditional expression>*]

If the specified resource exists at the specified point of the given resource space and the user has the authority to delete it, then it can be deleted by the following statement:

DELETE R **FROM** $RS_1, ..., RS_m$ [**AT** $URSL_1, ..., URSL_m$]
    [**WHERE** *<conditional expression>*]

The following update statement is used to change a resource index in a given resource space.

UPDATE *RS*
REPLACE R_1 **WITH** R_2
  [**WHERE** *<conditional expression>*]

1.2.5 View Definition

To define a view of a resource space, the name of the view as well as the query that computes the view is required. The view can be defined by the following command, where *<query expression>* is any valid query expression. The view name is represented by *v*.

CREATE VIEW *v* **AS** *<query expression>*

As an example, consider the view consisting of *m* axes of a resource space. We can define view *RS–view* as follows:

CREATE VIEW *RS–view* ($axis_1$, …, $axis_m$) **AS**
SELECT $X_1 = < c_{11},...,c_{1,k_1} >,...,X_m = < c_{m,1},...,c_{m,k_m} >$
FROM *RS*

The list of axis names can be omitted. We define a view over two resource spaces by using the merge operation as follows, where the new axis $axis_m$ is formed by $X_m \bigcup Y_m = < C_{X_m,1},...,C_{X_m,i}, C_{Y_m,1},...,C_{Y_m,j} >$.

CREATE VIEW *RS–view* ($axis_1$, …, $axis_m$) **AS**
SELECT $X_1, X_2,..., X_m < C_{X_m,1}, C_{X_m,2},..., C_{X_m,i} >$ **FROM** RS_1
MERGE
SELECT $Y_1, Y_2,..., Y_m < C_{Y_m,1}, C_{Y_m,2},..., C_{Y_m,j} >$ **FROM** RS_2
WHERE $X_1 = Y_1$, …, $X_{m-1} = Y_{m-1}$
AND $X_m.axis\_name = Y_m.axis\_name$.

We can define a view combining two resource spaces by joining the subspaces selected from them as follows:

CREATE VIEW *RS–view* ($axis_1$, …, $axis_m$) **AS**
SELECT $X_1, X_2,..., X_m < C_{X_m,1}, C_{X_m,2},..., C_{X_m,i} >$ **FROM** RS_1
JOIN

$$\textbf{SELECT}\ \ Y_1, Y_2, ..., Y_n < C_{Y_n,1}, C_{Y_n,2}, ..., C_{Y_n,j} > \textbf{FROM}\ \ RS_2$$
$$\textbf{WHERE}\ \ X_1 = Y_1, ..., X_i = Y_i\ \ (i \leq \text{minimum}(m,n))$$

1.2.6 Query Language

The following three clauses are components of a query:

1. The **SELECT** clause lists the resource attributes required in the answer.
2. The **FROM** $<RS\,(X_1, X_2, ..., X_m)>$ clause specifies the resource space RS to be used in the selection, where X_i is an axis.
3. The **WHERE** *<conditional expression>* clause conditions the answer in terms of coordinates of resources and semantic relationships between the coordinates.

A typical query takes the following form, where A_i represents a feature of the destination resource, and R_i names a source resource space. A **SELECT** * clause specifies that all attributes of all resources appearing in the **FROM** clause are to be selected. The compound name *resource_space.attribute* avoids ambiguity when an attribute appears in more than one resource space. However if an attribute appears in only one of the resource spaces in the **FROM** clause, the *resource_space* qualifier can be omitted.

> **SELECT** $A_1, A_2, ...\ A_n$
> **FROM** $R_1, R_2, ...\ R_m$
> **WHERE** *<conditional expression>*

Query can focus on either one point in the space or an area specified by more than one coordinates at one axis. An area consists of a set of points.

The *ACM Computing Classification System* can be constructed as a normalized 3-dimensional information space: *ACM–CCS(Category, Publication, Letter)*. The query "Find all journal papers in the resource space ACM–CCS which relate to Resource Space Model" can be expressed as follows:

> **SELECT** * **FROM** *ACM–CCS*

WHERE   *Category* ="Resource Space Model" **&** *Publication* =
"Journal"

1.2.7 Visualized Resource Locating

Locating resources is the basic operation of the Resource Space Model.
Users can accurately locate a set of resources by giving coordinates on
every axis. The underlying premise is that users know the structure of the
space or that users' viewpoint consists with the space designers on classification of resources. A visualized resource locator provides users with in-
tuitive knowledge on the underlying structure of the resource space.

Fig.1.5 shows a three-dimensional visualized resource locator for exhibiting Dunhuang culture. Points in the space correspond to the small
cubes in the 3-dimensional large cube. Each side of the cube can display
image, text and links. Users can see the details by clicking them. The operations are arranged as buttons in the up-row.

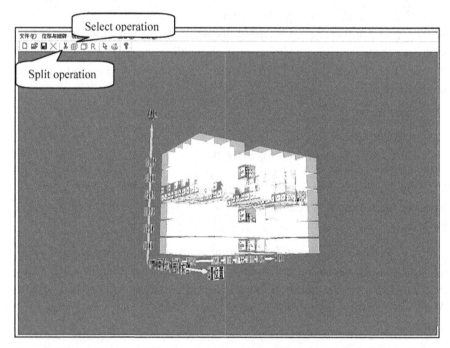

Fig. 1.5. The visualized 3-dimensional resource space locator.

Fig.1.6. shows an *n*-dimensional visualized resource locator. Users can create a view by selecting axes from the *n*-dimensional resource space.

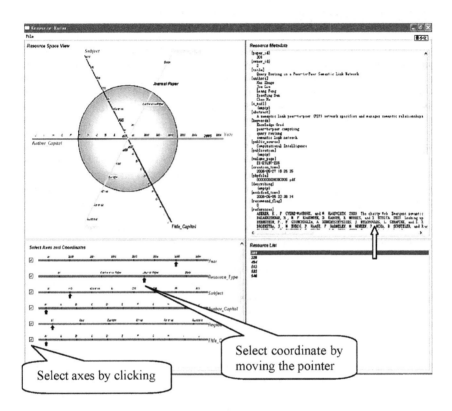

Fig. 1.6. Visualized *n*-dimensional resource locator.

1.3 Application Scenarios of the Resource Space Model

1.3.1 Management of Web Pages

The World Wide Web enables human to use browsers to display Web pages and jump from one page to another via hyperlink. How to efficiently index and manage the huge Web pages is an important issue.

The content of a Web page can be classified by topics such as news, finance, sport and health. Each topic can be further classified by time and language. This naturally corresponds to the classification characteristics of the Resource Space Model. A 3-dimensional resource space (*topic, time, language*) shown in Fig. 1.7 can be used to manage Web pages. The point (*Chinese, 2006-12-13, finance*) in the space contains a set of Web pages on finance (URLs). The resource space can provide classification semantics and distance measure between points that relational database cannot directly provide for better retrieval and learning on the Web.

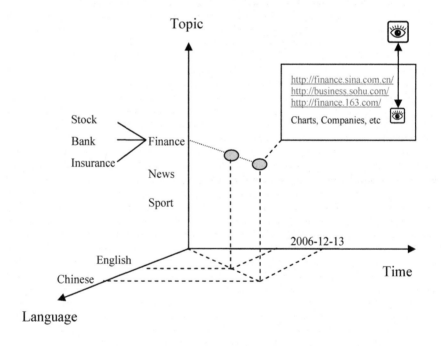

Fig. 1.7. A 3-dimensional resource space for managing the content of Web pages.

Entering into the point, users can obtain the required Web pages on finance — they do not need to input URL multiple times nor jump between URLs. The point includes more relevant statistic information on economics. The finance coordinate can be divided into finer coordinates, for example *stock*, *bank* and *insurance* information.   This refinement can express more detailed information when specifying resources, and can refine users' interest when retrieving resources. The Resource Space Model provides a new way to store and express Web resources.

The hierarchical classification characteristic of the resource space supports the management of a hierarchical Web structure from the hierarchical surface Web content to the underlying databases.

1.3.2 Managing Multi-layer Tables

Multi-layer tables provide integrated information of multiple abstraction levels from different analysis. The higher layers provide more abstract information. The lower layers constitute a fine classification of the higher layer, for example, *professor*, *associate professor* and *assistant professor* constitute a fine classification of the *teacher* class. Table 1.1 shows such a table on university human resources.

The traditional relational data model excludes this type of tables since the first normal form of relational data model requires the flat table and atomic fields. Many relational tables are needed to decompose the multilayer table if we use relational data model to realize the management of human resources with this form.

The table naturally corresponds to a 2-dimensional resource space as shown in Fig. 1.8. A point represents a set of persons of certain department and certain rank. Moreover, a *name* axis in alphabetical order can be added to form a 3-dimensional resource space.

Table 1.1. A multi-layer table of university human resources.

			School of Science			School of Engineering			School of Business	
			Dept. of Mathematics	Dept. of Physics	Dept. of Chemistry	Dept. of Chemical Engineering	Dept. of Computer Science & Engineering	Dept. of Mechanical Engineering	Dept. of Accounting	Dept. of Economics
Academic Staff	Professor									
	Associate Professor									
	Assistant Professor									
Student	Graduated	PhD								
		MPhil				University Human Resources				
	Under-graduate									
Support Staff										
Visiting Staff										

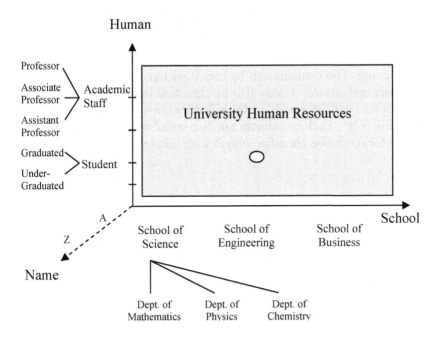

Fig. 1.8. A resource space for specifying university human resources.

The more layers the table has, the more advantages of the resource space model shows.

1.3.3 Management of Photos

A software tool that can efficiently manage and locate photos is very useful. Usually, we store photos in folders of a file system (the directories of a file system actually constitutes a 1-dimensional resource space). To efficiently locate resources, we can choose database systems to record information about photos such as place, time, and the path of storing photos.

However, people concern content of photos rather than their names when retrieving. The contents can be classified into three categories: *human*, *artifact* and *nature*. It can also be classified by *time* and *place*. So photos' content can be specified by a 3-dimensional resource space as shown in Fig. 1.9. Each coordinate can be a coordinate tree, for example, coordinate *China* can be classified into *Beijing, Shanghai, Xi'an*, etc.

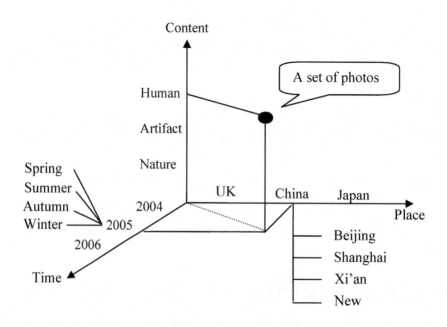

Fig.1.9. A 3-dimensional resource space for specifying photos.

This application proposes a new requirement: adding new coordinates during use, as we cannot estimate future visiting places and photos are added to the resource space after visiting.

New coordinates can be added to the resource space if its original normal forms can be retained. But a Resource Space Model system needs to update its schemas at all levels in this case.

1.3.4 Geographical Resource Space

A geographical Resource Space system can reflect multiple content layers over the same region, for example, geographical, ecological, economical and social information of the same region determined by longitude and latitude as shown in Fig. 1.10.

Every point (regional information) can further define a resource space specifying details, for example, the 3-dimensional resource space (*population, religion, occupation*). The system can display the statistical data about the population of different religions and the population of different occupation in various charts.

This example shows a characteristic of the resource space — the single semantic entry point of machine-understandable and human-understandable content.

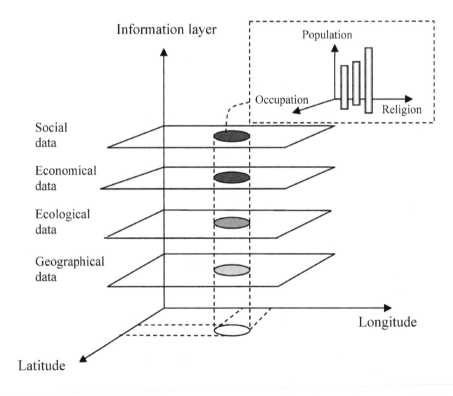

Fig.1.10. An embedded resource space for layered geographical information.

1.3.5 Multi-dimensional ACM Computing Classification System

The Resource Space Model can be used to reform the HTML-based ACM Computing Classification System into a normalized 3-dimensional information space: (*Category, Publication, Letter*) as shown in Fig.1.11.

The space satisfies the third normal form. The category axis contains eleven categories marked by the letters from "A" to "K", each of which corresponds to a coordinate hierarchy. Each coordinate at the category axis corresponds to a 2-dimensional slice (*Publication, Letter*), so users could retrieve the required information according to the publication types and/or the alphabet sequence in the given category. This feature is not provided by the existing classification system.

The Resource Space Model enables information retrieval in a 3-dimensional space. For the purpose of raising the retrieval efficiency, we can add a new axis: *topic*=(*methodology, theory, application, product*) to refine the space.

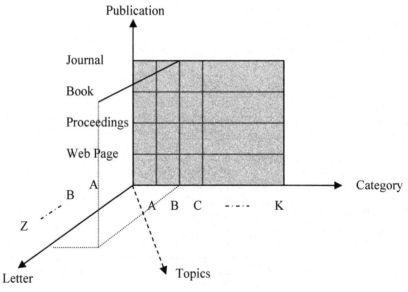

Fig. 1.11. The resource space of normalizing the "ACM Computing Classification System".

1.3.6 Management of Bio-information

The bio-information on the Web is currently managed by versatile data-bases developed by different countries. The Resource Space Model can be used to reform the existing bio-information retrieval and management sys-tems. All the bio-information databases can be uniformly and normally specified in the resource space. Bio-information can be specified by a two-dimensional resource space as shown in Fig.1.12, where "PubMed", "Structure", "Genome" and "PopSet" respectively stand for: biomedical literature, macromolecular structure, complete genome assemblies, and population study data sets.

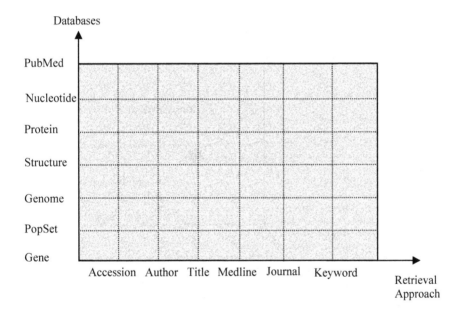

Fig. 1.12. A 2-dimensional resource space for uniformly and normally managing bio-information.

1.3.7 Media Content Space

A four-dimensional Dunhuang cave content space can be designed by classifying the cave content according to the following four axes: *dynasty, artifact type* (*wall painting, color statue, calligraphy*), *media type* (*text, video, image*) and *cave number* as shown in Fig. 1.13. The dynasty axis can be classified by the following sequential coordinates: *Tang, Song, Yuan, Ming,* and *Qing.* Any coordinate can be refined, for example, the *Tang* dynasty can be further divided into three sequential stages: *early, middle* and *late.* Given a set of coordinates on every axis, a set of contents can be accurately located.

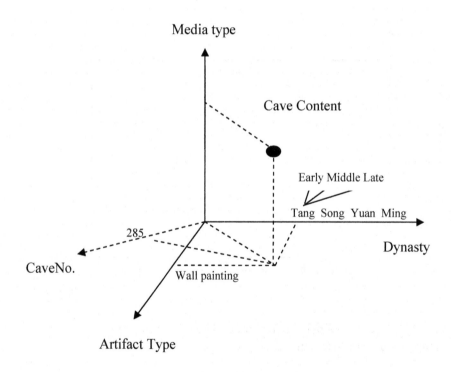

Fig. 1.13. A resource space for normalizing media content.

1.3.8 Automatically Add New Resources to the Resource Space

A resource has external feature and internal feature. The internal feature reflects the content of resources. The external feature helps distinguish one resource from the other resources. Usually the internal feature is not easy to be accurately obtained or expressed, while the external features can be accurately captured.

There could be no intersection between the external feature and the internal feature. For example, the publication date does not reflect the content of a paper.

A resource space represents the designer's viewpoint of classification on resources. If its user has stored some resources in the space, the resource space containing resources also reflects the user's classification viewpoint. Such classification viewpoint can help classify new resources.

The approach to automatically adding resources to resource space varies with the features of resources. To automatically add new papers to the resource space depends on the comparison between the external features and internal features of the new paper and the features of the point.

The keywords of papers in a point of the existing resource space represent authors' viewpoint on the classifications of the contents of papers. Information such as the publisher and the publication type (journal or proceeding) available from the publishers' website is the external feature.

The following process helps add new papers to the paper resource space.

1. Extract keywords from the papers in every point of the resource space, and unite a point p's keyword set with its coordinates to form a set K_p. An empty point K_p only consists of the coordinates of p. Information retrieval techniques like TF-IDF can help find important words in text (Salton, 1989; Salton, 1991).

2. Extract the keywords from the new paper and put them into set K_I representing the internal features.

3. Obtain the external features about the new paper such as journal name, publisher, publishing date and impact factor, and put them into set K_E. The main external features are usually available from the metadata of journals.

4. Unite the external features and the internal features on the new paper $K=K_I \cup K_E$.

5. For every point p in the space, compare K with K_p, if K can best match K_p according to some criteria (e.g., share a certain number of keywords in the meaning of domain ontology), the paper is likely to match the point and therefore put the new paper into the point, otherwise put it into the candidate pool awaiting additional techniques.

The citation relation reflects a kind of content inheritance relation. The citing and cited papers in the known classification can help determine the classification of a paper. If a paper in a point is cited by or cites the new paper, then the two papers probably belong to the same category. The more papers in a point cite or are cited by the new paper, the higher probability of the new paper belongs to that point.

We observed two phenomena from experiments of using TF-IDF to extract keywords and match the new paper and the point:

1. The more resources evenly distributed in the resource space, the better the effect of automatically adding new resources to the space; and,

2. The best effect (approximately 80%) can be reached when the weight of the external features reaches 90%.

That is to say, the external features play a more important role.

Fig.1.14 depicts the way to automatically classify papers by using the resource space.

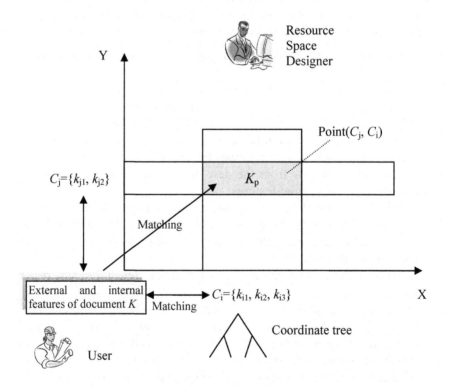

Fig. 1.14. Using resource space to automatically classify documents.

1.4 Design Method

Designing a resource space for application depends on the following three technical factors:

1. knowledge on the Resource Space Model,
2. domain knowledge, and,
3. design experience.

A resource space design consists of the following steps:

1. resource analysis;
2. top-down resource partition;
3. design low dimensional resource spaces like 2- or 3-dimensional resource spaces;
4. increase dimensionality by joining resource spaces or adding a new dimension to the existing resource space according to application requirement;
5. decrease dimension by splitting a resource space according to application requirement; and,
6. check normal forms of the resource spaces.

1.4.1 Resource Analysis

Resource analysis is to determine the application scope, to know the resources to be managed, and then to specify the resources in a *Resource Dictionary*.

Resources usually share some common attributes, for example {*name, author, owner, abstract, version, location, privilege, access-approach, effective-duration, semantic relevant resources*}. The *abstract* attribute (can be formal or informal) represents content abstraction, or the function description of a service.

Access privilege concerns:

1. *public* — any user can access to it;
2. *group* — only group members can access to it; and,
3. *private* — only the creator can access to it.

The Resource Dictionary enables designers to collect and edit resources and finally forms the axes of the resource space by defining resource classification hierarchy. A Resource Dictionary includes the following operations:

1. *Consistency checking* — check the semantic consistency between descriptions.
2. *Redundancy checking* — check redundancy and delete the redundant descriptions and redundant resources.
3. *Classification* — classify resources according to the specialization relationship determined by existing taxonomy, existing classification standard, available domain ontology, and user judgement.

1.4.2 Top-down Resource Partition

Yin-Yang is a representative of traditional Chinese understanding of how things are formed and work. Yin represents the following abstract concepts generalized from the real world: dark, passive, downward, cold, contracting and weak, while Yang represents the following abstract concepts generalized from the real world: bright, active, upward, hot, expanding and strong. Yin and Yang represent two energies that cause everything to happen. Yin and Yang are meta concepts in ancient Chinese philosophy.

Different epistemologies have different meta concepts.

Due to the difference of epistemology and culture, designers could have different partition solutions on the same set of resources, so a uniform viewpoint on resource partition is needed. The first step is to reach a top-level partition consensus.

Human, information and *natural (or artificial) object* can be the resource partition of human society at the epistemological level. The top-level resource partition of a domain is a special case of this epistemological level, for example, the top-level resources of an institute can be classified as three independent categories:

1. *human resources,*
2. *information resources,* and
3. *service resources* (including facilitates).

Each category can be refined until the categories are small enough for applications as shown in Fig.1.15. (Zhuge, 2004b).

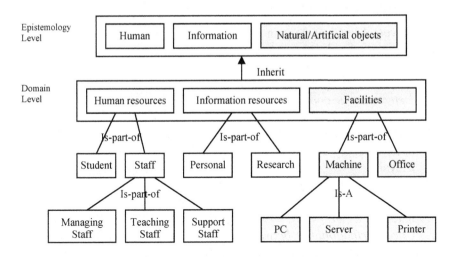

Fig. 1.15. An example of top-down resource partition.

1.4.3 From Low Dimension to High Dimension

Designers can easily handle low-dimensional spaces. So we can first design low dimensional resource spaces then add a new dimension to the existing space or integrate low-dimensional spaces into higher dimensional resource spaces.

A multi-layer table like Table 1.1 is suggested to help design a 2-dimensional resource space.

The design process is as follows:

1. *Determine the number of resource spaces* according to the number of top-level resource categories in the domain. For example, three resource spaces can be established for human resources, inheritance resources and faciliate resources.

2. *Determine axes' names* according to the resource categories at the universal level or domain level. An axis name represents a category of the domain-level partition.
3. *Determine the first-level coordinate names.* Each coordinate reflects one of the categories of the axis.
4. *Determine the coordinate hierarchies.* For each first-level coordinate, determine its low-level coordinates top-down until the basic category according to the resource partition hierarchy. The granularity of the basic category depends on the application requirement on resource retrieval.
5. *Check independency between coordinates.* If the independency is not satisfied, re-consider resource-partition at this level and adjust coordinates.
6. *Check orthogonality between axes.* If the orthogonality is not satisfied, re-consider the coordinate settings, and then adjust relevant coordinates.

According to the above process, designers can construct two resource spaces as shown in Fig.1.16 for the resource partition example of Fig.1.15.

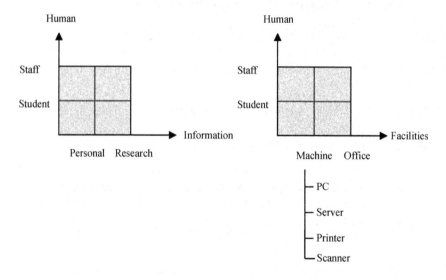

Fig. 1.16. Example of designing 2-dimensional resource spaces.

The Resource Space Model allows existing spaces to be joined into one to achieve the effect of the global resource view. Whether we need to join multiple resource spaces into one depends on application requirement.

To implement the join operation, we need to check the condition of the join operation first. It is important to ensure that different spaces to be joined to specify the same type of resources.

For example, the two resource spaces of Fig.1.16 share a common axis and specify the same type of resources. So they can be joined into one 3-dimensional resource space as shown in Fig.1.17.

The join operation may create new spaces, e.g., joining two two-dimensional resource spaces will generate one three-dimensional resource space where there exists a new two-dimensional space. The points in the new space should be defined together with the new space. For non-empty resource spaces, the following two strategies can be adopted:

1. Place the common resources in the old points sharing common coordinates of different spaces into the new points and keep the rest resources in the original space (i.e., the subspace of the new space); and,

2. Keep old resources in the original spaces (i.e., the subspace of the new space) and establish the mapping between the new points and the old points.

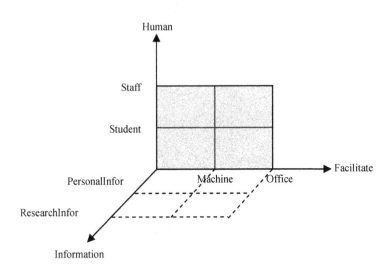

Fig. 1.17. A 3-dimensional resource space constructed by joining two 2-dimensional spaces.

Another example of creating a high dimensional space from two low dimensional spaces is shown in Fig. 1.18.   The two 3-dimensional resource spaces specifies the same type of resources—human; and, they share two axes—*Journal* and *Responsibility*. So they can be joined into a 4-dimensional resource space to finely classify the resources.

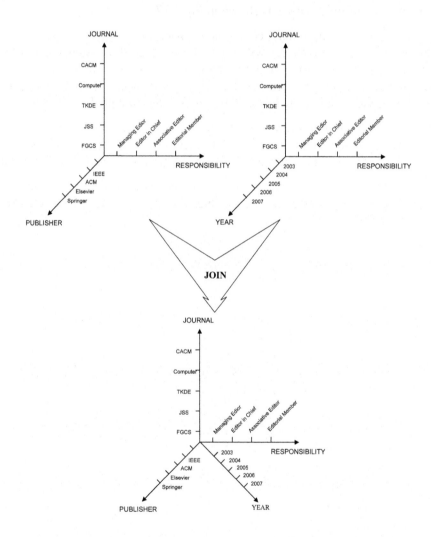

Fig.1.18. Example of creating high dimensional space from low dimensional spaces.

1.4.4 Abstraction and Analogy in Designing Resource Space

Examples play an important role in learning and design processes. People learn the process and the pattern of design by example. To design for a new application, a designer often recalls his/her experience or others' experience (examples) when planning and evaluating a design.

A good designer often makes abstraction when matching examples with the new application requirement. Abstraction also generates experience of matching so that more relevant examples can emerge during design.

Abstraction and analogy represent human problem-solving ability. If we regard the design of resource space as problem-solving, abstraction and analogy can play an important role in raising the efficiency of resource space design. By abstraction, two seemly different concepts can be classified into the same category if a common ancestor can be found.

The following describes the process of using experience to design a resource space. The pre-requisite condition is that experience is available either in assistant tool or in organization.

1. Find a domain D in the ontology repository (a kind of experience of community) similar to the new domain D'.
2. Map ontology of D into ontology of D' with abstraction. Existing methods of ontology mapping can help this step.
3. Map the resource space RS of D into the resource space of the new domain RS' according to the mapping between ontologies.
4. Add the new ontology to the ontology repository and then make necessary abstraction.
5. Check the new resource space.
    a) Check the independency between coordinates according to the synonym relationship between coordinates in the context of domain ontology. The resource dictionary and domain ontology are the basis of determining the independency between coordinates. An independency checking tool can be designed to help designers with such checking.
    b) Check the orthogonal relationship between axes. To check the refinement relation is the basis of orthogonality checking. Let $X=(C_1, \ldots, C_n)$ and X' be two axis, X' is a fine classification of X if X' is the common attributes of C_i. The independency checking should be carried out before the checking of orthogonality. An orthogonality checking tool can be designed to help designers with such checking.

6. Verify the new resource space *RS'* and make necessary modifications according to the query requirement.
7. Terminate the process if the designer satisfies with the new resource space, otherwise go to step 1.

Fig. 1.19 depicts the above process. Analogical reasoning can help derive out new relations (Zhuge, 2007).

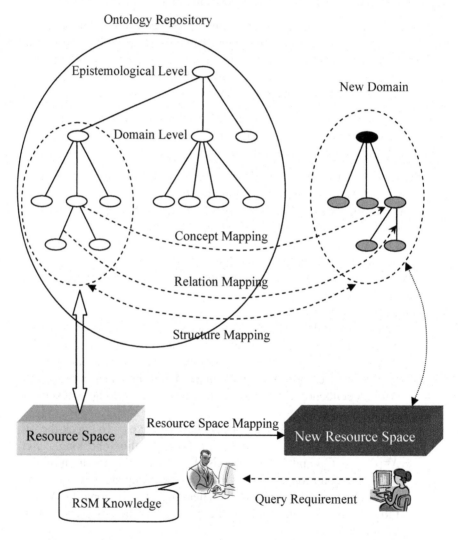

Fig. 1.19. Design by analogy and abstraction.

The creation of a new resource space depends on the following factors:

1.   the existing examples of well-design resource spaces and correspond-
      ing domain ontology mechanisms;
2.   the domain ontology of the new domain;
3.   matching between the existing domain ontology and the new domain
      ontology; and,
4.   query requirement in the new domain.

Given a domain ontology, it is possible to automatically generate the resource space of this domain. But, the automatically generated resource
space may not be suitable for the domain application if the users' query requirement is neglected. Take human resources in a university for example,
some users may expect to locate a student according to department and
grade, but some other users may expect to locate a student according to
gender and home address. Query requirement regulates the domain relevant classification.

1.5 Use Resource Space to Manage Relational Tables

A relational table can be transformed into a Resource Space Model. A table consists of one or several keys and a set of attributes dependent on the
key(s). It can be transformed into a Resource Space Model with a key
dimension and an attribute dimension denoted as follows:

Table$_1$(*Key*, A_1, A_2, .., A_n) $\Rightarrow$ *RSM*(*Key*, *Attribute*(A_1, ..., A_n)), where *attribute* denotes the axis name and (A_1, ..., A_n) denotes coordinates.

Coordinates of the attribute dimension are the attributes, and the coordinates of the key dimension are the values of the key as shown in Fig.1.20.

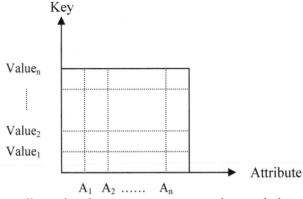

Fig. 1.20. A two-dimensional resource space managing a relational table.

For a first-normal-form table with one key: $table_1(Key, A_1, A_2, .., A_n)$, we can transform it into $RSM(Key, A(A_1, ..., A_n))$. Since any attribute is atomic in a first-normal-form relational table, there does not exist name duplication between A_1, A_2, ..., and A_n. Therefore the resource space satisfies the first-normal-form of the Resource Space Model.

If a table has more than one key, it can be transformed into a resource space with one attribute dimension and more dimensions for the keys. For example, a table with two keys can be transformed into a 3-dimensional resource space as shown in Fig.1.21.

$Table_2(Key_1, Key_2, A_1, A_2, .., A_n) \Rightarrow RSM(Key_1, Key_2, A(A_1, ..., A_n))$.

This 3-dimensional space can be split into two 2-dimensional resource spaces, each of which has only one key-dimension.

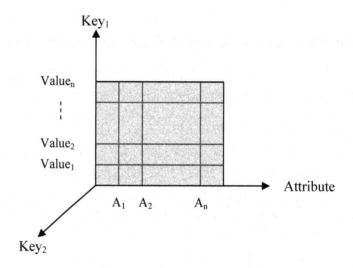

Fig. 1.21. A 3-dimensional resource space transformed from a relational table with two keys.

Multiple relational tables can be managed by a 3-dimensional space as shown in Fig.1.22, where the table-name dimension denotes all the tables that need to be managed. Each coordinate at the table-name dimension corresponds to a 2-dimensional space slice with a key dimension and an attribute dimension that represent a relational table.

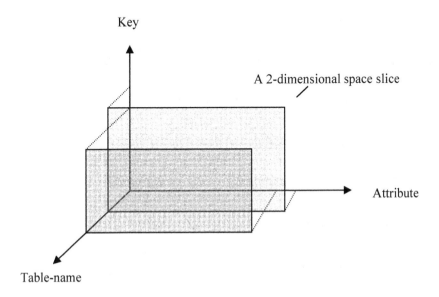

Fig. 1.22. Manage multiple tables by using a 3-dimensional resource space.

1.6 The Semantic Link Network

Anything in the world is not isolated, has its existence condition — certain relations with others. That is why children are often trained to learn concepts by filling in blanks with a given context.

The Semantic Link Network (in short SLN) is a semantic model for describing the appearance, abstraction or implied relations between resources. Although sometimes it seems no clear relations between two resources, abstraction semantic relations may be derived out by semantic relation reasoning.

As shown in Fig. 1.23, a Semantic Link Network usually consists of an abstraction level and an instance level (Zhuge, 2007). An abstraction Semantic Link Network is the abstraction of several instance Semantic Link Networks.

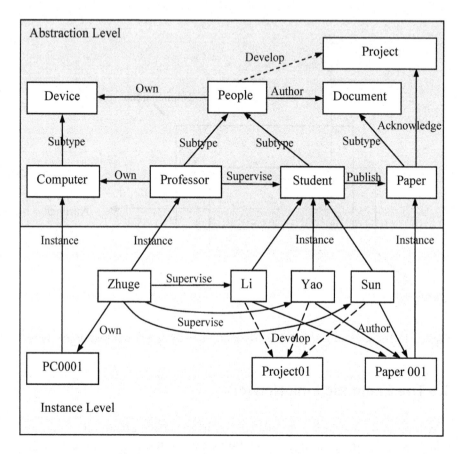

Fig. 1.23. An example of the Semantic Link Network.

The semantic link is the natural extension of the hyperlink. A semantic link connects two semantic nodes with certain semantics. A semantic node can be an identity, a semantic description and even a Semantic Link Network. A Semantic Link Network naturally supports semantic reasoning based on the semantic linking rules.

A semantic link can be reinterpreted to suit particular applications. For example, *reference* relation can be explained as the *citation* relation between papers, explained as the *call* relation between programs, and can be also explained as the *foreign key* relation between relational tables.

Application-specific semantic links need to be defined to support domain applications. For example, the layout relation is useful in specifying the relations between wall-paintings. Browsers for Semantic Link Network can be developed according to application requirements (Zhuge et al., 2004e).

Fig.1.24 shows the interface of a semantic relation search mechanism for exhibiting Dunhuang culture. Users can see the interested resources, the relevant resources and the relations between them.

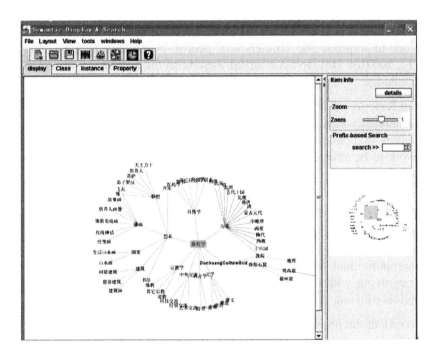

Fig. 1.24. The interface of a semantic search mechanism.

Semantic link was initiated for describing the relations between models for improving model retrieval (Zhuge, 1998). It was then extended to construct Active Document Framework (ADF) as a new e-document model

(Zhuge, 2003). It was systematically introduced in The Knowledge Grid (Zhuge, 2004d), where a *single semantic image* integrates Resource Space Model and Semantic Link Network, and a unified single semantic image query language was suggested.

The Semantic Link Network has been proved useful in Web page pre-fetching and object pre-fetching (Pons, 2005; Pons, 2006). As a semantic model, the *Semantic Link Network concerns typical semantic relations and relation reasoning*. Developers need to design application-specific relations to support applications.

A *Semantic Link* represents the semantic relation of a property or a set of properties between two semantic nodes. A semantic link can be of the following types: *cause-effect* (*ce*), *implication* (*imp*), *subtype* (*st*), *similar-to* (*sim*), *instance* (*ins*), *sequential* (*seq*) and *reference* (*ref*).

The Semantic Link Network naturally supports a semantic peer-to-peer network to improve the efficiency of peer-to-peer query routing (Zhuge and Li, 2007b). How to automatically establish the semantic links is a major challenge.

The Resource Space Model focuses on the classification on the content of resources, while the Semantic Link Network focuses on the external semantics of resources. It is not realistic to expect the Semantic Link Network to be able to describe complicated semantics that requires expert knowledge in such areas as natural language processing, logics and mathematics.

A Semantic Link Network can be established autonomously by incorporating logical reasoning, analogical reasoning, inductive reasoning and assistant tools. A large-scale Semantic Link Network can be formed by integrating individual Semantic Link Networks. Semantic Link Networks keep evolving with the execution of the up-level applications and human behaviors of using the network.

To reflect the probable relations, the Semantic Link Network can be extended to a probabilistic Semantic Link Network: *One node can link to any other semantically relevant node with a probability*. The uncertain semantic link can be represented as $A \text{---} <\alpha, p> \rightarrow B$, where α is a semantic factor and p is the probability of α.

Metcalfe's Law states that "The power of the network increases exponentially by the number of computers connected to it. Therefore, every computer added to the network both uses it as a resource while adding resources in a spiral of increasing value and choice."

What is the effect of the Semantic Link Network?

The importance of a Semantic Link Network depends on the number of people defining and maintaining semantic links rather than the definition of semantic links itself.

The evolution of the Semantic Link Network will form a kind of semantic effect that helps promote decentralized applications.

In daily life, people often ask neighbors/friends when they have questions so neighbors/friends are likely to hold relevant contents. For scientific papers, citation relations are dense between papers of the same area. This semantic relevancy leads to a semantic community phenomenon in pursuing efficiency.

The semantic communities can help promote the efficiency of searching relevant concepts by focusing on a specific semantic community.

Semantic locality requests to store relevant contents in semantically close places.

The storage mechanism of the Resource Space Model concerns the semantic locality to ensure search efficiency. It is also a criterion to implement a P2P semantic overlay to support semantic-rich decentralized applications.

The Semantic Link Network is a general semantic space. The Resource Space Model focuses only on one type of relation—the classification relation, so it can be regarded as a special case of the Semantic Link Network.

The Resource Space Model and the Semantic Link Network follow different rules. The theories on the Resource Space Model are not suitable for the Semantic Link Network. However, a resource space can be transformed into a Semantic Link Network, and a special Semantic Link Network can also be transformed into a resource space. Moreover, they can be integrated to provide views of different layers: the Resource Space Model placed over the Semantic Link Network provides with a classification view while the Semantic Link Network provides with a scalable semantic link network view.

1.7 Comparison between RSM and RDBM

Recognizing the attributes of an object and knowing the classification of objects are two basic approaches to understanding the real world. The two approaches support each other in recognizing the real world.

An object has attributes of many aspects like physical and chemical characteristics. Objects sharing the same set of attributes can be classified into the same category. Different aspects can form different classification methods. Existing classifications can be refined with the development of knowledge on classifications and attributes.

The Relational Database Model is based on the attributes of objects. Just like previous data models such as the network model and object-oriented model, both the Resource Space Model and the Relational Database Model support application systems. An ideal data model should be simple, capable and close to human thinking.

The Resource Space Model and the relational database can be further compared as follows.

1. The Resource Space Model focuses on the classification on objects (resources in the digital world). It allows designers and users to observe resources as a whole and then classifies them top-down by commonsense for high-level classification and domain specific knowledge for low-level classification. The relational database model focuses on attributes of objects (entities). In representation, the Resource Space Model is a uniform coordinate system, while the data model of the RDBMS is a relational table. Usually, an application needs to select (search) from many tables so operations on multiple tables are inevitable. The cost of operations on multiple table needs to be reduced.

2. A basic request of the classic relational database model is the atomicity of data. Attributes are defined by datatypes. The Resource Space Model does not request this atomicity in nature. A coordinate in the Resource Space Model can be defined by semantic description including basic datatype, keyword set, or a coordinate tree representing fine classification at different levels. So resources managed by the Resource Space Model can be any form of resources, while the classical relational data model only manages atomic data.

3. The normalization approaches of the Resource Space Model and the Relational Database Model are different in nature. The relational database model normalizes the functional dependence relation, while the Resource Space Model normalizes the classification relation. The Resource Space Model enables a uniform and universal resource view when operating resources. It is suitable for class operations since to retrieve a class is equivlent to locate a point in a resource space. To retrieve a class of data, the relational database system needs to check

all of the records unless it is indexed. The RDBMS essentially supports the view of one or more tables.

4. The Relational Data Model requests that application developers are the same as the database designer or that the applicatoin developers are very familiar with the database design because they need to know the table schemas for coding. The Resource Space Model also request the application develpers know the structure of the resource space. In applications, users should be familar with one-dimensional classification of the resources in the application domain. This is the basis of understanding the multi-dimensional resource space. In an organization, high-rank users are interested in high-level classifications, low-rank users are responsible for low-level classifications. The resource space actually provides a type of domain knowledge, which supports various applicaion systems.

5. The basic semantics of the Relational Database Model relies on the Data Definition Language (DDL). The DDL is used to create and destroy databases and database objects. These commands will primarily be used by database administrators during the setup and terminate phases of a database project. The basic semantics of the Resource Space Model is the commonsense on classification at high-level and the domain knowledge on classification at low level. Domain ontology helps explain low-level semantics.

6. For normalization, the Relational Database Model introudces artificial attributes like identity to differentiate one object from the others. Otherwise, the key does not exist in natural attributes in many cases. The Resource Space Model does not have this limitation.

7. Relational table raises its search efficiency by establishing one- dimensional index on attributes. The resource space uses one multi-dimensional index on the whole space. This multi-dimensional nature requires special storage mechanism different from relational database. As a descrete multi-dimensional index, the resource space has advantages in search efficiency.

8. Complex resources are properties if they are correctly stored. The existing resources bring users' classification viewpoint so they can be used to enrich the semantics of axes, coordinates and even points. In relational table, data does not contain such rich semantics as complex resources.

Above differences determine that the Resource Space Model concerns the contents (semantics) of resources and the content-based classification so it supports content-based operation. The relational database model concerns the attributes of the objects being managed so it supports attribute-based operation.

Differences exist between the design method for the relational databases and the design method for the Resource Space Model. The design method for the Resource Space Model does not have the conceptual model so experience plays an important role when designing an appropriate resource space. The Resource Space Model's conceptual model is actually the same as its data model. Its hierarchical resource organization approach is in line with the top-down resource partition and the "from general to special" thinking characteristic.

The classification-based normalization requires the Resource Space Model to have a special design method and tools, which are different from the Relational Database Model. The design of a resource space concerns the resource dictionary, independency checking of coordinates, and orthogonal checking of axes. The design of the relational database concerns the data dictionary and the balance between the normal forms and the retrieval efficiency with respect to the application requirement.

A basic semantic overlay should be able to describe basic semantic relations and can further find potential semantic relations. Just like relational database only focuses on very basic relations such as attribute-value relation and functional dependence relation, the Resource Space Model focuses on the classification relations. It is an interesting issue to find a way to integrate different types of semantics. The Resource Space Model, UML, OWL, and database can be mapped from one into another and integrated with each other to enhance and support each other.

1.8 Questions and Answers

Question 1. We have the relational database model and many commercial database systems. Do we still need Resource Space Model?

Answer 1. Different models have different application scopes. The relational database model is useful in many applications, especially in pure data management. The Resource Space Model aims at managing contents of various resources rather than pure data.

Question 2. What are the distinguished characteristics of the Resource Space Model compared with existing data models.

Answer 2. The Resource Space Model is based on content classification reflecting human classification commonsense and thinking on recognizing real-world objects. Coordinates at each axis are discrete and any coordinate can be a tree structure. Using the multi-dimensional index, the Resource Space Model supports efficient searching.

Question 3. Resource Space Model designers may not clearly know the classification of resources. For example, some cross-area book could belong to two categories.

Answer 3. The Resource Space Model is good at managing the content that can be clearly classified. Designers can design resource spaces of different normal forms according to different applications. The following approaches can be used to deal with this issue:

1. add undetermined coordinates to specify those un-determined resources;
2. add a cross-class coordinate to appropriate axis;
3. introduce fuzzy theory to establish a fuzzy Resource Space Model as introduced in (Zhuge, 2004c); and,
4. introduce probability into Resource Space Model to reflect the probability world (see chapter 9).

Question 4. Can Resource Space Model change structure during use?

Answer 4. The original Resource Space Model is designed for specific applications just like databases, so it is inappropriate to change structure after design. On the other hand, the normal form would be damaged if we change the structure of the Resource Space Model. There are two ways to resolve this issue. One is that we can design a more stable resource space since diverse resource spaces can be designed for an application. The second is that we can design a Resource Space Model system that can adapt to change.

Question 5. Can we use existing database systems to realize a resource space system?

Answer 5. Existing data structure and indexing techniques can be used to implement a resource space system. The XML file can be used as the intermediate of storing resources. However, a special approach that makes use of the characteristics of the Resource Space Model is needed. Chapter 6 presents an approach to the storage of resource space.

Question 6. Are resources stored in the resource space?

Answer 6. A resource space includes three parts: the structure of the space including axes and their coordinates, the specification of the content (including identity, path and semantic description) of resources, and the entity resources. The strategy of storing these parts depends on the resource space system. Based on the Resource Space Model, different types of re-source space systems can be developed.

Question 7. What is the relationship between the Resource Space Model and the Knowledge Grid?

Answer 7. The original idea of the Knowledge Grid is for effective knowl-edge sharing (Zhuge, 2002). Semantics is the basis for knowledge sharing. The Resource Space Model is suitable for managing knowledge resources by knowledge classification, for example, (*concept, relation, axiom, rules, method* and *theory*) can be one axis, and discipline can be another axis of a knowledge space. A decentralized Resource Space Model can be the un-derlying infrastructure of the Knowledge Grid.

Question 8. What is the relationship between the Resource Space Model and P2P networks?

Answer 8. P2P is a scalable decentralized resource management mecha-nism. A resource space can be either centralized or decentralized. A one-dimensional resource space can be implemented as a structured P2P net-work by partitioning a set of resources and enabling a peer to manage a class of resources. Semantic locality requires resources of the same class to be stored in the same place or close places and managed by one peer. It is an interesting issue to realize efficient routing in a multi-dimensional P2P resource space. Chapter 8 and Chapter 9 present two solutions to con-struct P2P resource spaces.

1.9 Summary

Like Yin-Yang in ancient Chinese philosophy, *normalization* and *auton-omy* are two aspects of an ideal organization model. The Resource Space Model represents the normalization. The Semantic Link Network repre-sents the autonomy. Integration of the Resource Space Model and the Se-mantic Link Network can form a semantic overlay with the characteristics of normalization and autonomy.

A Resource Space Model can be distributed onto a network to meet the needs of distributed applications. The method and technology of the dis-tributed databases are good references in developing the distributed Re-source Space Model.

The Resource Space Model can be deployed onto a peer-to-peer net-work in a certain manner for decentralized applications. The peer-to-peer

Resource Space Model is a way to realize the synergy of normalization and autonomy.

The storage of the resource space is to map the discrete multi-dimensional resource space into a multi-dimensional index on a linear storage space by using a specific index structure. The peer-to-peer computing can be regarded as a decentralized storage mechanism that distributes a linear disk space onto a network.

This book arranges its content as follows:

Chapter 1 presents the general methodology of the Resource Space Model. Readers can know its general idea, concept, characteristic and method of the Resource Space Model. Readers could understand and start to design resource spaces for applications after reading this chapter.

Chapter 2 investigates the relationship between the Resource Space Model and the Semantic Link Network, and proposes an approach to integrate the two models to construct a richer semantic overlay synergying the normalization and autonomy for managing resources in the future interconnection environment.

Chapter 3 studies the expressiveness of query languages for Resource Space Model and introduces the completeness and necessity theory for query operations on resource spaces.

Chapter 4 introduces the algebra and calculus theory for the Resource Space Model. They are important parts of the theory of the Resource Space Model and the basis of its query language.

Chapter 5 analyzes the complexity of searching in the resource space. It unveils the relationship between the searching efficiency and the number of dimensions as well as the relationship between the searching efficiency and the distribution of coordinates.

Chapter 6 introduces an approach to physically store the resource space and its resources. The storage approach should reflect the characteristics of the resource space and efficiently support flexible query.

The next two chapters are on a decentralized Resource Space Model. Chapter 7 presents an approach to deploy the Resource Space Model onto peer-to-peer network to obtain the scalability. Chapter 8 presents an approach to make use of classification semantics to improve the efficiency of unstructured peer-to-peer network.

Chapter 9 constructs the probabilistic Resource Space Model to deal with uncertainty in applications by introducing the probability into the Resource Space Model. The motivation is similar to the fuzzy Resource Space Model (Zhuge, 2004c). The probabilistic Resource Space Model can be regarded as a more general Resource Space Model.

Chapter 2 A Semantic Overlay Integrating Normalization with Autonomy

Classifying objects into categories at different granularity levels, establishing semantic links between known objects, and discovering semantic clues between known and unknown objects are essential for understanding. Incorporating the Resource Space Model and the Semantic Link Network can form a semantic overlay synergy normalization and autonomy for managing resources in the future interconnection environment.

2.1 The Basic Idea

The Semantic Web is to improve the World Wide Web by extending HTML Web pages to descriptions with machine-understandable semantics, better enabling computers and people to work in cooperation (Berners-Lee et al., 2001; Heflin and Hendler, 2001). The success of the HTML guides researchers to develop more powerful markup languages like the Resource Description Framework (RDF, www.w3c.org/RDF), which is often used to integrate various applications by using the eXtensible Markup Language (XML) for syntax and URIs for naming (www.w3c.org/XML).

Grid computing research influences the development of the Semantic Web from the computing ideal, infrastructure and model aspects (Foster, 2000, www-fp.mcs.anl.gov/~foster/). Artificial intelligence research influences the development of the Semantic Web towards a wisdom Web (Hoschek et al, 2000; Zhong et al, 2002).

Knowledge representation and logics are the basis of traditional artificial intelligence. To introduce rules and description logics into the Semantic Web is a natural idea to enable the Semantic Web to support intelligent applications. An appropriate representation of semantics is also the key to solve the service discovery and matching issues in the service-oriented computing.

To find a good representation approach is only one aspect of realizing the Semantic Web. Cross-domain understanding needs domain ontology. However, how to efficiently organize, use and maintain the semantic content is a major challenge to realize an efficient Semantic Web.

Relational Data Base Model is a semantic model to effectively organize and manage attribute-value semantics (Chen, 1976; Codd, 1970; Codd, 1971b). With the normal form theories, it ensures the efficiency and accuracy of operations on data (Mok, 2002; Ullman, 1988; William, 1983). But the function dependence relationship between attributes of objects and the relationship between attributes and values are limited in semantic ability to organize and manage versatile resources in a large-scale dynamic interconnection environment.

Object-oriented databases and object-relational databases extend the application scope of the relational databases by borrowing the advantages of the object-oriented methodologies and programming languages like inheritance and encapsulation to enable complex objects to be normally managed (Abiteboul et al, 1995; Kim, 1990; Rumbaugh et al., 1991; Ullman, 1988). Several graph-based semantic models built on the traditional hierarchical and network data models have been proposed (Gyssens et al, 1994; Levene and Loizou, 1995; Levene and Poulovassilis, 1990; Poulovassilis and Levene, 1994). But, these data models are incapable of effectively managing heterogeneous, distributed and ocean resources in a large, open and dynamic network environment. Semantic rich data models are required for achieving the efficiency and efficacy of resource management in the future interconnection environment.

Human recognizes the objective world by classifying objects, establishing links between known objects, and discovering clues between known and unknown objects. Orthogonal classification is a way to normalize the classification of resources. For example, people are used to finding books in library by classifications on topics, publishers, or alphabets, which are orthogonal with each other. If they are integrated into one classification model as shown in Fig. 2.1, then people can locate a book by given three coordinates of corresponding axes in the three-dimensional classification space. Locating resources will be more efficient than only use one type of classification or separately use these classifications. Further, semantic links like citation relationships (e.g., "The Knowledge Grid" cites "Weaving the Web" as shown in Fig. 2.1) and *common-author* relationships can be established between books — the entries in nodes. The incorporation of the classification semantics with the link semantics can form a richer semantic image (overlay) for locating resources.

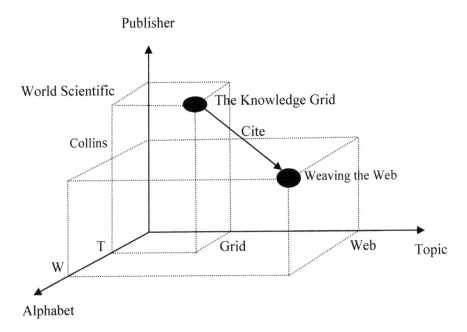

Fig.2.1. An example of integrating orthogonal classification semantics with link semantics.

The Resource Space Model RSM is a semantic data model for uniformly, normally and effectively specifying and managing resources by normalizing classification semantics (Zhuge, 2004a). Its theoretical basis is the normal forms and integrity constraints on resources (Zhuge et al., 2005c).

The characteristic of the Resource Space Model is the normalization on classification semantics.

Semantic Link Network SLN is a semantic model that links resource descriptions by semantic links (Zhuge, 2003). The SLN model supports semantic representation, reasoning, execution, referential search, and normalization. An SLN can represent any semantic relationships between resources.

The characteristic of the SLN is its autonomy: any node (resource) can link to any semantic relevant node.

Are there any intrinsic rules between RSM and SLN? To know these rules can better develop the theory of the semantic overlay for the future interconnection environment.

2.2 Integrating Resource Space Model with Semantic Link Network

A resource space is an n-dimensional space $RS(X_1, X_2, \ldots, X_n)$, where $X_i = \{C_{i1}, C_{i2}, \ldots, C_{im}\}$ is an axis defined by a set of coordinates. A point $p(C_{1,j1}, C_{2,j2}, \ldots, C_{n,jn})$ is determined by the coordinate values at every axes. It can uniquely determine a resource set, where each element is called a resource entry. Point and resource entry are two fundamental operation units of the Resource Space Model.

Fig.2.2 is an example of a 3-dimentional resource space *Spec-Apart-Gen(Specialization, Apartment, Gender)* specifying the student information of a college. Three axes are *Specialization* = {*math, chemistry, physics*}, *Apartment* = {*1#, 2#, 3#*} and *Gender* = {*male, female*}. Each point denotes a class of students, for example, the point (*math, 1#, male*) represents all the male students who belong to the department of math and live in apartment no.1 in this college. And each resource entry in this point corresponds to a student in the college.

Class hierarchy can be defined top-down from any coordinate at an axis. Take Fig.2.2 for example, the coordinate *chemistry* on axis *Specialization* is classified into g_1, g_2 and g_3 in terms of *grade*, and then they can be further classified according to *class*. The label of each node is determined by a full path from the root, so the leaf node *chemistry.g_1.c_1* can be distinguished from *chemistry.g_2.c_1*.

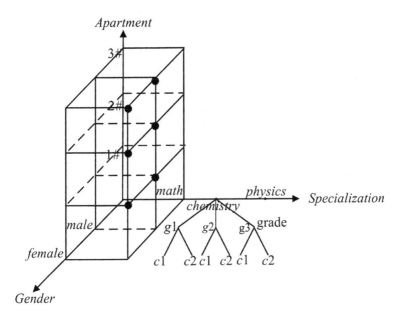

Fig.2.2. A 3-dimentional Resource Space *Spec-Apart-Gen.*

A Semantic Link Network consists of a semantic node set *Semantic-Nodes*, a semantic link set *SemanticLinks* and a reasoning rule set *SLNRules*, denoted as *<SemanticNodes, SemanticLinks, SLNRules>*. Any semantic link in the *SemanticLinks* is a binary relation between two semantic nodes in the *SemanticNodes*. For any three semantic nodes *A*, *B* and *C* in the semantic node set if there exist two semantic links *A—α→B* and *B—β→C* in the semantic link set, and there exists a semantic link rule *X—α→Y, Y—β→Z ⇒ X—γ→Z* (denoted as *α·β=γ* in simple) in the *SLNRules*, then *A —γ→C* can be derived out and added to *SemanticLinks* (Zhuge, 2003). Two semantic link networks can be merged into one by common nodes or by adding semantic links between nodes of different networks.

Normal forms of the Semantic Link Network are to guarantee the correctness of its semantics and operations. For example, *X–is-part-of→ Y* and *X–isn't-part-of→ Y* may exist in the same Semantic Link Network because different users may operate on the same Semantic Link Network. The following normal forms of Semantic Link Network are to resolve the redundancy and inconsistency issues.

1. If there does not exist semantic-equivalent nodes in a given Semantic Link Network, then we say that the Semantic Link Network is the first normal form *SLN* (1NF-SLN).

2. If a Semantic Link Network is 1NF and there does not exist inconsistent semantic links and duplicate semantic links between the same pair of nodes, then we say that the Semantic Link Network is the second normal form Semantic Link Network (2NF-SLN).

3. If a Semantic Link Network is a 2NF and there does not exist isolated nodes (accessible from each other), then we say that the Semantic Link Network is the third normal form Semantic Link Network (3NF-SLN).

An ideal Semantic Link Network is a semantic "map" of distributed versatile resources to enable people to autonomously publish, manage and browse resources according to semantic links in the map.

Each resource defined in the Resource Space Model can have a mapping image in the Semantic Link Network. The purpose is different from the knowledge portals that only provide knowledge services (Mack et al., 2001). Users can make and use the orthogonal classification semantics and the link semantics according to their cognition on the real world. The orthogonal classification semantics can help users focus their operation destination. The Semantic Link Network reflects the semantic clues between versatile resources. The integration of the Resource Space Model and the Semantic Link Network combines the classification semantics and relational semantics.

The normalization theories of Resource Space Model and Semantic Link Network support a kind of single semantic point of accessing relevant semantic content, i.e., single semantic image (Zhuge, 2004d). Knowledge portals are difficult to realize this function. Abstract knowledge like traditional semantic network and rule base can be derived from the Semantic Link Network by generalization, can be organized according to the orthogonal semantics in the up-level space, and thus enable the future interconnection environment to implement intelligent services.

A Global Semantic Overlay Grid can be built by integrating the Resource Space Model and Semantic Link Network as shown in Fig.2.3.

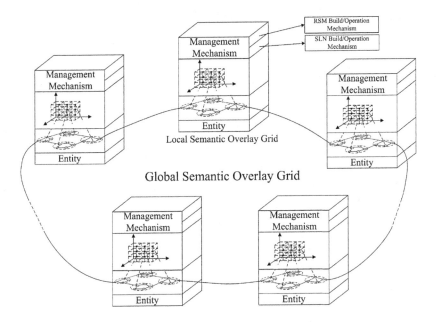

Fig.2.3. Building a Semantic Overlay Grid by integrating the Resource Space Model and the Semantic Link Network.

A local Semantic Overlay Grid has four layers: the entity layer, the local Semantic Link Network, the local resource space layer, and the management mechanism of the resource space and the Semantic Link Network. The integration of the Resource Space Model and the Semantic Link Network lays the foundation of the Local Semantic Overlay Grid. A normalized Local Semantic Overlay Grid requires that both the Resource Space Model and the Semantic Link Network satisfy the normal forms. The Global Overlay Semantic Grid consists of many Local Semantic Overlay Grids connected by the semantic links. A Normalized Global Semantic Overlay Grid requires that all Local Semantic Overlay Grids are normalized and that the global Semantic Link Network is normalized.

The Semantic Overlay Grid integrates the advantages of the normalization (the normalization of both Resource Space Model and Semantic Link Network) and self-organization (local Semantic Overlay Grids interconnect with each other autonomously). The normalization reflects the optimization ideal of the Grid.

2.3 Relationship between RSM and SLN

2.3.1 Transformation from Semantic Link Network to Resource Space Model

Definition 2.1. For a Semantic Link Network SLN (N, SL), (1) if for some nodes n_1, $n_2 \in N$ (SLN), there exists a directed path $p(n_1, n_2)$ from n_1 to n_2, then we call n_1 can reach n_2; (2) if for any pair of nodes n_1, $n_2 \in N$ (SLN), n_1 can reach n_2 or n_2 can reach n_1, then we call SLN (N, SL) is unilaterally connected; (3) if for any n_1, $n_2 \in N$ (SLN), n_1 can reach n_2 and n_2 can reach n_1, then SLN (N, SL) is called strongly connected; and (4) let SLN' be the underlying undirected graph of SL (N, SL), then SLN (N, SL) is called weakly connected if SLN' is connected; (5) if at least one semantic link (or can be derived from existing links) points from n_1 to n_2, we say that n_2 is semantically reachable from n_1, and that n_1 and n_2 are accessible each other by browsing (regardless of direction).

The weak connectedness is about the reachability of browsing. If we have $n_1 - \alpha \rightarrow n_2$, $n_2 - \alpha \rightarrow n_3 \Rightarrow n_1 - \alpha \rightarrow n_3$ ('$\Rightarrow$' means by implication), then we say that α or the α-link is transitive, and that there exists a semantic chain from n_1 to n_3. Then we can see that the unilateral and strong connectness is about the reachability of the semantic links by induction.

Definition 2.2. A sub-graph SLN' of SLN (N, SL) is called a (weak, unilateral, strong) connected component of SLN (N, SL) if (1) SLN' is (weakly, unilaterally, strongly) connected; and (2) if SLN'' is (weakly, unilaterally, strongly) connected too, and $SLN' \cap SLN'' \neq \Phi$, then $SLN' \supseteq SLN''$, i.e., SLN' is a maximal subset which is (weakly, unilaterally, strongly) connected.

A semantic component can be viewed as a point in the high-level resource space, then we can get the corresponding high-level resource space from a semantic link network as follows:

For a Semantic Link Network SLN (N, SL), let $SLN = \{C_1, C_2, ..., C_m\}$, where C_i represents a strongly connected component of SLN and $C_i \cap C_j = \Phi$. Then N $(SLN) = \cup N(C_i)$, where $N(C_i)$ denotes the nodes of C_i. A strongly connected component of SLN stands for a certain semantics that is independent from the semantics of other components. So a Semantic Link Network can be transformed to a Resource Space Model by mapping the strongly connected components into the points in the space. Fig.5 depicts such a transformation.

A transformation from a Semantic Link Network to a resource space exists because:

There exists an n-dimensional semantic space $RS(X_1, X_2, ..., X_n)$ to represent the semantics of a Semantic Link Network. The simplest case is a vector $(C_1, ..., C_n)$.

For each strongly connected semantic component C_i of the SLN, we can find projections on each axis $x_1, x_2, ..., x_n$, representing fine semantics on those axes. Each axis takes the projection of $C_1, ..., C_n$ on it as coordinates.

$C_i(x_1, x_2, ..., x_n)$ corresponds to a point in RS.

The rest points in RS can be assigned as null points.

Given a domain ontology, above steps can determine a resource space $RS(X_1, X_2, ..., X_n)$ by mapping axis and its coordinates onto concepts in the ontology hierarchy.

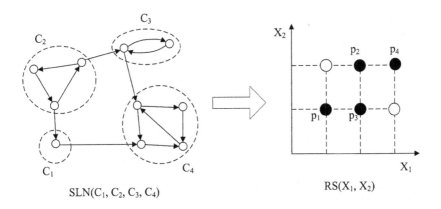

SLN(C_1, C_2, C_3, C_4)   RS(X_1, X_2)

Fig.2.4. Transformation from a Semantic Link Network to a resource space.

For a Semantic Link Network $SLN = \{C_1, C_2, C_3, C_4\}$ shown in Fig.2.4, C_i is the strong component, $1 \le i \le 4$. Then, we can get the resource space $RS(X_1, X_2) = \{p_1, p_2, p_3, p_4\}$ (other two unfilled points represent null points). We can see that when the high-level semantics are got in the resource space, the low-level semantics such as $p_1 \rightarrow p_4$, $p_3 \rightarrow p_4$, $p_2 \rightarrow p_3$, and $p_2 \rightarrow p_1$ in the Semantic Link Network are lost.

Corollary 2.1. A 1NF Semantic Link Network (1NF-SLN) can be transformed to a 1NF Resource Space Model (1NF-RSM).

Proof. If a Semantic Link Network is 1NF, then there do not exist semantic-equivalent nodes in it. From the definition of the strongly connected component, there should not exist the same strongly connected component in the Semantic Link Network. Suppose *RS* is the high-level resource space, then there should not exist the same sets of points in it. So, there does not exist name duplication between coordinates at any axis in the resource space. Then the resource space is also the 1NF. □

Corollary 2.2. A 2NF Semantic Link Network (2NF-SLN) can be transformed to a 2NF Resource Space Model (2NF-RSM).

Proof. If a Semantic Link Network is 2NF, then there do not exist inconsistent and duplicate semantic links between the same pair of nodes, this guarantees that the strongly connected components of Semantic Link Network are correct in semantics. Suppose $\{C_1, C_2, ..., C_m\}$ is the set of strongly connected components of the Semantic Link Network *SLN* and *RS* is the high-level resource space, then $RS = \{ p_1, p_2, ..., p_m \}$, where p_i corresponds to C_i, $1 \le i \le m$. If *RS* is not the second-normal-form, then there exist some points p_i and p_j are not independent from each other, i.e., $R(C_i) \cap R(C_j) \neq \Phi$, which means $C_i \cap C_j \neq \Phi$. This is not consistent with that C_i and C_j are different strongly connected components in *SLN*, so the *RS* is also a 2NF-RSM. □

Corollary 2.3. A 3NF Semantic Link Network (3NF-SLN) can be transformed to a 3NF Resource Space Model (3NF-RSM).

Proof. If a Semantic Link Network *SLN* is a 3NF, then there does not exist isolated nodes (accessible from each other), therefore all the strongly connected components of *SLN* are accessible from each other. Suppose *RS* is the high-level resource space, we can get that any of its point are reachable from others, then every axis X_i can represent all the resources in *RS*, which is equivalent to that any two axes of *RS* are orthogonal with each other (Zhuge et al., 2005c), so *RS* is also a 3NF. □

The above three corollaries show that the normal forms of the Resource Space Model and the Semantic Link Network have common properties in solving the redundancy and inconsistency.

2.3.2 Transformation from Resource Space to Semantic Link Network and Correlations

There are multiple ways to transform a resource space to a Semantic Link Network, but semantics may lose during transformation. So it is important to ensure the semantic equivalence of the transformation. The following is a semantically equivalent transformation. Fig.2.5 depicts the transformation process.

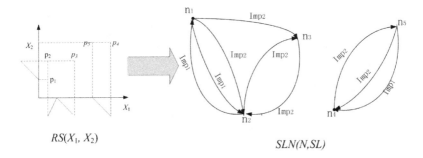

$$RS(X_1, X_2) \qquad\qquad SLN(N, SL)$$

Fig.2.5. An example of semantically equivalent transformation.

Take nodes in the resource space as nodes in the Semantic Link Network;

Define the semantic links between $n_1(x_1, \ldots, x_n)$ and $n_2(y_1, \ldots, y_n)$ as:

$$SL(x_i, y_i) = \begin{cases} imp_i & \text{if } < x_i, y_i > \in X_i \text{ or } x_i = y_i; \\ \Phi, & \text{otherwise.} \end{cases}$$

Where X_i is the axis of the resource space RS, and imp_i means that node $n_1(x_1, \ldots, x_n)$ implies $n_2(y_1, \ldots, y_n)$ on the semantics of axis X_i. Then we can get SL (SLN) from SL (SLN)$=\cup_{n1,n2 \in N} SL(n_1, n_2)$.

Because the semantic links are directed, $SL(x_i, y_i) \neq SL(y_i, x_i)$ in most cases. If $x_i = y_i$, then $SL(x_i, y_i) = SL(y_i, x_i) = Imp_i$. On the contrary, if $SL(x_i, y_i) = Imp_i$ and $SL(y_i, x_i) = Imp_i$, then $x_i = y_i$. It is clear that the link Imp_i is transitive. For any node $n(x_1, x_2, \ldots, x_n)$ in the resulting SLN (N, SL), we have $R(x_i) = \cup \{R(y_i) | SL(x_i, y_i) = Imp_i\}$. Then, from the steps of construction, it is clear that the resulting SLN (N, SL) is semantically equivalent to the resource space RS (P, E).

In a resource space *RS*, an axis with hierarchical coordinates can be transformed into an axis with flat coordinates if only the leaf nodes of each hierarchy are considered. So here focuses on the flat cases. In this case, the semantic link network *SLN* corresponds to resource space *RS* regularly. For any two points $p_1(x_1, x_2, ..., x_n)$ and $p_2(y_1, y_2, ..., y_n)$ in *RS*, we have $x_i = y_i$ or $R(x_i) \cap R(y_i) = \Phi$, $1 \le i \le$ n, i.e., both "x_i implies y_i" and "y_i implies x_i" hold or neither hold. Correspondingly, for any two nodes $n_1(x_1, x_2, ..., x_n)$ and $n_2(y_1, y_2, ..., y_n)$ in the *SLN*, $SL(x_i, y_i) = SL(y_i, x_i) = Imp_i$ or $SL(x_i, y_i) = SL(y_i, x_i) = \Phi$, i.e., there are no semantic links between x_i and y_i.

Given a resource space *RS*, there is a semantically equivalent Semantic Link Network SLN, so we can compare the normal forms of *RS* and the corresponding *SLN* to study the correlations between the normal forms of RSM and SLN.

Corollary 2.4. A 1NF-RSM can be transformed to a 1NF-SLN.

Proof. If *RS* is 1NF, then there does not exist name duplication between coordinates at any axis, so there cannot be the same points in *RS*. Suppose *SLN* is the corresponding semantic link network of *RS*, from $N (SLN) = P (RS)$, we can get that there does not exist semantic-equivalent nodes in *SLN*, so *SLN* is also the 1NF. □

Corollary 2.5. A 2NF-RSM can be transformed to a 2NF-SLN.

Proof. If *RS* is a 2NF, then for any axis, any two coordinates are independent from each other. Suppose *SLN* is the corresponding semantic link network of *RS*, then there do not exist semantic-equivalent nodes in *SLN*. And for any pair of nodes $n_1(x_1, x_2, ..., x_n)$ and $n_2(y_1, y_2, ..., y_n)$ in the *SLN*, the semantic links between them fall into two cases: $SL(x_i, y_i) = SL(y_i, x_i) = Imp_i$ or $SL(x_i, y_i) = SL(y_i, x_i) = \Phi$, so there do not exist inconsistent semantic links and duplicate semantic links between n_1 and n_2, i.e., the *SLN* is the 2NF. □

Corollary 2.6. A 3NF-RSM can be transformed to a 3NF-SLN.

Proof. If *RS* is a 3NF, then any two axes of it are orthogonal with each other, in other words, every axis X_i can represent all the resources in *RS*, formally, $R(X_1) = R(X_2) = ... = R(X_n)$ (Zhuge et al., 2005c), this guarantees that any points in the form of $\{ p(x_1, x_2, ..., x_n) | x_i \in X_i \}$ are meaningful. Suppose *SLN* is the corresponding semantic link network of *RS*, from $N (SLN) = P (RS)$, we have: any nodes in *SLN* in the form of $\{ n(x_1, x_2, ..., x_n) | x_i \in X_i \}$ are also meaningful. Then, for any two nodes $n_1(x_1, x_2, ..., x_n)$ and $n_2(y_1, y_2, ..., y_n)$ in the *SLN*, if there exists some i, $1 \le i \le n$, such that $x_i = y_i$, then $SL(x_i, y_i) = SL(y_i, x_i) = Imp_i$, then n_1 and n_2 can be accessed from each

other. Else if $x_i \neq y_i$, for $1 \leq i \leq n$ hold, let $n_3 = n_3(x_1, x_2, ..., x_{n-1}, y_n)$, from $x_1 \neq y_1$ and $x_n \neq y_n$, we can get $n_3 \neq n_1$ and $n_3 \neq n_2$. Then there exist semantic links $n_1 - Imp_1 \rightarrow n_3$, and $n_3 - Imp_n \rightarrow n_2$, so n_1 and n_2 can also be accessed from each other by the chain $n_1 - Imp_1 \rightarrow n_3 - Imp_n \rightarrow n_2$. So any two nodes in the *SLN* are accessible from each other, i.e., the *SLN* is the third-normal-form.
□

The above three corollaries further confirm that the normal forms of the Resource Space Model and the Semantic Link Network have the common properties in solving the redundancy and inconsistency.

2.3.3 Topological Properties

Just as the quotient resource space defined in (Zhuge et al., 2005c), the quotient Semantic Link Network is the abstract of the original Semantic Link Network, and it reflects the higher level semantics. Here we will prove that the quotient Semantic Link Network keeps the three normal forms of the original one, which shows that the quotient Semantic Link Network is a "good" Semantic Link Network.

Definition 2.3. For a Semantic Link Network *SLN* (*N*, *SL*), if there exists an equivalent relation *R* on the set of nodes *N* (*SLN*), then the quotient Semantic Link Network of *SLN* (*N*, *SL*) is defined as *SLN* '(*N* ', *SL*'), where *N* '(*SLN*')= *N* (*SLN*)/*R*={$C_1, C_2, ..., C_m$}, where C_i is an equivalent class in *N* (*SLN*) under the relation *R*; and, *SL*'(C_i, C_j)=∪{ *SL*(n_i, n_j) | n_i, n_j ∈ *N* (*SLN*) and $n_i \in C_i$, $n_j \in C_j$ }, $1 \leq i, j \leq m$.

Theorem 2.1. Let *SLN* (*N*, *SL*) be a Semantic Link Network, and *SLN* '(*N* ', *SL*') is the quotient Semantic Link Network constructed as above, then *SLN'*(*N* ', *SL* ') keeps the three normal forms of *SLN* (*N*, *SL*).

Proof. (1) If *SLN* is 1NF, then there do not exist semantic-equivalent nodes in it. For the quotient network *SLN'*(*N'*, *SL'*), *N'*(*SLN'*)= *N* (*SLN*)/*R*={$C_1, C_2, ..., C_m$}. According to the definition of the equivalence relation *R*, $C_i \cap C_j = \Phi$, $1 \leq i, j \leq m$. So there do not exist semantic-equivalent nodes in *SLN* '(*N* ', *SL* '), which means that *SLN* '(*N* ', *SL* ') is also 1NF. (2) If *SLN* is 2NF, then there do not exist inconsistent semantic links and duplicate semantic links between the same pair of nodes in *SLN*. According to the construction process of the quotient Semantic Link Network, *SL* '(C_i, C_j)=∪{*SL*(n_i, n_j) | n_i, n_j ∈ *N* (*SLN*) and $n_i \in C_i$, $n_j \in C_j$ }, we can get that *SL* '(*SLN* ')⊆ *SL* (*SLN*), so there do not exist inconsistent semantic links and duplicate semantic links, in *SLN* '(*N* ', *SL'*) either, which means that *SLN*

$'(N', SL')$ is also 2NF. (3) If SLN is 3NF, then there do not exist isolated nodes (accessible from each other), that is for any two nodes n_i, $n_j \in N$ (SLN), there exists a path $n_i\ n_1\ \ldots\ n_t\ n_j$ from n_i to n_j. Then in the case of SLN', for any two nodes C_i, $C_j \in N'(SLN')$, then there exists n_i, $n_j \in N$ (SLN) and $n_i \in C_i$, $n_j \in C_j$. Then we can consider the series $S = C_i\ C_1\ \ldots\ C_t\ C_j$, where C_k is the corresponding equivalence class of n_k, which means that $n_k \in C_k$, $1 \le k \le t$. Then in the series S, (a) if any two neighboring nodes C_k, C_p in it satisfying $C_k \ne C_p$, then S is a path from C_i to C_j; (b) if there exists two neighboring nodes $C_k = C_p$ in S, then we get a new series S' in which C_k C_p is C_k. Repeating this process finite times, we can get a new series S' with the property that any two neighboring nodes in it are not equal, so S' is a path, and obviously that it is from C_i to C_j. From (a) and (b), we can get that any two nodes in $N'(SLN')$ are accessible from each other, so SLN $'(N', SL')$ is 3NF. $\square$

We have proposed a method to transform a given Semantic Link Network to a resource space. In fact, the transformation process is to construct a quotient Semantic Link Network first, then to get the corresponding resource space from the quotient Semantic Link Network. According to the construction process and the definition of the quotient semantic link network, we only need to show that the "strongly connected component" is an equivalent relation among the nodes of the Semantic Link Network.

Corollary 2.7. Let SLN (N, SL) be a Semantic Link Network, and R be the relation that "in the same strongly connected component" on N (SLN), then R is an equivalent relation on N (SLN).

Because the quotient Semantic Link Network is the abstraction of the original Semantic Link Network, the construction process shows again that the resource space is the abstraction of the Semantic Link Network, reflects the higher-level semantics.

Given a resource space RS, we have constructed a Semantic Link Network SLN (N, SL) that is semantically equivalent to it, if we view SLN (N, SL) as the underlying undirected graph, then we can study the topological properties of it. Here we always assume that RS is 2NF and its coordinates are flat.

Let the weight on each edge $-Imp_i \rightarrow$ be 1, $1 \le i \le n$, then we can define the distance and diameter of SLN as (Bollobás, 1998).

Definition 2.4. For any two nodes n_1 and n_2 in SLN (N, SL), the distance $d(n_1, n_2)$ between n_1 and n_2 is the length of the shortest path between them.

Definition 2.5. The diameter of the graph SLN (N, SL) is $D(SLN)=$ Max$\{$ $d(n_1, n_2)|$ $n_1, n_2 \in N$ $(SLN)\}$.

For any two points $p_1(x_1, x_2, ..., x_n)$ and $p_2(y_1, y_2, ..., y_n)$ in the resource space $RS(X_1, X_2, ..., X_n)$, the distance $d(p_1, p_2) = (\sum_{i=1}^{n} d_i^2(x_i, y_i))^{\frac{1}{2}}$, where d_i is the distance on axis X_i, $1 \le i \le n$ (Zhuge et al., 2005c). We can see that the distance d on RS is the Euclidian sum of d_i, and from Definition 2.4, the distance on SLN is equivalent to $d=Min\{d_i | 1 \le i \le n\}$. As the existence of the semantic links, the distance between two nodes in SLN is much smaller than in the RS. From this perspective, the SLN is more suitable for the search and location of resources. The following theorem supports this view.

Theorem 2.2. Let RS be a 3NF resource space, and SLN (N, SL) is the corresponding Semantic Link Network, then SLN is an Euler graph, and the diameter of it is 2.

Proof. Since RS is 3NF, from Corollary 2.3, the SLN is 3NF too, then any two nodes in it are accessible from each other, i.e., SLN is a connected graph. For any node n in SLN, the edges $-Imp_i \rightarrow$ and $\leftarrow Imp_i-$ are present or absent simultaneously, so the degree of n is even. Because the degree of every node in SLN is even, it is an Euler graph. Suppose the distance $d(n_1, n_2)$ between two nodes $n_1(x_1, x_2, ..., x_n)$ and $n_2(y_1, y_2, ..., y_n)$ is the biggest in SLN, then $D(SLN)= d(n_1, n_2)$. Then $x_i \neq y_i$, for $1 \le i \le n$. Else if $x_i = y_i$ for some i, then there exists edge $-Imp_i \rightarrow$ between n_1 and n_2 such that $d(n_1, n_2)=1$. Let $n_3= n_3(z_1, z_2, ..., z_n)$, satisfying $x_i \neq z_i$, for $1 \le i \le n$, then there dose not exist any semantic link between n_1 and n_3, so $d(n_1, n_3)>1= d(n_1, n_2)$, this is inconsistent with the assumption that $d(n_1, n_2)$ is the biggest. So $x_i \neq y_i$, for $1 \le i \le n$ holds and therefore $d(n_1, n_2)> 1$. Let $n_4= n_4(x_1, x_2, ..., x_{n-1}, y_n)$, from $x_1 \neq y_1$ and $x_n \neq y_n$, we can get $n_4 \neq n_1$ and $n_4 \neq n_2$. Then there exist edges $n_1-Imp_1 \rightarrow n_4$, and $n_4 -Imp_n \rightarrow n_2$, so n_1 and n_2 are linked by the path $n_1-Imp_1 \rightarrow n_3-Imp_n \rightarrow n_2$, from the definition of $d(n_1, n_2)$, we can get that $d(n_1, n_2) \le 2$. And from $d(n_1, n_2)> 1$, we have $d(n_1, n_2)=2$. So $D(SLN)= d(n_1, n_2)=2$. $\square$

Theorem 2.2 implies that the distance between any two nodes in the 3NF (corresponding to a resource space) is either 1 or 2. And from Theorem 2.2 we can get the following corollary:

Corollary 2.8. Let RS be a 3NF resource space, and SLN (N, SL) is the corresponding Semantic Link Network, then for any two nodes $n_1(x_1, x_2,$

..., x_n) and $n_2(y_1, y_2, ..., y_n)$ in *SLN*, $d(n_1, n_2)=1 \Leftrightarrow$ "there exists some *i*, $1 \leq i \leq n$, such that $x_i=y_i$". And $d(n_1, n_2)=2 \Leftrightarrow x_i \neq y_i$, for $1 \leq i \leq n$.

Then we can see that the mean distance between two nodes in *SLN* is within 1 and 2, much smaller than in the resource space *RS*, which is related to the dimension *n* and the average number of coordinates on all axes, so we can say that the Semantic Link Network is more suitable for search and location of resources than Resource Space Model. But there is one more important factor that makes the distance in the Semantic Link Network much smaller, which is that there are too much semantic links in the corresponding Semantic Link Network constructed.

2.4 Union View of Resource Space and Semantic Link Network

Integrating the Resource Space Model's classification semantics with the Semantic Link Network's link semantics supports richer semantic modeling and applications. To facilitate the cooperation between the Resource Space Model and the Semantic Link Network, we propose the Union View of the Resource Space Model and the Semantic Link Network by introducing a structure called Resource Class Hierarchy, which can be derived from the Resource Space Model. The Union View has the following three advantages:

1. Providing an efficient mapping mechanism from the Resource Space Model to the Semantic Link Network;
2. Facilitating quick and easy modeling of Semantic Link Network; and,
3. Enhancing the interoperability between Semantic Link Networks.

2.4.1 The Framework

Fig.2.6 describes the cooperation between the Resource Space Model and the Semantic Link Network for a simple teaching system. A node in this graph represents a resource or a set of resources. The dotted circles represent *resource class hierarchies*, each of which corresponds to a resource space. The rectangles in dotted circles denote the *resource classes* corresponding to a class of resources in the Resource Space Model. Both the circle and the triangle represent generic classes defined in the original Semantic Link Network. And the rounded rectangles denote the *printable classes*, the system-defined classes similar to the basic types in programming languages (Hull and King, 1987; Ullman, 1988). Using the printable classes, the atomic value of attributes can be precisely represented. The only *String* class has three duplications for clarity. The edges and edge labels in this graph are used to represent the relationships between nodes. Note that the edges without labels in the dotted circles represent the *inclusion relationships* between *resource classes*.

Fig.2.6 has two *resource class hierarchies*: *Human-Resource* and *Score-Course* derived from the corresponding resource spaces *Human-Resource* and *Score-Course* in the RSM. The resource space *Human-Resource* is used to store the information about all teachers and students. And the resource space *Score-Course* is used to manage the information about the test scores of the students.

Definition 2.6. The Union View of the Resource Space Model and the Semantic Link Network is a triple $S = (VE, RE, RCH)$, where VE is a finite set of nodes in the Union View which could include resources, generic classes, printable classes and *resource classes* derived from the Resource Space Model; RE is a finite set of triple $<v_1, v_2, re>$, where re represents the relationship between nodes v_1 and v_2 coming from VE; and, RCH is a finite set of *resource class hierarchies* each of which corresponds to a resource space in the meaning of the Resource Space Model.

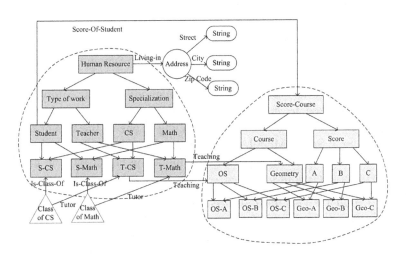

Fig.2.6. Example of incorporating Semantic Link Network with the resource space.

The Union View has the following three advantages:

(1) *The Union View provides an efficient mapping mechanism from Resource Space Model to Semantic Link Network.* The Semantic Link Network is a general-purpose semantic-rich model for the representation of resources and can provide a semantic overlay for many data models in the style of map. Since each *resource class hierarchy* corresponds to a resource space, by introducing the *resource class hierarchies* into the original Semantic Link Network, the Union View provides an efficient and effective mapping from the Resource Space Model to the Semantic Link Network. The efficiency and effectiveness of the mapping depend on the following two points:

a) The Union View of Resource Space Model and Semantic Link Network increases the granularity of the mapping from Resource Space Model to Semantic Link Network. In the original Semantic Link Network, each resource defined in the Resource Space Model has a mapping image in the Semantic Link Network. However in the Union View, a point, an axis and even a resource space in the Resource Space Model can be mapped to a node in the Semantic Link Network. Thus, many operations can be applied to a batch of resources.

b) The Union View of Resource Space Model and Semantic Link Network provides not only resource mappings but also operation mappings from the Resource Space Model to the Semantic Link Network.

(2) *The Union View of Resource Space Model and Semantic Link Network makes use of the Resource Space Model to make the Semantic Link Network modeling easier.* Many traditional methods such as entity-relation model can be used to help modeling with the Semantic Link Network (Chen, 1976). Since quick and easy modeling is one of the salient features of the Resource Space Model, the *resource class hierarchies* in the Union View make the Semantic Link Network modeling easier without conflicting with other approaches.

(3) *The Union View of the Resource Space Model and the Semantic Link Network can enhance the interoperability between Semantic Link Networks.* Semantic Link Network operations are mainly based on the structure information. The Union View has introduced some new RSM-based operations, which emphasize on not only the structure but also the semantics of Semantic Link Networks. Thus, the Union View of Resource Space Model and Semantic Link Network can enhance the interoperability between Semantic Link Networks.

2.4.2 The Core Component of Union View: Resource Class Hierarchy

We use δ to represent a resource space, an axis, a point or a coordinate of the RSM and $R(\delta)$ represents the resources that δ can contain. Let $RS(X_1, X_2, \ldots, X_n)$ be a resource space. Its axes $X_i = \{C_{i1}, C_{i2}, \ldots, C_{im}\}$ can be extended to $X_i^* = \{C_{i1}, C_{i2}, \ldots, C_{im}, \pi_i\}$, $1 \leq i \leq n$. A point taking the coordinate value π_i on the axis X_i means that the axis X_i has no restriction on that point. For example, if a student belongs to the point $(\pi_{Specialization}, 3\#, male)$ in the resource space *Spec-Apart-Gen*, then he/she may major in math, chemistry, physics or any other specialization. Meanwhile, we introduce a constant γ_i at each axis X_i that is equivalent to the union of $C_{i1}, C_{i2}, \ldots, C_{im}$ in semantics, i.e. $R(\gamma_i) = R(C_{i1}) \cup R(C_{i2}) \cup \ldots \cup R(C_{im})$. Thus, we say that γ_i is derived from $C_{i1}, C_{i2}, \ldots, C_{im}$. So $R(\gamma_i) \subseteq R(\pi_i)$ holds.

Definition 2.7. Let $RS(X_1, X_2, \ldots, X_n)$ be a resource space and X_i^*, $1 \leq i \leq n$ be its extended axes. The set of resources represented by $(\pi_1, \ldots, \pi_{i-1}, \gamma_i, \pi_{i+1}, \ldots, \pi_n)$ is defined as the *axis resource class* of axis X_i, denoted as ac_i. Axis resource class and each relation in the Cartesian product $X_1^* \times X_2^* \times \ldots \times X_n^*$ are generally called *resource classes*. Particularly, the relation $(\pi_1, \pi_2, \ldots, \pi_n)$ is called *base resource class*, denoted as $root_{RS}$.

In fact, the resource class $(C_{1,j1}, C_{2,j2}, \ldots, C_{n,jn})$ is the set of resources which simultaneously satisfies all the conditions $C_{1,j1}, C_{2,j2}, \ldots,$ and $C_{n,jn}$ on corresponding axes in the resource space. And the base resource class $(\pi_1, \pi_2, \ldots, \pi_n)$ actually represents the whole resource space. Take the resource space *Spec-Apart-Gen* as an example, the base resource class $(\pi_{Specialization}, \pi_{Apartment}, \pi_{Gender})$ denotes all the students concerned by this resource space. Regardless the gender, the resource class $(physics, 3\#, \pi_{Gender})$ represents all the students who are major in physics and live in 3# apartment.

For any two resource classes $c = (C_{1,j1}, C_{2,j2}, \ldots, C_{n,jn})$ and $c' = (C_{1,j1}', C_{2,j2}', \ldots, C_{n,jn}')$ in a resource space, if $R(C_{1,j1}) \subseteq R(C_{1,j1}')$, $R(C_{2,j2}) \subseteq R(C_{2,j2}')$, $\ldots$, $R(C_{n,jn}) \subseteq R(C_{n,jn}')$ hold respectively, then the resource class c is called the subclass of the resource class c' and the resource class c' is called the superclass of the resource class c. And this inclusion relationship is denoted as $c \subseteq_c c'$.

The inclusion relationship existing between c and c' is a particular case of the subtype relationship defined in (Zhuge, 2003). Since the inclusion relationship exists only between resource classes in the *resource class hierarchy*, for the sake of representation simplicity we also name the inclusion relationship as the internal relationship and any other relationships as external relationships.

Theorem 2.3. Let $RS(X_1, X_2, \ldots, X_n)$ be a resource space and X_i^* ($1 \le i \le n$) be its extended axes. Any axis resource class ac_i of axis X_i is one of the subclasses of the base resource class $root_{RS}$ of RS. And the axis resource class ac_i is one of the super-classes of any of the resource classes ($x_1, \ldots, x_{i-1}, x_i, x_{i+1}\ldots, x_n$), where x_j belongs to X_j^* ($1 \le j \le i-1$ or $i+1 \le j \le n$) and x_i belongs to X_i.

Proof. (1) For the axis resource class $ac_i = (\pi_1, \ldots, \pi_{i-1}, \gamma_i, \pi_{i+1}, \ldots, \pi_n)$ and the base resource class $root_{RS} = (\pi_1, \pi_2, \ldots, \pi_n)$, we have $R(\pi_1) \subseteq R(\pi_1), \ldots, R(\pi_{i-1}) \subseteq R(\pi_{i-1}), R(\gamma_i) \subseteq R(\pi_i), R(\pi_{i+1}) \subseteq R(\pi_{i+1}), \ldots R(\pi_n) \subseteq R(\pi_n)$ hold respectively. So the axis resource class ac_i is one of the subclasses of the base resource class $root_{RS}$. (2) For any resource class $c = (x_1, \ldots, x_{i-1}, x_i, x_{i+1}\ldots, x_n)$ in RS where x_j belongs to X_j^* ($1 \le j \le i-1$ or $i+1 \le j \le n$) and x_i belongs to X_i. It is obvious that c is one of the subclasses of the *resource class* $c' = (\pi_1, \ldots, \pi_{i-1}, x_i, \pi_{i+1}\ldots, \pi_n)$. According to the definition of γ_i, we have $R(x_i) \subseteq R(\gamma_i)$. Thus c' is one of the subclass of ac_i. So the axis resource class ac_i is one of the superclasses of the resource class ($x_1, \ldots, x_{i-1}, x_i, x_{i+1}\ldots, x_n$). $\square$

Theorem 2.3 indicates that the introduction of axis resource classes will not break the inclusion relationships in the *resource class hierarchy* of a certain resource space. The resource class set of the resource class hierarchy is defined as follows:

Definition 2.8. Let $RS(X_1, X_2, \ldots, X_n)$ be a resource space and X_i^*($1 \le i \le n$) be its extended axes. The set $CS = X_1^* \times X_2^* \times \ldots \times X_n^* \cup \{(\pi_1, \ldots, \pi_{i-1}, \gamma_i, \pi_{i+1}, \ldots, \pi_n) \mid 1 \le i \le n\}$ is called the *resource class set* of RS.

In the *resource class hierarchy* of a given resource space, only the inclusion relationships between resource classes are concerned. The inclusion relationship is reflexive, asymmetric and transitive, and it supports multi-inheritance. Thus, the *resource class hierarchy* of a given resource space can be viewed as a directed graph consisting of its resource class set and these inclusion relationships. In a directed graph, $\Gamma(v_1, v_2, \ldots, v_n)$ will be used to denote one path from v_1 to v_n. The *resource class hierarchy* of a given resource space can be defined as follows:

Definition 2.9. Let $RS(X_1, X_2, \ldots, X_n)$ be a resource space. The *resource class hierarchy* of RS is defined as the directed graph $RSG(CS, E)$, where
1. CS is the resource class set of RS;
2.   For any resource classes $c_1, c_2 \in CS$, if $<c_1, c_2> \in E$, then $c_2 \subseteq_c c_1$ holds;

3. For any resource classes c_1, $c_2 \in CS$, if $c_2 \subseteq_c c_1$ holds, then there exists at least one path $\Gamma(c_1, c_{j1}, c_{j2}, \ldots, c_{jm}, c_2)$.

The second condition in definition 2.9 is used to guarantee that **RSG**(*CS*, *E*) can only include the valid inclusion relationships in **RS**. And the third condition implies that all inclusion relationships in **RS** should be implicitly included in **RSG**(*CS*, *E*). Fig.2.7 is the illustration of a flat resource space and a part of its resource class hierarchy.

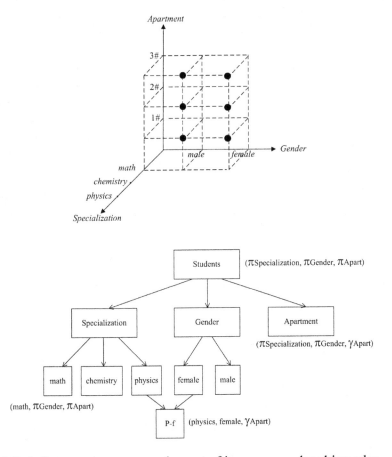

Fig.2.7. A flat resource space and a part of its resource class hierarchy.

2.4.3 Operations on Resource Class Hierarchy

The Resource Space Model's Join, Disjoin, Merge and Split operations can also be applied to the Resource Class Hierarchy. The following theorem defines the Join operation on resource class hierarchies of resource spaces:

Theorem 2.4. Let $RS_1(X_1, \ldots, X_t, X_{t+1}, \ldots, X_m)$ and $RS_2(X_{t+1}, \ldots, X_m, X_{m+1}, \ldots, X_n)$ be two resource spaces that can be joined together to form the resource space $RS(X_1, \ldots, X_t, X_{t+1}, \ldots, X_m, X_{m+1}, \ldots, X_n)$. Assume that $RSG_1(CS_1, E_1)$ and $RSG_2(CS_2, E_2)$ are the resource class hierarchies of RS_1 and RS_2 respectively. We construct the directed graph $RSG(CS, E)$ such that:

(1) $CS = X_1^* \times X_2^* \times \ldots \times X_n^* \cup \{(\pi_1, \ldots, \pi_{i-1}, \gamma_i, \pi_{i+1}, \ldots, \pi_n) \mid 1 \le i \le n\}$;

(2) For any two classes $c = (C_1, \ldots, C_t, C_{t+1}, \ldots, C_m, C_{m+1}, \ldots, C_n)$ and $c' = (C_1', \ldots, C_t', C_{t+1}', \ldots, C_m', C_{m+1}', \ldots, C_n')$ in CS, $<c, c'> \in E$ holds if and only if both $<(C_1, \ldots, C_t, C_{t+1}, \ldots, C_m), (C_1', \ldots, C_t', C_{t+1}', \ldots, C_m')> \in E_1$ and $<(C_{t+1}, \ldots, C_m, C_{m+1}, \ldots, C_n), (C_{t+1}', \ldots, C_m', C_{m+1}', \ldots, C_n')> \in E_2$ hold.

Then, the directed graph $RSG(CS, E)$ is the resource class hierarchy of resource space RS.

Proof. According to the definition 2.8, it is obvious that CS is the resource class set of resource space RS. We will prove that E satisfies the last two conditions mentioned in definition 2.9.

(1) For any two resource classes $c = (C_1, \ldots, C_t, C_{t+1}, \ldots, C_m, C_{m+1}, \ldots, C_n)$ and $c' = (C_1', \ldots, C_t', C_{t+1}', \ldots, C_m', C_{m+1}', \ldots, C_n')$ in CS, if $<c, c'> \in E$ holds, then $<(C_1, \ldots, C_t, C_{t+1}, \ldots, C_m), (C_1', \ldots, C_t', C_{t+1}', \ldots, C_m')> \in E_1$ and $< (C_{t+1}, \ldots, C_m, C_{m+1}, \ldots, C_n), (C_{t+1}', \ldots, C_m', C_{m+1}', \ldots, C_n')> \in E_2$ hold. Since $RSG_1(CS_1, E_1)$ and $RSG_2(CS_2, E_2)$ are the resource class hierarchies of RS_1 and RS_2 respectively, $R(C_1) \subseteq R(C_1')$, $R(C_2) \subseteq R(C_2')$, ..., $R(C_n) \subseteq R(C_n')$ hold. So $c \subseteq_c c'$ holds.

(2) For any two resource classes $c = (C_1, \ldots, C_t, C_{t+1}, \ldots, C_m, C_{m+1}, \ldots, C_n)$ and $c' = (C_1', \ldots, C_t', C_{t+1}', \ldots, C_m', C_{m+1}', \ldots, C_n')$ in CS, if $c' \subseteq_c c$ holds, we can prove that there exists one path from c to c' in $RSG(CS, E)$. Clearly, both $(C_1, \ldots, C_t, C_{t+1}, \ldots, C_m) \subseteq_c (C_1', \ldots, C_t', C_{t+1}', \ldots, C_m')$ and $(C_{t+1}, \ldots, C_m, C_{m+1}, \ldots, C_n) \subseteq_c (C_{t+1}', \ldots, C_m', C_{m+1}', \ldots, C_n')$ hold. Let x_i $(t+1 \le i \le m)$ be a coordinate from the axis X_i $(t+1 \le i \le m)$. And this coordinate satisfies: $R(C_i') \subseteq R(x_i) \subseteq R(C_i)$ and there does not exist a coordinate x_i' such that both $R(x_i) \subseteq R(x_i') \subseteq R(C_i)$ and $x_i \ne x_i'$ hold. Thus, both $<(C_1, \ldots, C_t, C_{t+1}, \ldots, C_m), (C_1, \ldots, C_t, x_{t+1}, \ldots, x_m)> \in E_1$ and $<(C_{t+1}, \ldots, C_m, C_{m+1}, \ldots, C_n), (x_{t+1}, \ldots, x_m, C_{m+1}, \ldots, C_n)> \in E_2$ hold. So $<c, (C_1, \ldots, C_t, x_{t+1}, \ldots,$

x_m, C_{m+1}, ..., C_n)> $\in E$ holds. By analogy, through limited steps we can construct one path from c to c' in $RSG(CS, E)$.

According to 1) and 2), we can conclude that the directed graph $RSG(CS, E)$ is the resource class hierarchy of resource space RS. $\Box$

According to theorem 2.4, the resource class hierarchy of resource space RS deriving from the Join operation of resource spaces RS_1 and RS_2 can be easily constructed.

The Disjoin operation on the resource class hierarchy of a given resource space complies with the following theorem.

Theorem 2.5. Let $RS_1(X_1, ..., X_t, X_{t+1}, ..., X_m)$ and $RS_2(X_{t+1}, ..., X_m, X_{m+1}, ..., X_n)$ be two resource spaces which derive from the Disjoin operation on the resource space $RS(X_1, ..., X_t, X_{t+1}, ..., X_m, X_{m+1}, ..., X_n)$. Assume that $RSG(CS, E)$ is the resource class hierarchy of RS. We construct the directed graph $RSG_1(CS_1, E_1)$ such that:
(1) $CS_1 = X_1^* \times X_2^* \times ... \times X_m^* \cup \{(\pi_1, ..., \pi_{i-1}, \gamma_i, \pi_{i+1}, ..., \pi_m) \mid 1 \le i \le m\}$;
(2) For any two resource classes $c = (C_1, ..., C_t, C_{t+1}, ..., C_m)$ and $c' = (C_1', ..., C_t', C_{t+1}', ..., C_m')$ in CS_1, $<c, c'> \in E_1$ holds if and only if there exists at least a pair of resource classes $(C_1, ..., C_t, C_{t+1}, ..., C_m, C_{m+1}, ..., C_n)$ and $(C_1', ..., C_t', C_{t+1}', ..., C_m', C_{m+1}', ..., C_n')$ in $RSG(CS, E)$ such that $<(C_1, ..., C_t, C_{t+1}, ..., C_m, C_{m+1}, ..., C_n), (C_1', ..., C_t', C_{t+1}', ..., C_m', C_{m+1}', ..., C_n')> \in E$ holds.
    Then, the directed graph $RSG_1(CS_1, E_1)$ is the resource class hierarchy of resource space RS_1.

Proof. We prove that $RSG_1(CS_1, E_1)$ satisfies the three conditions as the resource class hierarchy of resource space RS_1 as follows:
(1) According to the definition of the resource class set of a given resource space, it is obvious that CS_1 is the resource class set of resource space RS_1.
(2) For any two resource classes $c = (C_1, ..., C_t, C_{t+1}, ..., C_m)$ and $c' = (C_1', ..., C_t', C_{t+1}', ..., C_m')$ in CS_1, if $<c, c'> \in E_1$ holds, then there exists one pair of resource classes $(C_1, ..., C_t, C_{t+1}, ..., C_m, C_{m+1}, ..., C_n)$ and $(C_1', ..., C_t', C_{t+1}', ..., C_m', C_{m+1}', ..., C_n')$ in $RSG(CS, E)$ such that $<(C_1, ..., C_t, C_{t+1}, ..., C_m, C_{m+1}, ..., C_n), (C_1', ..., C_t', C_{t+1}', ..., C_m', C_{m+1}', ..., C_n')> \in E$ holds. Thus, $R(C_1) \subseteq R(C_1')$, $R(C_2) \subseteq R(C_2')$, ..., $R(C_m) \subseteq R(C_m')$ hold. It is obvious that $c \subseteq_c c'$ holds.
(3) Suppose that two resource classes $c_1 = (C_1, ..., C_t, C_{t+1}, ..., C_m)$ and $c_1' = (C_1', ..., C_t', C_{t+1}', ..., C_m')$ in CS_1 satisfy $c_1 \subseteq_c c_1'$. There exist two resource classes c and c' in CS such that they have common coordinates on X_1, X_2, ..., and X_m with c_1 and c_1' respectively and $c \subseteq_c c'$ holds. So there

must exist one path $\Gamma(c, v_1, v_2, ..., v_p, c')$ connecting c with c' in $\boldsymbol{RSG}(CS, E)$. For any v_i $(1 \leq i \leq p)$, there must exist a class v_i' in CS_1 such that v_i' has common coordinates on $\boldsymbol{X}_1, \boldsymbol{X}_2, ..., \boldsymbol{X}_m$ with v_i. Thus, there must exist the path $\Gamma(c_1, v_1', v_2', ..., v_p', c_1')$ connecting c_1 with c_1' in $\boldsymbol{RSG}_1(CS_1, E_1)$.

According to 1), 2) and 3), we have: the directed graph $\boldsymbol{RSG}_1(CS_1, E_1)$ is the resource class hierarchy of resource space $\boldsymbol{RS}_1$. $\square$

Theorem 2.5 provides a method to obtain the resource class hierarchy of a resource space deriving from the Disjoin operation on another resource space.

The following theorem defines the Merge operation on resource class hierarchies of resource spaces:

Theorem 2.6. Let $\boldsymbol{RS}_1(\boldsymbol{X}_1, \boldsymbol{X}_2, ..., \boldsymbol{X}_m, \boldsymbol{X'})$ and $\boldsymbol{RS}_2(\boldsymbol{X}_1, \boldsymbol{X}_2, ..., \boldsymbol{X}_m, \boldsymbol{X''})$ be two resource spaces that can be merged into a resource space $\boldsymbol{RS}(\boldsymbol{X}_1, \boldsymbol{X}_2, ..., \boldsymbol{X}_m, \boldsymbol{X})$ by merging $\boldsymbol{X'}$ and $\boldsymbol{X''}$ into $\boldsymbol{X}$. Assume that $\boldsymbol{RSG}_1(CS_1, E_1)$ and $\boldsymbol{RSG}_2(CS_2, E_2)$ are the resource class hierarchies of $\boldsymbol{RS}_1$ and $\boldsymbol{RS}_2$ respectively and that ac, ac' and ac'' are the axis resource classes corresponding to axes $\boldsymbol{X}$, $\boldsymbol{X'}$ and $\boldsymbol{X''}$ respectively. We construct the directed graph $\boldsymbol{RSG}(CS, E)$ that satisfies:

1. $CS = CS_1 \cup CS_2 \cup \{ac\} - \{ac', ac''\}$; and,
2. $E = E_1 \cup E_2 \cup \{<ac, c> \mid <ac', c> \in E_1$ or $<ac'', c> \in E_2\} \cup \{<c, ac> \mid <c, ac'> \in E_1$ or $<c, ac''> \in E_2\} - \{<ac', c> \mid <ac', c> \in E_1\} - \{<ac'', c> \mid <ac', c> \in E_2\}$.

If $\boldsymbol{RS}$ is in 2NF, then the directed graph $\boldsymbol{RSG}(CS, E)$ is the resource class hierarchy of resource space $\boldsymbol{RS}$.

Proof. Let CS^* be the resource class set of $\boldsymbol{RS}$.

(1) Assume that the resource class $c = (\boldsymbol{C}_{1,i1}, \boldsymbol{C}_{2,i2}, ..., \boldsymbol{C}_{m,im}, \boldsymbol{C}) \in CS$ holds. If c equals to either ac or the base resource class of $\boldsymbol{RS}$, then $c \in CS^*$ holds. Otherwise, either $c \in CS_1$ or $c \in CS_2$ holds. Thus the coordinate $\boldsymbol{C}$ is on either $\boldsymbol{X'}$ or $\boldsymbol{X''}$. So we conclude that the coordinate also belongs to $\boldsymbol{X}$. It is obvious that $c \in CS^*$. So $CS \subseteq CS^*$ holds. For any resource class $c = (\boldsymbol{C}_{1,i1}, \boldsymbol{C}_{2,i2}, ..., \boldsymbol{C}_{m,im}, \boldsymbol{C}) \in CS^*$, If c is equal to either ac or the base resource class of $\boldsymbol{RS}$, then $c \in CS$ holds. Otherwise, the coordinate $\boldsymbol{C}$ must be on $\boldsymbol{X}$. Thus the coordinate $\boldsymbol{C}$ is on either $\boldsymbol{X'}$ or $\boldsymbol{X''}$. So either $c \in CS_1$ or $c \in CS_2$ holds. It is obvious that $c \in CS$. So $CS^* \subseteq CS$ holds. Thus, we have $CS = CS^*$ holds. So CS is the resource class set of $\boldsymbol{RS}$.

(2) It is easy to prove that for any $<c, c'> \in E$, $c \subseteq_c c'$ holds. For any two resource classes c and c' in $\boldsymbol{RS}$ that satisfy $c \subseteq_c c'$, we will prove that there

exists one path from c' to c in $\textbf{RSG}(CS, E)$ (here excludes the case where c is equal to c'): (a) Firstly, we suppose that $c \in \textbf{CS}_1$ holds. If c' is equal to ac, then we can conclude that $c \subseteq_c ac'$ holds. So there must exist one path $\Gamma(ac', v_1, v_2, ..., v_p, c)$ from ac' to c in $\textbf{RSG}_1(CS_1, E_1)$. Thus, the path $\Gamma(ac, v_1, v_2, ..., v_p, c)$ must exist in $\textbf{RSG}(CS, E)$. If c' is not equal to ac, $c' \in CS_1$ must hold. Otherwise, the $\textbf{RS}$ arising from the merge of $\textbf{RS}_1$ and $\textbf{RS}_2$ cannot be in 2NF. So there must exist a path $\Gamma(c', v_1, v_2, ..., v_p, c)$ from c' to c in $\textbf{RSG}_1(CS_1, E_1)$. There must exist a path Γ' from c' to c in $\textbf{RSG}(CS, E)$ which is obtained by replacing ac' with ac in $\Gamma(c', v_1, v_2, ..., v_p, c)$. (b) Similarly, we can draw the same conclusion when $c' \in CS_1$ holds.

According to 1) and 2), we can conclude that the directed graph $\textbf{RSG}(CS, E)$ is the resource class hierarchy of resource space $\textbf{RS}$. $\square$

The Split operation on the resource class hierarchy of a given resource space complies with the following theorem.

Theorem 2.7. Let $\textbf{RS}_1(X_1, X_2, ..., X_m, X')$ and $\textbf{RS}_2(X_1, X_2, ..., X_m, X'')$ be two resource spaces deriving from the Split operation on the resource space $\textbf{RS}(X_1, X_2, ..., X_m, X)$ in 2NF. Assume that $\textbf{RSG}(CS, E)$ is the resource class hierarchy of $\textbf{RS}$ and that ac, ac' and ac'' are the axis resource classes of axes X, X' and X'' respectively. We construct the directed graph $\textbf{RSG}_1(CS_1, E_1)$ satisfying:

1. $CS_1 = X_1^* \times X_2^* \times ... \times X_m^* \times X'^* \cup \{(\pi_1, ..., \pi_{i-1}, \gamma_i, \pi_{i+1}, ..., \pi_m, \pi) \mid 1 \le i \le m\} \cup ac'$; and,
2. $E_1 = \{<c, c'> \mid c \in CS_1 \wedge c' \in CS_1 \wedge <c, c'> \in E\} \cup \{<ac', c> \mid c \in CS_1 \wedge <ac, c> \in E\} \cup \{<c, ac'> \mid c \in CS_1 \wedge <c, ac> \in E\}$.

Then, the directed graph $\textbf{RSG}_1(CS_1, E_1)$ is the resource class hierarchy of resource space $\textbf{RS}_1$.

2.4.4 Operations on the Union View of Resource Space and Semantic Link Network

The Union View of resource space and Semantic Link Network not only maps resource spaces into resource class hierarchies but also inherits all operations of the RSM. The informal description of the four RSM-based operations on the Union View is as follows:

Join: Assume that $\textbf{RSG}_1(CS_1, E_1)$ and $\textbf{RSG}_2(CS_2, E_2)$ are two resource class hierarchies which correspond to the resource spaces $\textbf{RS}_1(X_1, ..., X_t, X_{t+1}, ..., X_m)$ and $\textbf{RS}_2(X_{t+1}, ..., X_m, X_{m+1}, ..., X_n)$ respectively. And $\textbf{RSG}(CS, E)$ is derived from the Join operation on $\textbf{RSG}_1(CS_1, E_1)$ and $\textbf{RSG}_2(CS_2, E_2)$ with axes $X_{t+1}, ..., X_m$ as described in theorem 2.4. For any resource class $c_1 = (C_1, ..., C_t, C_{t+1}, ..., C_m)$ in $RSG_1(CS_1, E_1)$, there must exist the corresponding resource class $c = (C_1, ..., C_t, C_{t+1}, ..., C_m, \pi_{m+1}, ..., \pi_n)$ in $RSG(CS, E)$ according to the definition of resource class hierarchy. Then, any external relationships starting from or ending at c_1 should be transferred to c.

Disjoin: Assume that $RSG(CS, E)$ is a resource class hierarchy corresponding to the resource space $RS(X_1, ..., X_t, X_{t+1}, ..., X_m, X_{m+1}, ..., X_n)$. $RSG_1(CS_1, E_1)$ and $RSG_2(CS_2, E_2)$ are derived from the Disjoin operation on $RSG(CS, E)$ with axes $X_{t+1}, ..., X_m$ as described in theorem 2.5. For any resource class $c = (C_1, ..., C_t, C_{t+1}, ..., C_m, \pi_{m+1}, ..., \pi_n)$ in $RSG(CS, E)$, there must exist corresponding resource class $c_1 = (C_1, ..., C_t, C_{t+1}, ..., C_m)$ in $RSG_1(CS, E)$ according to the definition of resource class hierarchy. Then, any external relationships starting from or ending at c should be transferred to c_1. Any resource class $c' = (C_1, ..., C_t, C_{t+1}, ..., C_m, C_{m+1}, ..., C_n)$ in $RSG(CS, E)$ satisfies: there at least exits one i ($m+1 \leq i \leq n$) such that $C_i \neq \pi_i$, if there exists any external relationship starting from or ending at c', then insert c' and all external relationships starting from or ending at c' into the destination SLN and insert the subtype relationship between c' and the resource class $(C_1, ..., C_t, C_{t+1}, ..., C_m, \pi_{m+1}, ..., \pi_n)$.

Merge: Assume that $RSG_1(CS_1, E_1)$ and $RSG_2(CS_2, E_2)$ are two resource class hierarchies corresponding to the resource spaces $RS_1(X_1, X_2, ..., X_m, X')$ and $RS_2(X_1, X_2, ..., X_m, X'')$ respectively. And $RSG(CS, E)$ is derived from the Merge operation on $RSG_1(CS_1, E_1)$ and $RSG_2(CS_2, E_2)$ by merging X' and X'' into X as described in theorem 2.6. Let ac, ac' and ac'' be the axis resource classes corresponding to axes X, X' and X'' respectively. For any resource class $c_1 = (C_1, C_2, ..., C_m, C')$ in $RSG_1(CS_1, E_1)$, if c_1 is not equal to ac', then we can find the resource class $c = (C_1, C_2, ..., C_m, C')$ in $RSG(CS, E)$. Any external relationships starting from or ending at c_1 should be transferred to c. If c_1 is equal to ac', then any external relationships starting from or ending at c_1 should be transferred to each of the immediate successors of ac in $RSG(CS, E)$.

Split: Assume that $RSG(CS, E)$ is one resource class hierarchy corresponding to the resource space $RS_1(X_1, X_2, ..., X_m, X)$. $RSG_1(CS_1, E_1)$ and $RSG_2(CS_2, E_2)$ are derived from the Split operation on $RSG(CS, E)$ by splitting X into X' and X'' as described in theorem 2.7. Let ac, ac' and ac'' be the axis resource classes corresponding to axes X, X' and X'' respectively. For any resource class $c = (C_1, C_2, ..., C_m, C)$ in $RSG(CS, E)$, if c is not equal to ac, then we can find the resource class $c' = (C_1, C_2, ..., C_m, C)$ in $RSG_1(CS_1, E_1)$ or $RSG_2(CS_2, E_2)$. Any external relationships starting from or ending at c should be transferred to c'. If c is equal to ac, then any external relationships starting from or ending at c should be transferred to both ac' and ac''.

The following theorems indicate that the RSM-based operations keep some SLN normal forms.

Theorem 2.8. Both the Join operation and the Merge operation of the Resource Space Model keep 1NF-SLN, 2NF-SLN and 3NF-SLN of the original Semantic Link Network.

Neither the disjoin operation nor the split operation increase semantic-equivalent nodes and links, so they keep 1NF and 2NF. But they may break accessibility, so they do not keep 3NF.

Theorem 2.9. Both disjoin operation and split operation of the Resourcce Space Model keep 1NF-SLN and 2NF-SLN of the original Semantic Link Networks.

2.5 Discussion and Summary

A data cube is a type of multidimensional matrix that lets users explore and analyze a collection of data from many perspectives (Agrawal, 1996; Gray, 1996). Data is usually organized in cube form. Cooperation with other tools in statistics or analysis, the data cube can support establishing trends and analyzing performance (Graefe, 1993).

The following are three major differences between data cube and the Resource Space Model:

1. The data cube is used to establish trends and analyze performance, while the Resource Space Model is to specify and manage resources by orthogonal classification semantics;
2. The data in a data cube has already been processed and aggregated into cube form, thus data cube is a read-only data model, while the Resource Space Model can deal with dynamic data; and,
3. A lot of calculations for view in data cube will be completed before hand, while the operations in the Resource Space Model are real-time.

A data warehouse is a specifically structured copy of transaction data for query and analysis (Inmon, 2002). The data in a data warehouse is usually organized by certain multidimensional data model. Cooperation with OLAP and data mining, data warehouse can provide decision support for enterprise management.

The main differences between data warehouse and the Resource Space Model are:

1. A data warehouse is mainly used to support decision-making, so it attaches more importance to historical, summarized and consolidated data (Kimball, 1996). In contrast, the Resource Space Model focuses mainly on online resource operation.
2. Data warehouses are usually not updatable. Since data warehouses are usually used to store historical data for query and analysis, data in data warehouses are read-only. While, the Resource Space Model, targeted at Internet applications, can be frequently operated.
3. The application scope of the Resource Space Model is broader than that of data warehouse. The application scope of a data warehouse is usually confined within a certain enterprise, while the Resource Space Model can uniformly specify and manage versatile resources on the whole network.

The comparison in table 2.1 shows that the integration of the Resource Space Model and the Semantic Link Network reserves the advantages of both models.

Table 2.1 A brief comparison.

Features	RSM	SLN	RSM+ SLN	Data Cube	RDBM
Semantics	Classification semantics	Link semantics	Classification semantics + Link semantics	Classification + Aggregation	Functional dependence
Normal Form	Yes	Yes	Yes	No	Yes
Integrity	Yes	Yes	Yes	No	Yes
Reasoning ability	No	Strong	Strong	No	middle
Search	Space locating	Relation search	Locating + Relation search	Space locating	Key-based search

The Resource Space Model and the Semantic Link Network reflect classification semantics and link semantics respectively. They can be transformed to each other under certain conditions. The integration of the two models can form a single semantic image to support semantic-based resource location. The operations on the union view can keep the normal forms. Further, the integration of the two models can construct a semantic overlay integrating the normalization and autonomy.

Chapter 3 Expressiveness of Query Languages for Resource Space Model

A great variety of query languages can be designed for operating resource spaces. But how many operations are complete or necessary? How to define "complete" or "necessary" formally? This chapter answers these questions by investigating the theoretical basis for determining how complete a selection capability is provided in a proposed resource sublanguage independently of any host language. The results are very useful to the design and analysis of the operating languages of the Resource Space Model.

3.1 The Problem

A number of operations on resource spaces such as Join, Disjoin, Merge and Split have been defined (Zhuge, 2004a). The principles in the design of a Resource Operation Language (ROL) of the Resource Space Model have been proposed (Zhuge, 2004d). The Resource Operation Language provides a uniform interface for programmers or application systems to operate the Resource Space Model through programs. The completeness of query operations on resource spaces is discussed in (Zhuge and Yao, 2006), where a set of complete operations and a set of necessary operations are also defined.

A relational algebra and a relational calculus are defined in the relational data model. The relational algebra is a collection of operations on relations, and a query language could be directly based on it. There are eight operations defined in the relational algebra, they are extended Cartesian product, traditional set operations (union, intersection and difference), projection, join, division and selection (Codd, 1970). The relational calculus is an applied predicate calculus which may also be used in the formulation of queries on any database consisting of a finite collection of relations in a simple normal form. A data sublanguage (called ALPHA), founded directly on the relational calculus, has been informally described in (Codd, 1971b). The equivalence of relational algebra and relational calculus is proved in (Codd, 1971b; Ullman, 1982). An algebra or calculus is relationally complete if, given any finite collection of relations R_1, R_2, ..., R_N in simple normal form, the expressions of the algebra or calculus permit definition of any relation definable from R_1, R_2, ..., R_N by alpha expressions (Codd, 1972). A relational database language SQL (Structured Query Language) based on the relational algebra and calculus is proposed by Boyce and Chamberlin (ANSI SQL, 1986; Boyce et al., 1975; Chamberlin and Boyce, 1974; Chamberlin et al., 1976).

A great variety of languages could be designed for querying and updating resource spaces. This chapter investigates a theoretical basis which may be used to determine how complete a selection capability is provided in a proposed resource sublanguage independently of any host language in which the sublanguage may be embedded. We especially concern: *when are the defined operations sufficient for use and how many operations are necessary?*

3.2 Completeness of Query Languages on Resource Spaces

Completeness is a rather mathematical concept. In mathematics, it is commonly the closeness of a set under operations on the set. For example, the rational number field is complete under the operations addition, subtraction, multiplication and division. And we can also define the completeness of operations, for example on the rational number field, operations addition, subtraction, multiplication and division are complete but operations addition and subtraction are incomplete. It is because operations addition and subtraction can only get a subset of the rational number field, but not the whole field. If we regard the queries of the Resource Space Model as operations on resource spaces, then the completeness of query languages on resource spaces can be viewed as the completeness of operations as above. First we give an example in the traditional set theory.

3.2.1 Basic Idea

Given two sets A and B, if we only consider the set operations between them, then how many operations are sufficient for use? Experience tells us that three operations—union, intersection and difference are complete. But what is the reason? Can we define other operations in addition to the three operations?

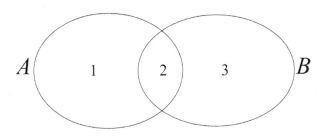

Fig.3.1. An example of set operations.

As shown in Fig.3.1, in general, A and B are divided into three parts according to the distribution of their elements (here we do not consider the simpler cases where some of the three parts are empty). Part 1 consists of elements which are in A but not in B. Part 2 consists of elements which are both in A and B. Part 3 consists of elements which are in B but not in A. If the empty set $\varnothing$ is also considered as a required result, then there are in all $2^3=8$ required sets, which are: {$\varnothing$, Part 1, Part 2, Part 3, Part 1 and Part 2, Part 1 and Part 3, Part 2 and Part 3, Part 1 and Part 2 and Part 3}, which actually are: {$\varnothing$, $A-B$, $A\cap B$, $B-A$, A, $A\oplus B$, B, $A\cup B$}, where $\oplus$ is always called symmetric difference (Robert, 1979). We can see that the operations set {$\cup$, $\cap$, $-$, $\oplus$} are sufficient, because from A and B, these operations can get all the required results. Among these four operations, only $\cup$ and $-$ are necessary, because $\cap$ and $\oplus$ can be represented by them, we can see it from: $A\cap B = A - (A-B)$, and $A\oplus B = (A-B)\cup (B-A)$.

This inspires us to explore the theoretical basis for the design and analysis of the resource space's query languages. An operation set is called sufficient when it can get all the required results, and an operation set is called necessary only when it is the smallest sufficient operation set.

3.2.2 Definition of Completeness of Query Operations

First, we need to make clear the definition of query operations on resource spaces. Because the operands are resource spaces and the results of operations are also resource spaces, we can view the query operations as the mappings on resource spaces. Suppose S is the discussed domain, an operation *op* on S is a mapping *op*: $S \times ... \times S \rightarrow S$, *op* $(s_1, ... , s_n) = s$, where s and $s_1, ... , s_n$ belong to S. When $n=1$, *op* is called unary operation like Disjoin and Split; when $n=2$, *op* is called binary operation like Join and Merge (Zhuge, 2004b). Here we only consider the unary and binary operations.

Then, how to define the completeness of operations on resource spaces? In applications, the number of resource spaces considered is finite, so for any given finite resource spaces, if an operation set can get all the possible query results on them, then the operation set is complete. Then we need to know what all the possible query results are of any given finite resource spaces.

For query in resource spaces, we only consider the information in single spaces or the correlations between many spaces. For a single resource space, the smallest unit is a coordinate of one point. So for any given finite collection of resource spaces RS_1, RS_2, ..., RS_N in simple normal form, we can get that all the possible query results are in the form of $\{RS(x_1, ... , x_d)|$ $x_k \in RS_i(X_j)$, $1 \leq i \leq N$, $d \geq 1$ and $1 \leq k \leq d\}$, i.e., all the combinations of the coordinates of the resource spaces. So we can give the following definition:

Definition 3.1 An operation set OP on resource spaces is called complete, if: for any given finite collection of resource spaces RS_1, RS_2, ..., RS_N in simple normal form, OP can get all the resource spaces in the form of: $\{RS(x_1, ... , x_d)| x_k \in RS_i (X_j)$, $1 \leq i \leq N$, $d \geq 1$ and $1 \leq k \leq d\}$.

As discussed above, in a complete operation set, some operations can be represented by other operations, so they are not necessary, then the following definition can be given:

Definition 3.2 An operation set OP on resource spaces is called necessary, if it is complete and there does not exist a real subset of it which is also complete.

Since the definition of the completeness of operations is given, then we need to discuss the design and verification of a complete set of operations.

3.3 Complete set of Operations

In addition to existing operations, we first define several new operations. Then the completeness of the defined set of operations is verified, and we want to answer the question like: how many new operations can we define in addition to existing operations?

3.3.1 Design of Query Operations

The operations Join, Disjoin, Merge and Split, have been defined in (Zhuge, 2004a) as follows:

Operation 3.1 *Join* — Let $|RS|$ be the number of the dimensions of RS. If two resource spaces RS_1 and RS_2 store the same type of resources and have n ($n \geq 1$) common axes, then they can be joined together as one resource space RS such that RS_1 and RS_2 share these n common axes and $|RS|=|RS_1| + |RS_2| - n$. RS is called the join of RS_1 and RS_2, denoted as $RS_1 \cdot RS_2 \Rightarrow RS$.

According to the above definition, all the resources in the result resource space RS come from RS_1 and RS_2 and they can be classified by more axes. Join operation provides an approach to refining classification of resources.

Operation 3.2 *Disjoin* — A resource space RS can be disjoined into two resource spaces RS_1 and RS_2 that store the same type of resources as that of RS such that they have n ($1 \leq n \leq \min(|RS_1|, |RS_2|)$) common axes and $|RS| - n$ different axes, and $|RS| = |RS_1| + |RS_2| - n$ (denoted as $RS \Rightarrow RS_1 \cdot RS_2$). The Disjoin operation can clarify the classification of resources by separating a resource space with large number of axes into two smaller ones. Both Join and Disjoin operations keep 1NF, 2NF and 3NF of the Resource Space Model.

Operation 3.3 *Merge* — If two resource spaces RS_1 and RS_2 store the same type of resources and satisfy: (1) $| RS_1|=| RS_2|=n$; and (2) they have $n-1$ common axes, and there exist two different axes X' and X'' satisfying the merge condition, then they can be merged into one RS by retaining the $n-1$ common axes and adding a new axis $X^*=X' \cup X''$. RS is called the merge of RS_1 and RS_2, denoted as $RS_1 \cup RS_2 \Rightarrow RS$, and $|RS|= n$.

Operation 3.4 *Split* — A resource space RS can be split into two resource spaces RS_1 and RS_2 that store the same type of resources as RS and have $|RS| - 1$ common axes by splitting an axis X into two: X' and X'', such that $X=X' \cup X''$. This split operation is denoted as $RS \Rightarrow RS_1 \cup RS_2$.

By the split operation, the unconcerned coordinates on a certain axis can be filtered out and only the interested coordinates are preserved.

It is obvious that we can also define the set operations of the Resource Space Model, including operations like Union, Difference and Intersection. These operations are not the same with the traditional set operations. They should also satisfy more conditions. Suppose two resource spaces RS_1 and RS_2 have the same number of dimensions, and the corresponding axes are in the same domain ontology. Then, we can define the operations Union, Difference and Intersection as follows:

Operation 3.5 *Union* — The union of two resource spaces $RS_1(X_{11}, \ldots, X_{1n})$ and $RS_2(X_{21}, \ldots, X_{2n})$ is: $RS_1 \cup RS_2 = \{ (x_1, \ldots, x_n) | (x_1, \ldots, x_n) \in RS_1$ or $(x_1, \ldots, x_n) \in RS_2 \}$. The result is also a resource space with n axes, which consists of the points in RS_1 or RS_2.

Operation 3.6 *Difference* — The difference of two resource spaces $RS_1(X_{11}, \ldots, X_{1n})$ and $RS_2(X_{21}, \ldots, X_{2n})$ is: $RS_1 - RS_2 = \{ (x_1, \ldots, x_n) | (x_1, \ldots, x_n) \in RS_1$ and $(x_1, \ldots, x_n) \notin RS_2 \}$. The result is also a resource space with n axes, which consists of the points in RS_1 but not in RS_2.

Operation 3.7 *Intersection* — The intersection of two resource spaces $RS_1(X_{11}, \ldots, X_{1n})$ and $RS_2(X_{21}, \ldots, X_{2n})$ is: $RS_1 \cap RS_2 = \{ (x_1, \ldots, x_n) | (x_1, \ldots, x_n) \in RS_1$ and $(x_1, \ldots, x_n) \in RS_2 \}$. The result is also a resource space with n axes, which consists of the points both in RS_1 and RS_2.

In addition to these operations, we can also define two operations Extended Cartesian Product and Selection as follows:

Operation 3.8 *Extended Cartesian Product* — The extended Cartesian Product of two resource spaces $RS_1(X_{11}, \ldots, X_{1n})$ and $RS_2(X_{21}, \ldots, X_{2m})$ is a resource space with $n + m$ axes. The first n axes are the axes of RS_1 and the following m axes are axes of RS_2. If RS_1 has k_1 points and RS_2 has k_2 points, then the Extended Cartesian Product of RS_1 and RS_2 has $k_1 \times k_2$ points, we denote it as $RS_1 \times RS_2 = \{(x_{11}, \ldots, x_{1n}, x_{21}, \ldots, x_{2m}) | (x_{11}, \ldots, x_{1n}) \in RS_1$ and $(x_{21}, \ldots, x_{2m}) \in RS_2 \}$.

Operation 3.9 *Selection* — The selection is also called Restriction. It is for selecting the points satisfying the given conditions in the resource space RS, denoted as $\sigma_F(RS) = \{t \mid t \in RS$ and $F(t) = \text{'true'}\}$, where F represents the selecting conditions, it is a logic expression, it has binary value 'true' or 'false'. The logic expression F is composed of the logic operators $\neg, \wedge, \vee$ connecting every arithmetic expression. In fact the operation 'selection' is to select the points that make the logic expression F be true from the resource space RS.

It is clear that different users will also design new operations on different purposes and we cannot list all of them. Then, we will discuss the verification of the completeness of operations and prove that the nine operations defined above are a complete operation set for query on resource spaces.

3.3.2 Verification of Completeness of Operations

Before we verify the completeness of operations, two definitions about operations should be given first. Given two operations op_1 and op_2 on resource spaces, suppose op_1 is unary and op_2 is binary, we use $op_1 (RS_1)$ to represent the result of RS_1 under operation op_1, $RS_1 op_2 RS_2$ to represent the result of RS_1 and RS_2 under operation op_2.

Definition 3.3 Two unary operations op_1 and op_2 on resource spaces are called equivalent to each other if for any resource space RS, $op_1 (RS) = op_2 (RS)$. Two binary operations op_1 and op_2 on resource spaces are called equivalent to each other if for any resource spaces RS_1 and RS_2, $RS_1 op_1 RS_2 = RS_1 op_2 RS_2$.

For example, if we define a binary operation '*' as: $*: RS_1 * RS_2 = RS_1 \cap (RS_1 \cap RS_2)$, then '*' is equivalent to the operation '$\cap$', denoted as $* = \cap$. If two operations are equivalent to each other, they are the same from the perspective of mapping, so they are the same operation. We define the equivalence of operations is to show that the operations elaborately designed by users may be the same with existing operations in essence.

As we can see, the operation '*' is composed of operation '$\cap$', then we can say that operation '*' can be represented by operation '$\cap$'. Then we have the following definition.

Definition 3.4 Suppose OP is an operation set on resource spaces, an unary (or binary) operation op is called can be represented by OP, if op (RS) (or $RS_1 op RS_2$) can be represented as an expression of OP.

For example, we have $RS_1 \cap RS_2 = RS_1 - (RS_1 - RS_2)$, so operation '$\cap$' can be represented by operation '-'. Equivalence and representation are the two basic relations between operations discussed in this paper.

Because we cannot give all possible operations, the completeness of operations can only be proven in theory and cannot be proven by giving examples. But the incompleteness of operations can be proven by giving examples. So we give an example to show that operations set {Union, Difference, Intersection} is not complete. For example, suppose the resource spaces considered are $\{RS_1(X_1, X_2), RS_2(X_1, Y_2)\}$, then it is clear that space $RS_3(X_1, X_2, Y_2)$ is in the required results. But from $\{RS_1(X_1, X_2), RS_2(X_1, Y_2)\}$, the operations {Union, Difference, Intersection} cannot get the space $RS_3(X_1, X_2, Y_2)$. It is because the precondition of these traditional set operations is that the operated spaces have the same dimensions, and the result spaces also have the same dimension. So from two 2-

dimensional spaces we cannot get a 3-dimensional space. Then, it is clear that operations set {Union, Difference, Intersection} is not complete.

Then we will prove that the nine operations defined above are complete for query on resource spaces.

Theorem 3.1. The nine operations Union, Difference, Intersection, Extended Cartesian Product, Selection, Join, Disjoin, Merge and Split are complete for query in resource spaces.

Proof. According to definition 3.1, an operation set OP on resource spaces is complete if: for any given finite collection of resource spaces RS_1, RS_2, ..., RS_N in simple normal form, and OP can get all the resource spaces in the form of: $\{RS(x_1, \dots ,x_d)|\ x_k \in RS_i\ (X_j),\ 1 \leq i \leq N,\ d \geq 1$ and $1 \leq k \leq d\ \}$. So, we only need to show that the nine operations can get the result spaces as above.

We use mathematical induction to prove this. When $N=1$, for a single resource space $RS_1(x_1, \dots ,x_d)$, we can use the unary operation Selection to get the spaces in the form of $\{RS(x_1, \dots , x_n)|\ (x_1, \dots , x_n) \in RS_1\}$, then use the unary operation Disjoin to select any axes we need, then we can get the spaces in the following form $\{RS(x_1, \dots , x_d)|\ x_k \in RS_1\ (X_j)\ ,\ 1 \leq j \leq$ n and $1 \leq k \leq d\ \}$, which means that when $N=1$ the conclusion holds. Suppose when $N=m$ the conclusion holds, i.e., the nine operations can get all the result spaces in the form of $\{RS(x_1, \dots , x_d)|\ x_k \in RS_1\ (X_j)\ ,\ 1 \leq j \leq$ n and $1 \leq k \leq$ $d\ \}$, next we will show that when $N=m+1$ the conclusion also holds. Now we divide these $m+1$ resource spaces into two parts: $RS_1, RS_2, \dots, RS_m$ and RS_{m+1}, for the preceding m spaces, from the assumption we can get that the nine operations can get the result spaces in the following form: $\{RS(x_1, \dots , x_d)|\ x_k \in RS_i\ (X_j),\ 1 \leq i \leq m,\ d \geq 1$ and $1 \leq k \leq d\ \}$; for the resource space RS_{m+1}, as the above using operations Selection and Disjoin we can get: $\{RS(x_1, \dots , x_d)|\ x_k \in RS_{m+1}\ (X_j)\ ,\ 1 \leq j \leq$ n and $1 \leq k \leq d\ \}$. For these two spaces, using the set operations Union, Difference, Intersection and operation Extended Cartesian Product we can get the correlations between them: $\{RS(x_1, \dots , x_d)|\ x_k \in RS_i\ (X_j),\ 1 \leq i \leq m+1,\ d \geq 1$ and $1 \leq k \leq d\ \}$. So when $N=m+1$ the conclusion also holds. Then we can get for any given finite collection of resource spaces $RS_1, RS_2, \dots, RS_N$ in simple normal form, the nine operations can get all the resource spaces in the form of: $\{RS(x_1, \dots ,x_d)|\ x_k \in RS_i(X_j),$ $1 \leq i \leq N,\ d \geq 1$ and $1 \leq k \leq d\}$. So, the nine operations Union, Difference, Intersection, Extended Cartesian Product, Selection, Join, Disjoin, Merge and Split are complete for query in resource spaces. □

From the above proof process we can see that, in fact the operation set {Union, Difference, Extended Cartesian Product, Selection, Disjoin} is already complete and the other four operations can all be represented by it. Then are these five operations necessary? The answer is yes. We only need to show that any of these five operations cannot be represented by the other operations. For this negative conclusion, we only need to give a counter-example. Then we will give an example to show that operation Extended Cartesian Product cannot be represented by operations {Union, Difference, Selection, Disjoin}. Suppose RS is a 2-dimensional resource space, then $RS \times RS$ is a 4-dimensional resource space. But the operations {Union, Difference, Selection, Disjoin} can only maintain or decrease the dimensionality of resource spaces, so from the 2-dimensional resource space RS, the four operations cannot get a resource space whose dimensionality is larger than 2. So space $RS \times RS$ cannot be got from RS under operations {Union, Difference, Selection, Disjoin}, which means that operation Extended Cartesian Product cannot be represented by operations {Union, Difference, Selection, Disjoin}. Then we can get the following corollary.

Corollary 3.1. The five operations Union, Difference, Extended Cartesian Product, Selection and Disjoin are complete and necessary for query in resource spaces.

In theory, the definition of a complete and necessary operation set is enough, it is indeed from the perspective of expressiveness of query languages. But in applications, some new operations which can be represented by existing operations will also be defined, for the convenience of expression or operation. For example, from the Join operation, we can naturally introduce another useful operation: Division. And we can define another operation Projection from the operation Disjoin. Then how many new operations we can define in addition to the existing operations? The answer is infinite. The following example will show this.

Example 3.1 There exist infinite different operations. According to definition 3, we only need to show that there exist infinite operations which are not equivalent to each other. We define a sequence of operations $\{\Theta_1, \Theta_2, \Theta_3, \dots\}$ as follows:

Θ_1: $rs_1 \Theta_1 rs_2 = (rs_1 \cup rs_2) \times (rs_1 \cap rs_2)$,

Θ_2: $rs_1 \Theta_2 rs_2 = (rs_1 \Theta_1 rs_2) \Theta_1 (rs_1 \Theta_1 rs_2)$,

......

Θ_{i+1}: $rs_1 \Theta_{i+1} rs_2 = (rs_1 \Theta_i rs_2) \Theta_1 (rs_1 \Theta_i rs_2)$,

......

From the definition, we have:

$$\text{rs}_1 \; \Theta_2 \; \text{rs}_2 = (\text{rs}_1 \; \Theta_1 \; \text{rs}_2) \; \Theta_1 \; (\text{rs}_1 \; \Theta_1 \; \text{rs}_2)$$
$$= ((\text{rs}_1 \cup \text{rs}_2) \times (\text{rs}_1 \cap \text{rs}_2)) \; \Theta_1 \; ((\text{rs}_1 \cup \text{rs}_2) \times (\text{rs}_1 \cap \text{rs}_2))$$
$$= (((\text{rs}_1 \cup \text{rs}_2) \times (\text{rs}_1 \cap \text{rs}_2)) \cup ((\text{rs}_1 \cup \text{rs}_2) \times (\text{rs}_1 \cap \text{rs}_2))) \times$$
$$\quad (((\text{rs}_1 \cup \text{rs}_2) \times (\text{rs}_1 \cap \text{rs}_2)) \cap ((\text{rs}_1 \cup \text{rs}_2) \times (\text{rs}_1 \cap \text{rs}_2)))$$
$$= ((\text{rs}_1 \cup \text{rs}_2) \times (\text{rs}_1 \cap \text{rs}_2)) \times ((\text{rs}_1 \cup \text{rs}_2) \times (\text{rs}_1 \cap \text{rs}_2))$$
$$= (\text{rs}_1 \; \Theta_1 \; \text{rs}_2) \times (\text{rs}_1 \; \Theta_1 \; \text{rs}_2).$$

So we can see that $\Theta_2 = \Theta_1 \times \Theta_1$. And, we conjecture that $\Theta_i = \Theta_{i-1} \times \Theta_{i-1}$ for any $i \geq 2$.

$$\text{rs}_1 \; \Theta_i \; \text{rs}_2 = (\text{rs}_1 \; \Theta_{i-1} \; \text{rs}_2) \; \Theta_1 \; (\text{rs}_1 \; \Theta_{i-1} \; \text{rs}_2)$$
$$= ((\text{rs}_1 \; \Theta_{i-1} \; \text{rs}_2) \cup (\text{rs}_1 \; \Theta_{i-1} \; \text{rs}_2)) \times ((\text{rs}_1 \; \Theta_{i-1} \; \text{rs}_2) \cap (\text{rs}_1 \; \Theta_{i-1} \; \text{rs}_2))$$
$$= (\text{rs}_1 \; \Theta_{i-1} \; \text{rs}_2) \times (\text{rs}_1 \; \Theta_{i-1} \; \text{rs}_2).$$

So we have $\Theta_i = \Theta_{i-1} \times \Theta_{i-1}$ for any $i \geq 2$. Then, it is clear that operations $\{\Theta_1, \Theta_2, \Theta_3, \ldots\}$ are not equivalent to each other, so they are infinite and different operations.

This example tells that finding a "self-contained" operation set regardless of its applications is impractical.

After the study of the completeness of operations, we will discuss the expressiveness of query languages, and the emphasis is on the comparison between expressiveness of different query languages and the characteristics of expressiveness.

3.4 Expressiveness of Query Languages

The expressiveness of query languages is an abstract concept, it is difficult to be defined or depicted accurately. Here we have not defined the expressiveness of operations directly, we just study the comparison between expressiveness and some characteristics of it. For example, we want to answer questions like: given two operation languages, whose expressiveness is stronger? Or for two given operations P and Q, whose expressiveness is stronger?

3.4.1 Comparison between Expressiveness

Given two operations op_1 and op_2 on two resource spaces RS_1 and RS_2, suppose op_1 is unary and op_2 is binary. We use $op_1 (RS_1)$ to represent the result of RS_1 under operation $\boldsymbol{op_1}$, and use RS_1 $\boldsymbol{op_2}RS_2$ to represent the result of RS_1 and RS_2 under operation $\boldsymbol{op_2}$. Then, all the resource spaces we can get from the set $\{RS_1, RS_2\}$ under the set $\{$ $\boldsymbol{op_1}$, $\boldsymbol{op_2}\}$ can be listed as follows: $\{\boldsymbol{op_1}$ (RS_1), $\boldsymbol{op_1}(RS_2)$, $RS_1\boldsymbol{op_2}RS_2$, $\boldsymbol{op_1}$ $(\boldsymbol{op_1}(RS_1))$, $\boldsymbol{op_1}$ $(\boldsymbol{op_1}(RS_2))$, $\boldsymbol{op_1}(RS_1$ $\boldsymbol{op_2}$ $RS_2)$, ...$\}$. Then, a definition can be given as follows:

Definition 3.5 Given a set of resource spaces RSS and a set of operations OP on the resource spaces, we define RSS^{OP} as all the resource spaces that can be got from RSS under a sequence of operations in OP.

In general cases, when RSS and OP are both finite, RSS^{OP} is also finite. For example, for $RSS=\{RS_1, RS_2\}$, if $OP_s=\{\cup, \cap\}$, then $RSS^{OPs}=\{RS_1, RS_2, RS_1\cup RS_2, RS_1\cap RS_2\}$; if $OP_t=\{\cup\}$, then $RSS^{OPt}=\{RS_1, RS_2, RS_1\cup RS_2\}$. This example is very simple, but in many cases, it is not easy to compute RSS^{OP} given RSS and OP. For example, for $RSS =\{RS_1, RS_2\}$ and $OP=\{-\}$, one may think that $RSS^{OP} =\{RS_1\text{-}RS_2, RS_2\text{-}RS_1\}$. But in fact, $RS_1\text{-} RS_1=\varnothing$, $RS_1\text{-} \varnothing =RS_1$, $RS_2\text{-}\varnothing =RS_2$ and $RS_1\text{-} (RS_1\text{-} RS_2)= RS_1\cap RS_2$, now the generated spaces are $\{\varnothing, RS_1 , RS_2, RS_1\text{-}RS_2, RS_2\text{-}RS_1, RS_1\cap RS_2\}$. Are there more spaces that can be generated? The answer is no, because the results of these six spaces under the operation '-' are also included by themselves, for example, $RS_1\text{-} (RS_1\cap RS_2)=RS_1\text{-} RS_2$. So in fact now $RSS^{OP} =\{\varnothing, RS_1, RS_2, RS_1\text{-}RS_2, RS_2\text{-}RS_1, RS_1\cap RS_2\}$.

Intuitively, given any set of resource spaces RSS, if operation set OP_s can get more results than OP_t, i.e., $RSS^{OPs} \supset RSS^{OPt}$, then we can say that the expressiveness of OP_s is stronger than OP_t. So a definition can be given as follows:

Definition 3.6 Given two operation sets OP_s and OP_t on resource spaces, the expressiveness of OP_s is stronger (weaker) than OP_t, denoted by $OP_s>OP_t$ $(OP_s<OP_t)$, if for any given set of resource spaces RSS, $RSS^{OPs}\supset RSS^{OPt}$ $(RSS^{OPs}\subset RSS^{OPt})$ holds.

Here the "more results" does not mean the whole quantity of data in the result spaces, but the number of different spaces in the result spaces. For example, for $RSS =\{ RS_1 , RS_2\}$, $OP_s=\{\cup, \cap\}$ and $OP_t=\{\cup\}$, we have $RSS^{OPs} =\{RS_1, RS_2, RS_1\cup RS_2, RS_1\cap RS_2\}$ and $RSS^{OPt} =\{RS_1, RS_2, RS_1\cup RS_2\}$. The whole quantities of data are all of the resources included in space $RS_1\cup RS_2$, but the operation set OP_s gets one more result $RS_1\cap RS_2$, so we say that the expressiveness of OP_s is much stronger than OP_t.

3.4.2 Some Characteristics of Expressiveness

Some characteristics of expressiveness of operations are given as follows.

Characteristic 3.1 Given two operation sets OP_s and OP_t, it is possible that neither $OP_s > OP_t$ nor $OP_s < OP_t$ holds.

For example, for $RSS=\{RS_1, RS_2\}$, $OP_s=\{\cap\}$ and $OP_t=\{\cup\}$, we have $RSS^{OPs} =\{RS_1, RS_2, RS_1 \cap RS_2\}$ and $RSS^{OPt} =\{RS_1, RS_2, RS_1 \cup RS_2\}$. So $RSS^{OPs} \not\subset RSS^{OPt}$ and $RSS^{OPt} \not\subset RSS^{OPs}$, then both $OP_s > OP_t$ and $OP_s < OP_t$ do not hold, i.e., we cannot say which one is stronger than the other in expressiveness.

Characteristic 3.2 Given two different operation sets $\{OP_s\}$ and $\{OP_t\}$, the expressiveness of them can be the same.

For example, for $RSS=\{RS_1 , RS_2\}$, $OP_s=\{\cup, -\}$ and $OP_t=\{\cup, -, \cap\}$, we have $RSS^{OPs} =\{\emptyset, RS_1- RS_2, RS_1 \cap RS_2, RS_2- RS_1, RS_1, RS_1 \oplus RS_2, RS_2, RS_1 \cup RS_2\}=RSS^{OPt}$, so the expressiveness of them are the same.

Characteristic 3.3 Given two operation sets OP_s and OP_t, if $OP_s \supset OP_t$ then $OP_s > OP_t$.

Characteristic 3.4 If $OP_s > OP_t$ and $OP_r > OP_s$, then $OP_r > OP_t$.

Characteristic 3.5 Given an operation set OP_s, if OP is equivalent to or can be represented by some operations in OP_s, then $OP_s > OP$.

Characteristic 3.6 If $OP_s > OP_t$, then $(OP_s \cup OP_t)=OP_s$.

Characteristic 3.6 tells that if newly defined operations can be represented by existing operations, then the expressiveness of operations does not increase in essence.

3.5 Comparison and Analysis

Section 1.7 has made a comparion between the Resource Space Model and the Relational Data Model. Several differences influence the design of a query language. Relational data tend to have a regular structure, which allows the descriptive meta-data to be stored in a separate catalog. Resources in resource space, in contrast, are usually heterogeneous. Resource spaces often contain many levels of nested elements, whereas relational data are "flat." Relational data are usually "dense" (every column has a value). Resource spaces, in contrast, are often "sparse". So, the relational query languages are not suitable for querying resource spaces.

The Resource Space Model needs a resource-using mechanism to provide not only an operational browser for end users but also a programming environment for high-level developers (Zhuge, 2004d). It provides a set of specific programming language — Resource Operation Language ROL, and also provides a running platform for this language to be used for querying and operating resource spaces. The ROL could be embedded in other high-level programming languages supporting the call from other languages. In contrast, the SQL provides a programming language for relational database application systems to operate relational tables.

The ROL could be a programming environment. It adopts the SQL's SELECT-FROM-WHERE grammar. The ROL can execute the operations similar to the classic relational databases such as nesting query, aggregation and ordering the results. The ROL also borrows from the XML query language such characteristics as the management of the structured and semi-structured data, the support of abstract data types, the support of document selection and local path expression. The comparisons of the ROL with the XQL (XML Query Language) and the SQL are given in the following table.

Table 3.1 Comparisons of ROL with XQL and SQL

Feature Items	ROL	XQL	SQL
Abstract data types	Yes	No	No
SQL-like	Yes	No	Yes
Specific data model	Yes	No	Yes
Document selection	Yes	Yes	No
Partial specified path expression	Yes	Yes	No
Nested queries	Yes	No	Yes
Update language	Yes	No	Yes
Loop statement	Yes	No	Partially
Branch statement	Yes	No	Partially
Set operations	Yes	Yes	Yes
Aggregates	Partially	Partially	Yes
Join operation	Yes	No	Yes
Open operation	Yes	No	No
Support View	Yes	No	Yes
Create new elements	Yes	No	Yes
Query structure	Yes	No	No
Query content	Yes	Yes	Yes
Ordering results	Yes	No	Yes

3.6 Summary

This chapter investigates the completeness of resource space query languages. The completeness of operations is introduced to answer when the defined operations are sufficient. Several new operations are defined, and the verification of the completeness of the operations is discussed.

We conclude that:

1. {Union, Difference, Intersection, Extended Cartesian Product, Selection, Join, Disjoin, Merge and Split} is a set of complete operations for query on resource spaces; and,
2. {Union, Difference, Extended Cartesian Product, Selection and Disjoin} is a set of complete and necessary operations for query on resource spaces.

It is possible to define infinite new operations regardless of practical requirements, while the definition of a self-contained set of operations is impractical. The proposed framework can be used to compare the expressiveness of different resource sublanguages. The theoretical results are very useful in the design and analysis of resource space sublanguages, and they could be also applied to the operation theory of other data models like relational data model and XML.

Any general purpose query language of the Resource Space Model must have this completeness at least.

Chapter 4 Algebra and Calculus of the Resource Space Model

To know the query capability and make use of the potential expressive power of the Resource Space Model are essential issues. The query capability and expressive power of the Resource Space Model can be studied from two perspectives: resource space algebra and resource space calculus.

4.1 Basic Idea

The resource space algebra consists of a set of resource spaces and a set of operations of the Resource Space Model. Results of operations on resource spaces are also resource spaces. Users can use a series of operations in the resource space algebra to obtain the desired resources. The query completeness of the operations in the proposed resource space algebra has been discussed in chapter 3.

To lay the foundation of the query language for the Resource Space Model, we propose a non-procedural query style — a resource space calculus. The resource space calculus is a type of applied predicate calculus and a foundation for the declarative query language. By the alpha expressions defined in the resource space calculus, users can easily and clearly specify the desired resources.

The relational algebra and the relational calculus were proposed to depict the query capability of the relational model (Codd, 1971a; Ullman, 1982). A reduction algorithm is also proposed to transform a relation expression into a semantically equivalent expression of the relational algebra (Codd, 1972), though this reduction algorithm has a little defect (Date, 1989; Date 1992). The extended relational algebra and relational calculus with aggregate functions were discussed (Klug, 1982). Structured Query Language (SQL) has the features of both the relational algebra and the relational calculus (Boyce et al. 1975; Chamberlin and Boyce, 1976; Chamberlin et al., 1976).

A query algebra on Object-Oriented Database synthesizing relational query concepts with object-oriented databases as well as corresponding query languages were proposed (Alashqur et al., 1989; Shaw and Zdonik, 1990; Shipnan, 1981; Zaniolo, 1983). A conceptual model and its algebra and calculus have been introduced for OLAP-based applications (Gyssens and Lakshmanan, 1997).

4.2 Resource Space Algebra

Query operations on a given resource space may result in only some desirable points, but these resultant points cannot be operated further by the proposed resource space operations. To guarantee the query result to be a resource space, the following mechanism is employed. Any operation will result in a certain resource space and all undesired points in this resultant resource space will be maintained and marked as *null* points instead of being filtered out and all desired points marked as *non-null* points.

In the following discussion, $R(p)$ denotes the resources that point p can contain and $R_\Delta(p)$ denotes the resources that point p actually contains. In a resource space RS, for any *null* point p we have $R(p)=\varnothing$, $R_\Delta(p)=\varnothing$ and $p \notin RS$. For axis X_i and point p in RS, $p[X_i]$ is used to denote the projection of p on the axis X_i.

Two resource spaces $RS_1(X_1, X_2 \dots X_n)$ and $RS_2(Y_1, Y_2 \dots Y_n)$ are *union-compatible* if RS_1 and RS_2 have the same schema, i.e. $X_1=Y_1, \dots, X_n=Y_n$. Let p_1 and p_2 be two points in two union-compatible resource spaces $RS_1(X_1, X_2 \dots X_n)$ and $RS_2(X_1, X_2 \dots X_n)$ respectively. If $p_1[X_i]=p_2[X_i]$ for $1 \leq i \leq n$ holds, then we say that p_1 has the same coordinates with p_2, denoted as $p_1 =_p p_2$.

4.2.1 Definitions of Operations

All operations in this algebra fall into two categories: the traditional set operations (union, intersection, difference and Cartesian product) and the

RSM-specific operations (join, disjoin, merge, split, division, selection, and projection).

The set operations of the Resource Space Model can be defined as follows:

Union. For two union-compatible resource spaces RS_1 and RS_2, the union of RS_1 and RS_2, denoted as $RS_1 \cup RS_2$, has the same resource space schema as RS_1 and RS_2, and $RS_1 \cup RS_2 = \{p \mid (p_1 \in RS_1 \vee p_2 \in RS_2) \wedge p =_p p_1 \wedge p =_p p_2\}$. This means that p is *non-null* in RS if and only if either p_1 is *non-null* in RS_1 or p_2 is *non-null* in RS_2. For any point p in $RS_1 \cup RS_2$ and its counterparts p_1 in RS_1 and p_2 in RS_2, we have $R_\Delta(p) = R_\Delta(p_1) \cup R_\Delta(p_2)$. Fig. 4.1 is an example of union operation.

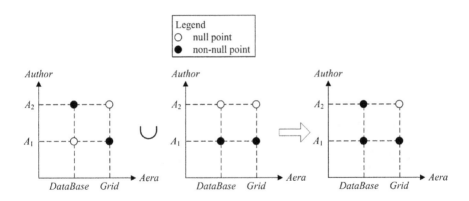

Fig. 4.1. An example of Union operation.

Intersection. For two union-compatible resource spaces RS_1 and RS_2, the intersection of RS_1 and RS_2, denoted as $RS_1 \cap RS_2$, has the same resource space schema as RS_1 and RS_2. And $RS_1 \cap RS_2 = \{p \mid p_1 \in RS_1 \wedge p_2 \in RS_2 \wedge p =_p p_1 \wedge p =_p p_2\}$. This means that p is *non-null* in RS if and only if both p_1 is *non-null* in RS_1 and p_2 is *non-null* in RS_2. For any point p in $RS_1 \cap RS_2$ and its counterparts p_1 in RS_1 and p_2 in RS_2, we have $R_\Delta(p) = R_\Delta(p_1) \cap R_\Delta(p_2)$. Fig. 4.2 is an example of the intersection operation.

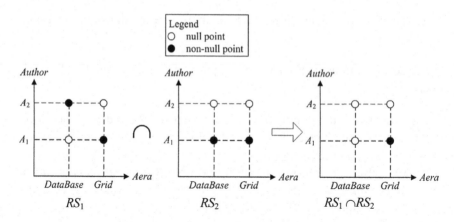

Fig. 4.2. An example of the Intersection operation.

Difference. For two union-compatible resource spaces RS_1 and RS_2, the difference of RS_1 and RS_2, denoted as RS_1-RS_2, has the same resource space schema as RS_1 and RS_2. For any point p in RS_1-RS_2, let p_1 and p_2 be two points having the same coordinates as p in RS_1 and in RS_2 respectively. Then $R_\Delta(p)=R_\Delta(p_1) - R_\Delta(p_2)$. p is *non-null* if and only if either (1) p_1 is *non-null* and p_2 is *null*, or (2) $R_\Delta(p)$ is non-null. Otherwise, p is *null*.

Cartesian product. Let $RS_1(X_1, X_2 \ldots X_n)$ and $RS_2 (Y_1, Y_2 \ldots Y_m)$ be two resource spaces that store the same type of resources. The Cartesian product of RS_1 and RS_2 is defined as $RS_1 \times RS_2 = RS(X_1, X_2 \ldots X_n, Y_1, Y_2 \ldots Y_m)$. For any point $p(x_1, x_2 \ldots x_n, y_1, y_2 \ldots y_m)$ in RS, there exist $p_1(x_1, x_2 \ldots x_n)$ and $p_2(y_1, y_2 \ldots y_m)$ in RS_1 and RS_2 respectively. Then p is *non-null* if and only if both p_1 and p_2 are *non-null*. If $n=m$, $X_i=Y_i$ $(1{\le}i{\le}n)$ and $x_j=y_j$ $(1{\le}j{\le}n)$, then $R_\Delta(p)=R_\Delta(p_1){\cup}R_\Delta(p_2)$. Otherwise, $R_\Delta(p)=R_\Delta(p_1){\cap}R_\Delta(p_2)$.

The RSM-specific operations Join, Disjoin, Merge and Split have been defined in (Zhuge, 2004a). The following definitions are given from the view of resources.

Join. Let $|RS|$ be the number of the dimensions of the RS. If two resource spaces $RS_1(X_1, \ldots, X_m, Y_1, \ldots, Y_n)$ and $RS_2(Y_1, \ldots, Y_n, Z_1, \ldots,Z_k)$ store the same type of resources and have n common axes, then they can be *joined* together as one resource space $RS(X_1, \ldots, X_m, Y_1, \ldots, Y_n, Z_1, \ldots,Z_k)$ such that RS_1 and RS_2 share these n common axes and $|RS|=|RS_1| + |RS_2| - n$. For any point $p(x_1, \ldots, x_m, y_1, \ldots, y_n, z_1, \ldots,z_k)$ in RS, p is *non-null* if and only if both point $p_1(x_1, \ldots, x_m, y_1, \ldots, y_n)$ in RS_1 and point $p_2(y_1, \ldots, y_n, z_1, \ldots,z_k)$ in RS_2 are *non-null*. If RS_1 and RS_2 are union-compatible, then

$R_\Delta(p)=R_\Delta(p_1)\cup R_\Delta(p_2)$. Otherwise, $R_\Delta(p) = R_\Delta(p_1)\cap R_\Delta(p_2)$. *RS* is called the join of RS_1 and RS_2, denoted as $RS_1 \cdot RS_2 \Rightarrow RS$.

According to the above definition, all the resources in the new resource space *RS* come from RS_1 and RS_2 and can be classified by $X_1, \ldots, X_m, Y_1, \ldots, Y_n, Z_1, \ldots, Z_k$. The Join operation provides an efficient method to refine classification of resources.

Disjoin. A resource space $RS(X_1, \ldots, X_m, Y_1, \ldots, Y_n, Z_1, \ldots, Z_k)$ can be *disjoined* into two resource spaces $RS_1(X_1, \ldots, X_m, Y_1, \ldots, Y_n)$ and $RS_2(Y_1, \ldots, Y_n, Z_1, \ldots, Z_k)$ that store the same type of resources as that of *RS* such that they have n ($1 \le n \le \min(|RS_1|, |RS_2|)$) common axes and $|RS| - n$ different axes, and $|RS|=|RS_1| + |RS_2| - n$. For any point p_1 in RS_1, there exists a set P of points in *RS*, each element of which has the same projections on $X_1, \ldots, X_m, Y_1, \ldots, Y_n$ as p_1. Then p_1 is *non-null* if and only if there exists at least one *non-null* point in P. $R_\Delta(p_1)=\cup R_\Delta(p)$ for any $p \in P$. RS_1 and RS_2 are called disjoin of *RS*, denoted as $RS \Rightarrow RS_1 \cdot RS_2$.

Different from the Join operation, the disjoin operation can clarify the classification of resources by separating large number of axes into two overlapped parts.

Based on the disjoin operation, we can naturally introduce another useful operation: *projection*. The projection of the RSM has almost the same definition as disjoin except that projection results in only one resource space which includes all the desirable axes. For resource space $RS(X_1, \ldots, X_m, X_{m+1}, \ldots, X_n)$, $\pi_{X1, \ldots, Xm}(RS)$ will be used to denote the projection of the resource space *RS* on axes $X_1, \ldots,$ and X_m. From the definition of disjoin, it is clear that the projection provides an algebraic counterpart to the existential quantifier.

Merge. If two resource spaces $RS_1(X_1, \ldots, X_{n-1}, X')$ and $RS_2(X_1, \ldots, X_{n-1}, X'')$ store the same type of resources and satisfy: 1) $|RS_1|=|RS_2|=n$; and, 2) they have $n-1$ common axes, and there exist two different axes X' and X'' satisfying the merge condition, then they can be merged into one *RS* by retaining the $n-1$ common axes and adding a new axis $X^*=X' \cup X''$. *RS* is called the merge of RS_1 and RS_2, denoted as $RS_1 \cup RS_2 \Rightarrow RS$, and $|RS|= n$. For any point p in *RS*, there exists a set P of points in RS_1 and RS_2, each element of which has the same projections on all axes as p. Then p is *non-null* if and only if there exists at least one *non-null* point in P. The formal definition is $RS_1 \cup RS_2 = \{p(X_1, \ldots, X_{n-1}, X^*) \mid p \in RS_1 \vee p \in RS_2 \wedge X^* = RS_1.X \cup RS_2.X"\}$.

It is obvious that the Union operation is the special case of the merge operation where all axes are common. The above definition can be easily extended to a more general situation where resource spaces RS_1 and RS_2 have *n-m* common axes and *m* different axes satisfying the merge condition.

Split. A resource space *RS* can be *split* into two resource spaces RS_1 and RS_2 that store the same type of resources as *RS* and have $|RS|-1$ common axes by splitting an axis *X* into two: *X'* and *X"*, such that $X = X' \cup X"$. This split operation is denoted as $RS \Rightarrow RS_1 \cup RS_2$. For any point p_1 in RS_1, there exists a point *p* in *RS*, which has the same projections on all axes as p_1. Then p_1 is *non-null* if and only if *p* is *non-null*. The formal definition is $RS_1(X_1, \ldots, X_{n-1}, X[C]) = \{p(X_1, \ldots, X_{n-1}, X^*) \mid p \in RS \wedge X^* = X[C]\}$, where $X[C]$ represents the axis *X* containing only the coordinates in coordinate set *C*.

By using the split operation, the unconcerned coordinates on a certain axis can be filtered out and only the interesting coordinates are preserved.

Selection. For a resource space *RS*, the *Selection* operation is used to select the desirable points according to the given restriction. It is denoted as $\sigma_F(RS) = \{p \mid p \in RS \wedge F(p)\}$, where *F* is a logical expression. Any point in *RS* making *F* true will be marked with *non-null* and other points will be marked with *null*. *F* has the following four forms:

1. $p_m[X_i] \; \theta \; Y$, where *Y* may be $p_n[X_j]$ or just a noun and noun phrase in domain ontology and θ represents $=, \neq, <, \leq, \geq$ or $>$. It is a type of restrictions on the projections on axes of points.
2. $p_m[X_i] \; \theta \; Y$, where *Y* is just a set of nouns or noun phrases in domain ontology and θ represents $\in$ or $\notin$.
3. $R_\Delta(p_m[X_i]) \; \theta \; R_\Delta(p_n[X_j])$, where θ represents $=, \neq, \supset, \supseteq, \not\subset, \subset$ and $\subseteq$. It is a type of restrictions on the set of resources that points contain.
4. $f_c(p_i) \; \theta \; Y$, where f_c is the function to calculate the cardinality of the given point and θ represents $=, \neq, <, \leq, \geq$ and $>$. It is a type of restrictions on the quantity of resources that points contain.

Division. Let $RS_1(X_1, \ldots, X_m, Y_1, \ldots, Y_t)$ and $RS_2(Y_1, \ldots, Y_t, Z_1, \ldots, Z_n)$ be two resource spaces. Dividing RS_1 by RS_2 (denoted as $RS_1[\div Y_1, \ldots, Y_t]RS_2$)

is a resource space $\pi_{X1, ..., Xm}(RS)$, and for any point p in $\pi_{X1, ..., Xm}(RS)$, p is *non-null* if and only if for any *non-null* point p'' in RS_2 there exists a *non-null* point p' in RS_1 such that $p[X_1, ..., X_m]=p'[X_1, ..., X_m]$ and $p''[Y_1, ..., Y_t]=p'[Y_1, ..., Y_t]$.

The division operation provides an algebraic counterpart of the Universal Quantifier. Its role is similar to the division operation in relational algebra.

4.2.2 Relationships among Operations

Given a resource space RS, the following situation often occurs: there usually exist some resource-entries (for example r) and points (for example p) in RS such that $r \in R(p)$ but $r \notin R_\Delta(p)$.

In Fig. 4.3(a), there exists a resource-entry id_1 to appear in both point p_1 and point p_2 (3NF is not satisfied in this case). So we can conclude that $r \in R(a_1)$ from $r \in R_\Delta(p_1)$ and $r \in R(b_2)$ from $r \in R_\Delta(p_2)$. So $r \in R(p_3)$ but $r \notin R_\Delta(p_3)$. An issue of this situation is that a user could not obtain the resource-entry r when users only query the point p_3.

To solve this issue, we suppose that all resource spaces satisfy the following restriction. For any resource space $RS(X_1, ..., X_n)$, any point p in RS and any resource r, $r \in R_\Delta(p)$ holds if and only if there exist n points p_1, p_2, ..., and p_n in RS such that both $r \in R_\Delta(p_i)$ and $p[X_i]=p_i[X_i]$ hold for any $1 \le i \le n$.

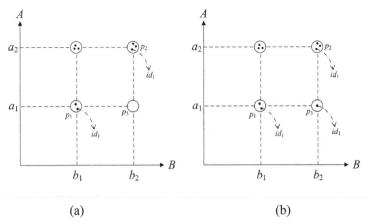

(a)   (b)

Fig. 4.3. An example of full resource space.

Theorem 4.1. For any resource space $RS(X_1, \ldots, X_n)$ satisfying the above restriction, $RS(X_1, \ldots, X_n) = (\pi_{X1}(RS) \times \pi_{X2}(RS) \times \ldots \times \pi_{Xn}(RS)) \cdot RS$ holds.

Proof. It is clear that the resource space RS and the resource space $(\pi_{X1}(RS) \times \pi_{X2}(RS) \times \ldots \times \pi_{Xn}(RS)) \cdot RS$ have the same schema. For any point p in RS and p' in $(\pi_{X1}(RS) \times \pi_{X2}(RS) \times \ldots \times \pi_{Xn}(RS)) \cdot RS$ such that $p =_p p'$, we will prove that p is non-null if and only if p' is non-null, and that $R_\Delta(p) = R_\Delta(p')$ holds. (1) If p is non-null, then there exist n non-null points $p_1, p_2, \ldots, p_n$ in $\pi_{X1}(RS)$, $\pi_{X2}(RS)$, $\ldots$, $\pi_{Xn}(RS)$ respectively such that $p[X_i] = p_i[X_i]$ hold for any $1 \le i \le n$. So there exists a non-null point p'' in $\pi_{X1}(RS) \times \pi_{X2}(RS) \times \ldots \times \pi_{Xn}(RS)$ such that $p =_p p''$. Since both p and p'' are non-null, p' is non-null point. It is obvious that if p is a null point then p' is also a null point. So p is non-null if and only if p' is non-null. (2) Since RS satisfies the given restriction, for any resource r if $r \notin R_\Delta(p)$ holds then there exists at least one axis X_i ($1 \le i \le n$) in RS such that $r \notin R_\Delta(p[X_i])$. So for resource space $\pi_{Xi}(RS)$, $r \notin R_\Delta(p[X_i])$. Since $p[X_i] = p'[X_i]$ holds, $r \notin R_\Delta(p[X_i])$ holds. Thus $r \notin R_\Delta(p')$ holds. On the other hand, if $r \in R_\Delta(p)$ holds, we can easily conclude that $r \in R_\Delta(p')$ holds. So $R_\Delta(p) = R_\Delta(p')$ holds. Thus $RS(X_1, \ldots, X_n) = (\pi_{X1}(RS) \times \pi_{X2}(RS) \times \ldots \times \pi_{Xn}(RS)) \cdot RS$ holds. □

According to theorem 4.1, for any resource space $RS(X_1, \ldots, X_n)$, the above restriction can be easily satisfied by setting RS as $(\pi_{X1}(RS) \times \pi_{X2}(RS) \times \ldots \times \pi_{Xn}(RS)) \cdot RS$.

Theorem 4.2. Let $A = X_1, \ldots, X_m$, $B = Y_1, \ldots, Y_t$ and $C = Z_1, \ldots, Z_n$. For any resource space $RS_1(A, B)$ and resource space $RS_2(B, C)$, $RS_1(A, B)[\div B]RS_2(B, C) = \pi_A(RS_1) - (\pi_A(RS_1) \cdot \pi_A(\pi_A(RS_1) \times \pi_B(RS_2) - \pi_A(RS_1) \times \pi_B(RS_2) \cdot RS_1))$ holds.

Proof. (1) Let p and p' be two points in resource spaces $RS_1(A, B)[\div B]RS_2(B, C)$ and $\pi_A(RS_1) - (\pi_A(RS_1) \cdot \pi_A(\pi_A(RS_1) \times \pi_B(RS_2) - \pi_A(RS_1) \times \pi_B(RS_2) \cdot RS_1))$ respectively. We will prove that if $p =_p p'$ holds, then p is non-null if and only if p' is non-null. Suppose that p is a null point in the resource space $RS_1(A, B)[\div B]RS_2(B, C)$. Then there exits a null point p_1 in $RS_1(A, B)$ and a non-null point p_2 in $RS_2(B, C)$ such that $p_1[A] = p[A]$ and $p_1[B] = p_2[B]$ hold. Let p_3 be the point in $\pi_A(RS_1)$ having the same coordinates as p. If p_3 is null, then it is obvious that the point p' is a null point. The following is the case that p_3 is a non-null point in $\pi_A(RS_1)$. Let p_4 be the point in $\pi_A(RS_1) \times \pi_B(RS_2)$ having the same coordinates as p_1. Since p_3 in $\pi_A(RS_1)$ and p_2 in $\pi_B(RS_2)$ are non-null points, p_4 is a non-null point. Since point p_1 is a null point in RS_1, the point p_1' in $\pi_A(RS_1) \times \pi_B(RS_2) \cdot RS_1$

satisfying $p_1 =_p p_1'$ is also a null point. Let p_5 be the point in $(\pi_A(RS_1) \cdot \pi_A(\pi_A(RS_1) \times \pi_B(RS_2) - \pi_A(RS_1) \times \pi_B(RS_2) \cdot RS_1))$ having the same coordinates as p. So p_5 is also a non-null point. Since both p_3 and p_5 are non-null point, p' is a null point. (2) In the same way, we can prove that p' is also a non-null point when p is a non-null point. □

Theorem 4.3. Merge, Difference, Cartesian product, Projection and Selection are sufficient and necessary. And other operations can be represented as follows:

1. Union is the special case of Merge;
2. $RS_1 \cap RS_2 = RS_1 - (RS_1 - RS_2)$;
3. $RS_1(X_1, ..., X_m, Y_1, ..., Y_t) \cdot RS_2(Y_1, ..., Y_t, Z_1, ..., Z_n) = \pi_{X1, ..., Xm, Y1, ..., Yt, Z1, ..., Zn}(RS_1 \times RS_2)$;
4. $RS(X_1, ..., X_{n-1}, X[C]) = \sigma_{p[X] \in C}(RS)$, where C represents a set of coordinates; and,
5. $RS_1(A, B)[\div B]RS_2(B, C) = \pi_A(RS_1) - (\pi_A(RS_1) \cdot \pi_A(\pi_A(RS_1) \times \pi_B(RS_2) - \pi_A(RS_1) \times \pi_B(RS_2) \cdot RS_1))$, where $A=X_1, ..., X_m$, $B=Y_1, ..., Y_t$ and $C=Z_1, ..., Z_n$.

Theorem 4.4. In the five basic operations (Merge, Difference, Cartesian product, Projection and Selection), Difference, Cartesian product, Projection and Selection keep 1NF (the first normal form), 2NF (the second normal form) and 3NF (the third normal form) of the Resource Space Model. Merge keeps 1NF and 2NF, but it does not keep 3NF. As a special Merge operation, Union keeps 1NF, 2NF and 3NF.

4.3 Resource Space Calculus

Having the resource space algebra, we now introduce an applied predicate calculus which can be used to construct declarative queries on any resource space system consisting of a finite set of resource spaces.

4.3.1 Definition

The resource space calculus consists of several classes of objects. They include *variables, terms, formulas* and *alpha expressions*.

The set V of *variables* is the countable sets $\{p, p_1, p_2, p_3 \ldots\}$, where each p_i stands for a point variable. A point variable p is a *free variable* if p does not occur within the scope of any quantifier ($\exists$ or $\forall$). Otherwise p is a *bound variable*.

The set T of *terms* is composed of the following six parts.

1. Any noun or noun phrase in ontology qualified to name coordinates is in T.
2. Any axis of a certain resource space, the split of an axis or the merge of two axes belong to T.
3. For any point variable p_i and its any axis X_j, $p_i[X_j]$ is a term.
4. For every point variable p_i, the set $R_\Delta(p_i[X_j])$ is a term.
5. For every point variable p_i, $f_c(p_i[X_j])$ is a term.
6. Integers not less than 0 belong to T.

The set RF of *range formulas* is defined as follows.

1. Let RS_i be a resource space and point variable $p \in V$, then $RS_i(p)$ belongs to RF (The monadic predicate $RS_i(p)$ is used to state that the point variable p has the range of resource space RS_i.)
2. If point variable p is the only point variable in a range formula, then this range formula is called a *range formula over p*. Let Δ, Γ be two range formulas over p. Then $\Delta \wedge \neg \Gamma$ belongs to RF.
3. Let Δ, $\Gamma \in RF$. For any point variable p in Δ and Γ, if all resource spaces specifying the range of p in Δ and Γ are union-compatible, then both the disjunction $\Delta \vee \Gamma$ and the conjunction $\Delta \wedge \Gamma$ are in RF.

The set F of *formulas* includes the following six types of formulas.

1. Any range formula in RF is in F.
2. *Coordinate formula* has one of the two forms (a) $p_m[X_i] \, \theta \, Y$, where Y may be $p_n[X_j]$ or just a noun and noun phrase in T and θ represents any of the relations $=, \neq, <, \leq, \geq$ and $>$; (b) $p_m[X_i] \, \theta \, Y$, where Y is a set of nouns and noun phrases in T and θ represents $\notin$ or $\in$.
3. Let θ be any of the relations $=, \neq, \supset, \supseteq, \not\subset, \subset$ and $\subseteq$. *Set formula* has the form of $R_\Delta(p_m[X_i]) \, \theta \, R_\Delta(p_n[X_j])$.
4. Let θ be any of the relations $=, \neq, <, \leq, \geq$ and $>$. *Cardinality formula* has the form of $f_c(p_i) \, \theta \, Y$, where Y may be $f_c(p_j)$ or just an integer not less than 0.
5. If Δ, $\Gamma \in F$, then the negation $\neg \Delta$, the disjunction $\Delta \vee \Gamma$ and the conjunction $\Delta \wedge \Gamma$ are in F. And,

6. Let Φ be a range formula over p. Then the quantification $(\exists\Phi)\Delta$ and $(\forall\Phi)\Delta$ are in **F**.

It is obvious that each qualifier ($\exists$ or $\forall$) in **F** must be associated with a range formula over a point variable. The expanded forms of $(\exists\Phi)\Delta$ and $(\forall\Phi)\Delta$ are as follows.

$$(\exists\Phi)\Delta = \exists p(\Phi \wedge \Delta)$$
$$(\forall\Phi)\Delta = \forall p(\neg\Phi \vee \Delta)$$

As with the relational calculus, the range of each point variable in a formula should be definitely specified (Codd, 1972). For any formula Γ in **F**, Γ is a *well-formed formula* (WFF in simple) *over p* if Γ has the form of $U_1 \wedge ... \wedge U_n \wedge V$, where

1. U_1 through U_n are range formulas over n point variables varying from one another;
2. V belongs to **F** and satisfies:
    a) The range of every free variable except p in V has been specified by a certain U_i;
    b) No rang formula occurs in V.

Then this WFF over p is denoted as $\Gamma(p)$.

Let $\Gamma(p)$ be a WFF formula over p and X_i ($1 \leq i \leq n$) be a group of axes. The *alpha expression* can be defined as follows:

1. $p(X_1, X_2, ..., X_n): \Gamma(p)$ is an alpha expression;
2. If both $p(X_1, X_2, ..., X_n): \Delta_1$ and $p(X_1, X_2, ..., X_n): \Delta_2$ are alpha expressions, then the following are alpha expressions.
    a) $p(X_1, X_2, ..., X_n): \Delta_1 \vee \Delta_2$;
    b) $p(X_1, X_2, ..., X_n): \Delta_1 \wedge \Delta_2$;
    c) $p(X_1, X_2, ..., X_n): \Delta_1 \wedge \neg\Delta_2$.

$p(X_1, X_2, ..., X_n)$ is called the target point and the logical expression following the colon is called the qualification. The semantics of the alpha expression $p(X_1, X_2, ..., X_n): \Gamma(p)$ is to construct a resource space RS consisting of axes $X_1, X_2, ...,$ and X_n where for any point p if p satisfies $\Gamma(p)$ then p is *non-null*, otherwise p is *null*.

The set **AE** is defined as the set of all alpha expressions, each of which can be used to represent a query in a certain resource space system.

4.3.2 From Resource Space Algebra to Resource Space Calculus

Each operation in the resource space algebra can be represented by a piece of alpha expression in the resource space calculus. Thus, we can draw the conclusion that the resource space calculus has at least as powerful query capability as the resource space algebra. The following is the alpha expressions corresponding to each operation in the resource space algebra.

Union. $RS_1 \cup RS_2 \Leftrightarrow \{p(X_1, X_2, ..., X_n): RS_1(p) \vee RS_2(p)\}$. This alpha expression means that each point in the new resource space of $RS_1 \cup RS_2$ is the union of the corresponding point in RS_1 and RS_2.

Intersection. $RS_1 \cap RS_2 \Leftrightarrow \{p(X_1, X_2, ..., X_n): RS_1(p) \wedge RS_2(p)\}$. This alpha expression means that each point in the new resource space of $RS_1 \cap RS_2$ is the intersection of the corresponding point in RS_1 and RS_2.

Difference. $RS_1 - RS_2 \Leftrightarrow \{p(X_1, X_2, ..., X_n): RS_1(p) \wedge \neg RS_2(p)\}$. This alpha expression means that each point in the new resource space of $RS_1 - RS_2$ is the difference operation on the corresponding point in RS_1 and RS_2.

Cartesian product. $RS_1 \times RS_2 \Leftrightarrow \{p(X_1, X_2, ..., X_n, Y_1, ... Y_m): (\exists RS_1(p_1))(\exists RS_2(p_2))(p[X_1]=p_1[X_1] \wedge ... \wedge p[X_n]=p_1[X_n] \wedge p[Y_1]=p_2[Y_1] \wedge ... \wedge p[Y_m]=p_2[Y_m])\}$. This alpha expression means that the axes of the new resource space of $RS_1 \times RS_2$ are the concatenation of the axes of RS_1 and RS_2. And each point in $RS_1 \times RS_2$ is the concatenation of the corresponding points in RS_1 and RS_2.

Join. $RS_1 \cdot RS_2 \Leftrightarrow \{p(X_1, ..., X_m, Y_1, ..., Y_n, Z_1, ..., Z_k): (\exists RS_1(p_1)) (\exists RS_2(p_2)) (p[X_1]=p_1[X_1] \wedge ... \wedge p[X_m]=p_1[X_m] \wedge p[Y_1]=p_1[Y_1]=p_2[Y_1] \wedge ... \wedge p[Y_n]=p_1[Y_1]=p_2[Y_n] \wedge p[Z_1]=p_2[Z_1] \wedge ... \wedge p[Z_k]=p_2[Z_k])\}$. This alpha expression means that the axes of the new resource space of $RS_1 \cdot RS_2$ are the union of the axes of RS_1 and RS_2. And each point in $RS_1 \times RS_2$ is the concatenation of the corresponding points in RS_1 and RS_2 without duplicate axes.

Disjoin. $RS(X_1, ..., X_t) \Leftrightarrow \{p(X_1, ..., X_t): (\exists RS(p_1))(p[X_1]=p_1[X_1] \wedge ... \wedge p[X_t]=p_1[X_t])\}$. This alpha expression means that the axes $X_1, ..., $ and X_t of the new resource space is a subset of the axes of RS. For each point p in the new resource space, p is *non-null* if and only if there exists one point p_1 in RS such that p and p_1 have the same projection on $X_1, ..., $ and X_t.

Merge. $RS(X_1, ..., X_n, X \cup Y) \Leftrightarrow \{p(X_1, ..., X_n, X \cup Y):$ $(\exists RS_1(p_1))(p[X_1]=p_1[X_1] \wedge ... \wedge p[X_n]=p_1[X_n] \wedge p[X \cup Y]=p_1[X]) \vee$ $(\exists RS_2(p_2))(p[X_1]=p_2[X_1] \wedge ... \wedge p[X_n]=p_2[X_n] \wedge p[X \cup Y]=p_2[Y])\}$. This alpha expression means that the first n axes of the new resource space are the same as RS_1 and RS_2 and the $(n+1)$th axis is the merge of the $(n+1)$th axes of RS_1 and RS_2. Each point in the new resource space is the union of the corresponding point in RS_1 and RS_2.

Split. $RS(X_1, ..., X_n, X[C]) \Leftrightarrow \{p(X_1, ..., X_n, X[C]): (\exists RS(p_1))(p[X_1]=p_1[X_1]$ $\wedge ... \wedge p[X_n]=p_1[X_n] \wedge p[X[C]]=p_1[X])\}$, herein C represents a set of coordinates. This alpha expression means that the first n axes of the new resource space are the same as RS and the coordinate set C of the $(n+1)$th axis is a subset of that of the $(n+1)$th axes of RS. Any point in the new resource space comes from RS.

Selection. $\sigma_F(RS(X_1, X_2, ..., X_n)) \Leftrightarrow \{p(X_1, X_2, ..., X_n): RS(p) \wedge (F \in \mathbf{F}) \wedge F\}$. This alpha expression means that each point in the new resource space should make F true.

Division. $RS_1(A, B)[\div B]RS_2(B, C) \Leftrightarrow \{p(A): (\forall RS_2(p_2)) (\exists RS_1(p_1)) (p[A]=p_1[A] \wedge p_2[B]=p_1[B])\}$, herein $A=X_1, ..., X_m, B=Y_1, ..., Y_t$ and $C=Z_1, ..., Z_n$. This alpha expression means that the axes of the new resource space of $RS_1(A, B)[\div B]RS_2(B, C)$ are axis list A. For any point p' in the new resource space, p' is *non-null* if and only if for any *non-null* point p'' in RS_2 there exists a *non-null* point p in RS_1 such that $p'[A]=p[A]$ and $p''[B]=p[B]$.

4.3.3 From Resource Space Calculus to Resource Space Algebra

Just as the relational calculus, the resource space calculus can be used to represent what is a query for, but it does not provide the process to answer the query. This section proposes an algorithm for converting any alpha expression in the resource space calculus to a corresponding series of operations in the resource space algebra.

For a given alpha expression $p(X_1, X_2, ..., X_n): \Delta$, where $p(X_1, X_2, ..., X_n)$ is the target point and Δ is the qualification, we use the following algorithm based on Codd's reduction algorithm to transform resource space calculus to resource space algebra (Codd, 1972).

(1) Suppose that X_1, X_2, ..., X_n come from RS_1, RS_2, ..., RS_n respectively, all of which are resource spaces in Δ. For RS_i ($1 \le i \le n$), we use RS_i^* to denote the union of all the resource spaces union-compatible with RS_i in Δ. Create a new resource space RS which is the projection of the resource space $RS_1^* \times RS_2^* \times ... \times RS_n^*$ on axes X_1, X_2, ..., and X_n. The qualification Δ is transformed into $\Delta'=RS(p) \wedge \Delta$.

(2) Since the qualification Δ' is the logical concatenation of a series of WFF over p using $\wedge$, $\vee$ and $\wedge\neg$, the qualification can be easily transformed into the disjunctive normal form. In this transformation process, any formula preceded by qualifiers ($\exists$ or $\forall$) is viewed as a whole and any logical operators in this type of formulas are not concerned. Each conjunctive clause in this disjunctive normal form is a WFF over p. For each conjunctive clause (WFF over p) $U_1 \wedge ... \wedge U_p \wedge V$ do from step (3) to step (8).

(3) In $U_1 \wedge ... \wedge U_p \wedge V$, for each U_j ($1 \le j \le p$) and the range formula U_i ($p+1 \le i \le q$) associated with each qualifier ($\exists$ or $\forall$), apply the following rewriting rules in the given order.

   (a) Substitute each rang formula $RS_k(p_k)$ over p_k by the resource space RS_k.

   (b) Substitute $\vee$ and $\wedge\neg$ by $\cup$ and $-$ respectively.

   (c) Substitute $\wedge$ by $\cap$.

   Then we can use a series of set-related operations (union, intersection and difference) to change U_j ($1 \le j \le q$) into S_j such that S_j only contains a new resource space. For example, if $U_j = RS_1(p) \vee RS_2(p)$, then $S_j = RS_1 \cup RS_2$.

(4) If there exists a S_j ($1 \le j \le p$) such that $S_j = \varnothing$, then make each point in RS *null* and jump to step (9). For each existence qualifier $\exists$, if its corresponding range formula S_j is equal to $\varnothing$, then replace the formula within the scope of this existence qualifier with Boolean constant F. For each universal qualifier $\forall$, if its corresponding range formula S_j is equal to $\varnothing$, then replace the formula within the scope of this universal qualifier with Boolean constant T.

   The replacement is based on the following two facts:

   (a)   If $S_j = \varnothing$, then $(\exists S_j)\Delta = \exists p(p \in S_j \wedge \Delta) = \exists p(F \wedge \Delta) = F$.

   (b)   If $S_j = \varnothing$, then $(\forall S_j)\Delta = \forall p(p \notin S_j \vee \Delta) = \forall p(T \vee \Delta) = T$.

(5) Transform V to its prenex disjunctive normal form V'. Assume that V' has q quantifiers ($\exists$ or $\forall$) and let each quantifier in V' be denoted as Q_j ($1 \le j \le q$) from left to right and the range formula associated with Q_j be S_{p+j}. For example, $V = \forall(RS_1(p_1))(p_1[X_i] \le '2000') \vee \exists(RS_2(p_2))$ $(p_2[X_j] \ne 'male')$ can be transformed into $V' = \forall(RS_1(p_1)) \exists(RS_2(p_2))$

$(p_1[X_i] \leq$'2000' $\vee$ $p_2[X_j] \neq$'male'). Each of the conjunctive clauses of V' will be denoted as P_i ($1 \leq i \leq n$). For each P_i ($1 \leq i \leq n$) do step (6).

(6) Construct a WFF over p, $S_1 \wedge ... \wedge S_p \wedge Q_{1+p}(S_{1+p}(p_{1+p}))...$ $Q_q(S_q(p_q))(P_i)$, for each P_i ($1 \leq i \leq n$). Without the loss of generality, we suppose that S_1 is the range formula of p. Let $Q_{1+p}(S_{1+p}(p_{1+p}))...$ $Q_q(S_q(p_q))(P_i)$ be denoted as V_i. For each $U_1 \wedge ... \wedge U_p \wedge V_i$ ($1 \leq i \leq n$), do the following steps.

(6.1) Form the defining equation $RS_i = S_1 \times ... \times S_{p+q}$.

(6.2) P_i consists of the conjunction of a series of coordinate formulas, set formulas and cardinality formulas. For resource space RS_i, execute the selection operation on the restrictions P_i: $\sigma_F(RS_i)=\{p \mid p \in RS_i \wedge P_i\}$. The result of the selection operation is denoted as RS_i'.

(7) Merge all the resource spaces RS_i' ($1 \leq i \leq n$) and the result is denoted as RS'.

(8) For any Q_j ($1 \leq j \leq q$) and the resource space S_{j+p} in its corresponding range formula, we use $RS'.X^*$ and $S_{j+p}.X^*$ to denote the sets of all axes of RS' and S_{j+p} respectively.

For j from q to 1, do the following iteration:

$$RS' = \pi_{RS'.X^* - S_{j+p}.X^*}RS' \qquad \text{if } Q_j = \exists$$
$$RS' = RS'[\div S_{j+p}.X^*]S_{j+p} \qquad \text{if } Q_j = \forall$$

After q step operations on RS', the eventual result is denoted as RS''. Then do the following transformation:

$$RS'' = S_1 \times \pi_{RS}(RS'')$$

Resource space RS'' is exactly the result resource space that one of the conjunctive clauses in step (2) desires.

(9) Merge all the resource spaces that all conjunctive clauses in step (2) produce through step (3) to step (8). The result resource space will be exactly the result resource space the original alpha expression desires.

Theorem 4.5. For any alpha expression $p(X_1, X_2, ..., X_n)$: Δ, after the above transformation any point satisfying Δ will appear in the result resource space and none of the points making Δ false will be in the result resource space.

Proof. For alpha expression $p(X_1, X_2, ..., X_n)$: Δ, we first construct RS as the target resource space according to $X_1, X_2, ...,$ and X_n. It is obvious that the desired resource space is a subset of RS. That is any point p making Δ true appears in RS. So transform Δ to $\Delta'=RS(p) \wedge \Delta$ and then the original alpha expression will be transformed into $p(X_1, X_2, ..., X_n)$: Δ'. After step

(1) and step (2) in the transformation, Δ' will be transformed into its disjunctive normal form involving m pieces of conjunctive clauses (WFFs over p).

If p satisfies Δ, we will prove that after the transformation p still exists in the result resource space. Since p makes Δ' true, there at least exists one conjunctive clause of Δ' that p satisfies. Let the conjunctive clause be $U_1 \wedge ... \wedge U_p \wedge V$. After step (3), (4) and (5) of the transformation, this conjunctive clause will become $S_1 \wedge ... \wedge S_p \wedge Q_1(S_{1+p}(p_{1+p}))...Q_q(S_{q+p}(p_{q+p}))(P_1 \vee P_2 \vee ... \vee P_n)$, where Q_j $(1 \le j \le q)$ represents qualifies ($\exists$ or $\forall$) and $Q_1(S_{1+p}(p_{1+p}))...Q_q(S_{q+p}(p_{q+p}))(P_1 \vee P_2 \vee ... \vee P_n)$ is the prenex disjunctive normal form of V. After step (6) and (7), we can get the resource space RS' corresponding to the above conjunctive clause $U_1 \wedge ... \wedge U_p \wedge V$. In step (8), we suppose that after the iteration from Q_q to Q_{j+1}, the resource space is transformed into RS'_{tmp} and the point p is still in RS'_{tmp}. Now, we will prove that after Q_j the point p still exists in the result resource space.

a) We firstly suppose that Q_j is an existence qualifier $\exists$. Since p is still in RS'_{tmp}, there at least exist one point p' in S_{p+j} such that there will exist a point p'' in RS'_{tmp} the projection of which on $RS.X^*$ is p and the projection on $S_{p+j}.X^*$ is p'. So point $p''[RS'.X^* - S_{j+p}.X^*]$ also appears in the resource space $\pi_{RS.X^* - Sj+p.X^*}RS'_{tmp}$.

b) Then we suppose that Q_j is a universal qualifier $\forall$. Since Q_j is a universal qualifier, for any point p' in S_{p+j} there will exist a point p'' in RS'_{tmp} such that the projection of p'' on $RS.X^*$ is p and the projection of p'' on $S_{p+j}.X^*$ is p'. So point $p''[RS'.X^* - S_{j+p}.X^*]$ also appears in the resource space $RS'_{tmp}[\div S_{j+p}.X^*]S_{j+p}$.

From a) and b), we can conclude that after step (8) of the transformation there at least exists one point p'' in RS'' such that the projection of p'' on $RS.X^*$ is p. So p will appear in the final result resource space RS.

Similarly, we can prove that any point making Δ false will not be in the result resource space. $\square$

The Resource Space Calculus proposed above has the following difference from the relational calculus (Codd, 1972).

1. The resource space calculus has different operational objectives with the relational calculus. The operational objectives in the resource space calculus includes resource space, axis, coordinate, point and resource-entry which represent different classification granularity of resources, while the relational calculus takes table, tuple, attribute and atomic value as the basic operational units.

2. In the relational calculus, there exists only one type of value-based comparison formulas called *join terms*. On the other hand, there exist three types of comparison formulas — *coordinate formula, cardinality formula* and *set formula*. Herein, coordinate formula and cardinality formula is value-based comparison formulas and set formula is set-based comparison formula. Richer semantics can be expressed by the resource space calculus.

3. The resource space calculus is used to express totally different semantics from the relational calculus. The classification semantics among resources can be efficiently expressed by using the Resource Space Model. As a basic element, a point in the resource space calculus is used to represent a class of resources. In the relational calculus, a tuple is used to represent just a single resource (a record).

4.3.4 Transformation from Relational Model to Resource Space

The Resource Space Model was proposed as a parallelism of the RDBM. In fact, a relational database system excluding null information can be represented by a set of resource spaces. Thus, the proposed resource space algebra and resource space calculus have at least as powerful expressiveness as the relational model. The following is the transforming process from a relational table to a resource space.

1. For each table $T(A_1, A_2, ..., A_n)$ in a given relational database system, create a resource space $RS(X_1, X_2, ..., X_n)$ by naming resource space after the table name, establishing a one-to-one relationship between the axes of the resource space and the attributes of the table (e.g., A_i corresponds to X_i), and naming each axis of this resource space after the corresponding attribute name. For each tuple $t(x_1, x_2, ..., x_n)$ in the table, insert x_i ($1 \leq i \leq n$) as a coordinate into the axis X_i if no coordinate duplication exists. And then insert a resource-entry into the point $p(x_1, x_2, ..., x_n)$ to represent the tuple $t(x_1, x_2, ..., x_n)$. If a tuple $t(x_1, x_2, ..., x_n)$ is deleted from the table, just delete the resource-entry residing in the point $p(x_1, x_2, ..., x_n)$ and leave this point and corresponding coordinates alone.

2. For each table $T(A_1, A_2, ..., A_n)$, let $A_1... A_m$ ($1 \leq m \leq n$) be the key of T. Then, the axes $X_1... X_m$ will be set as the key of RS. Thus, there do not exist any two different points $p(x_1... x_m, x_{m+1}...x_n)$ and $p'(x_1... x_m, x'_{m+1}...x'_n)$ such that both p and p' contain resource-entries simultaneously. The functional dependency in the relational database has been represented by the classification relationship in the RSM.

Since the one-to-one mapping between tables and resource spaces as well as between operations on relational table and operations on the resource space, the basic operations (Union, Difference, Cartesian Product, Selection and Project) in relational database can be easily simulated by Resource Space operations: Merge, Difference, Join, Selection and Projection (Zhuge, 2004a). Thus, any information represented by the relational model can be easily managed by the Resource Space Model.

Theorem 4.6. For any relational database system without null information, the generated resource spaces satisfy the first/second/third normal forms of the Resource Space Model.

Proof. Let $T(A_1, A_2, ..., A_n)$ be a relational table and $RS(X_1, X_2, ..., X_n)$ be the generated resource space. According to the creation process of RS, it is clear that RS satisfies the first and second normal forms. In the following, we prove that RS conforms to the third normal form. All resources (tuples) managed by RS come from the table T. For any axis X_i and any tuple t in T, there exists a coordinate on X_i such that this coordinate is the projection of t on X_i. So $t \in R(X_i)$ holds. On the other hand, $R(X_i)$ only contains the resources derived from the tuples in T. Thus, for any two axes X_i and X_j, $R(X_i)=R(X_j)$ holds. We can conclude that $X_i \perp X_j$ holds. So RS satisfies the third normal form. $\square$

4.4 Summary

The resource space algebra enables users or applications to directly and easily obtain the desired resources from the source resource spaces. The resource space calculus is a type of applied predicate calculus and provides a declarative style for describing the desired resources. The equivalence of the resource space algebra and the resource space calculus is discussed. We have shown that the Resource Space Model has at least as powerful expressive capability as the relational model by transforming relations into resource spaces. The algebra and calculus of the Resource Space Model are important part of the theory of the Resource Space Model. They are also the basis of the query language of the Resource Space Model.

Chapter 5 Searching Complexity of Resource Space Model

Given a resource space, it is important for us to know the relationship between the searching efficiency and its dimensions as well as the relationship between the searching efficiency and the coordinates at every axis. Is the dimension of a resource space the higher the better, the lower the better, or, other cases? Is the distribution of coordinates at every axis the evener the better? The answers help design, analyze and understand searching resource space.

5.1 Basic Concepts and Formulas

When a user gives a query $Q(X_1=q_1, ..., X_n=q_n)$, what is the complexity of searching the point $Q(X_1=q_1, ..., X_n=q_n)$ in resource space $RS(X_1, ..., X_n)$? The basic approach is to check the axis and coordinate for q_i ($i=1, ..., n$) one by one. Here focuses on the intrinsic complexity of searching in resource space based on comparison between names rather than any specific searching algorithms.

5.1.1 On Computation Complexity

The computation complexity studies intrinsic difficulty on the cost of computing resources (e.g., time and space) to solve problem. To study the computation complexity, first we need a computation model to illuminate which operations or steps are permissive and their cost. Turing machine and random access machine are common computing models. With common computing models, we can study the upper bound and lower bound of complexity of problems or seek the optimal algorithm (Aho et al., 1983).

The computation complexity of a problem is the function of the scale of the problem, so firstly we need to define the scale of a problem. For matrix operation, the order of matrix can be defined as the scale of problem. If the number of operations or steps needed to solve a problem is the exponential function of the scale of problem, then the problem is regarded as having the complexity of exponential time. If the number of operations needed is the polynomial function of the scale of problem, then the problem is regarded as having the complexity of polynomial time. The problems with polynomial time algorithm generally can be solved easily, and the algorithms with polynomial time complexity are regarded as good algorithms. In the theory of computation complexity, the class of problems with complexity of polynomial time is denoted as P. There are many problems for which the best algorithms known have complexity of exponential time. Such problems exist in such areas as combinatorial, graph theory and operation research, and we do not know whether there exist polynomial time algorithms for them. There is a big class of these problems in practice whose computation complexities are equivalent. If we can solve one of them in polynomial time then we can solve all of them in polynomial time. The class is called the NP-complete problem class.

For some problems, the upper bound of their complexity is the cost of the best algorithm known so far, but the lower bound can only be built by theoretical proof. To get the lower bound of complexity of a problem, we need to prove that there does not exist any algorithm whose complexity is smaller than the lower bound. It is obvious that building lower bound is much harder than building upper bound. To find the upper bound of the complexity of a given problem, we only need to study the complexity of one specific algorithm. But if we want to get the lower bound of complexity of the same problem, we must study all the algorithms which can solve this problem (this is usually impossible).

From the perspective of computation complexity, the main task of the design and analysis of algorithm is to build the upper bound (Knuth, 1997b). Suppose n is the scale of problem, the following are some common problems and the upper bounds of complexity:

1. In the worst case, the comparison-based sorting of n different elements needs $O(n \lg n)$ comparisons (Knuth, 1997c).
2. The multiplication of matrix of order n needs $O(n^{2.41})$ times multiplication operations (Robinson, 2005; Strassen, 1969; Cohn and Umans, 2003).
3. The decision of whether a number of n digits is prime needs time $O(n^{c \lg \lg \lg n})$ (Knuth, 1997b; Mairson, 1977).

The greatest lower bound and the least upper bound depict the intrinsic complexity of problem and the best solution known so far. In fact, the greatest lower bound is the best lower bound known theoretically and the least upper bound is the best solution known in the real world, i.e., the best existing algorithm. A problem's intrinsic complexity will not change with the newly discovered greatest lower bound or least upper bound. If the upper bound got from an algorithm is equal to the known greatest lower bound, then this upper bound (or lower bound) is exactly the intrinsic complexity of the problem. In this case, the algorithm is called optimal in this sense.

In the problem of sorting based on the comparison between names (suppose all of the names are different), suppose $S(n)$ (n is the scale of problem) is the number of comparisons must do at least in the worst case. By building a binary decision tree for this problem, we get a lower bound:

$$S(n) \geq \lceil \lg n! \rceil = n \lg n - \frac{n}{\ln 2} + \frac{\lg n}{2} + O(1).$$

Analyzing the algorithm Binary Insertion (suppose the number of comparisons in the worst case is $B(n)$), we get an upper bound:

$$B(n) = \sum_{k=1}^{n} \lceil \lg k \rceil = n \lceil \lg n \rceil - 2^{\lceil \lg n \rceil} + 1.$$

Combining these upper and lower bounds for $S(n)$ can reach:

$$\lim_{n \to \infty} \frac{S(n)}{n \lg n} = 1.$$

So any algorithm (including Binary Insertion) with complexity of $n \lg n$ is asymptotic optimal. But it is desirable to obtain more precise information, and from table 5.1 we can see that:

Table. 5.1 Comparison of lower bound and upper bound

$n=$	1	2	3	4	5
$\lceil \lg n! \rceil =$	0	1	3	5	7
$B(n)=$	0	1	3	5	8

When $n=5$, the lower bound given by $\lceil \lg n! \rceil$ is 7, but the upper bound given by $B(5)$ is 8, then $S(5)$ may be 7 or 8. The common algorithms we know which are asymptotic optimal, including Heap Sort, Merge Sort all give the upper bound 8 or 9. Then, how many comparisons are necessary for sorting five elements in the worst case? The answer is 7, but it is not easy to find a method which only needs 7 comparisons. This method is now called Merge Insertion due to the advantages of both Merge and Insertion. It was first proposed in (Demuth, 1956), and then generalized in (Ford and Johnson, 1959).

5.1.2 Searching Complexity and Formulas

For the type of problems whose inputs are non-deterministic (there are many cases of inputs), such as sorting and searching, generally we consider two types of complexity, the worst-case complexity and the average complexity, denoted as $W(n)$ and $A(n)$ respectively, supposing the scale of problem is n. Suppose the probability of the occurring of every element in the set is the same and the probability of a successful searching is 1, then we have the following conclusions (Baase and Gelder, 2000; Levitin, 2003):

Lemma 5.1 Searching an element K in a sorted set with n elements, any algorithm (based on the comparison between names) must do at least $\lceil \lg(n+1) \rceil$ comparisons in the worst case.

Lemma 5.2 Searching an element K in a sorted set with n elements, any algorithm (based on the comparison between names) must do at least $\lg n - 1$ comparisons on average.

Lemma 5.3 Searching an element K in an unsorted set with n elements, any algorithm (based on the comparison between names) must do at least n comparisons in the worst case.

Lemma 5.4 Searching an element K in an unsorted set with n elements, any algorithm (based on the comparison between names) must do at least $\dfrac{n+1}{2}$ comparisons on average.

The above lower bounds are all optimal. For example, the Binary Search algorithm can get the lower bounds in lemma 5.1 and 5.2, the Sequential Searching algorithm can get the lower bounds in lemma 5.3 and 5.4.

Here $\lg n$ is the base-2 logarithm, $\log n$ is the base-10 logarithm, $\ln n$ is the natural logarithm, and $\log_a^n$ is the base-a logarithm. $\lfloor x \rfloor$ is the floor of x, $\lceil x \rceil$ is the ceiling of x, and we have: $x - 1 < \lfloor x \rfloor \le x \le \lceil x \rceil < x + 1$. Specially, for natural number n, we have: $\lg n < \lceil \lg(n+1) \rceil \le \lg n + 1$ and $\lceil \lg(n+1) \rceil = \lfloor \lg n \rfloor + 1$ (Graham et al., 1989).

For $x_i \ge 0$, $1 \le i \le n$, there is a sequence of inequalities (Agarwal, 2000):

$$\frac{n}{\dfrac{1}{x_1} + \dfrac{1}{x_2} + \cdots + \dfrac{1}{x_n}} \le \sqrt[n]{x_1 x_2 \cdots x_n} \le \frac{x_1 + x_2 + \cdots + x_n}{n} \le \sqrt{\frac{x_1^2 + x_2^2 + \cdots + x_n^2}{n}}.$$

For a function $f(x)$ defined on the real domain, if $f''(x) > 0$ or $f''(x) < 0$, then $f(x)$ is a concave function (or convex function), $f(x)$ has a unique minimum (or maximum) on the definition domain, and we have the following formula (Agarwal, 2000):

$$f(\frac{1}{n}\sum_{i=1}^{n} x_i) \le \frac{1}{n}\sum_{i=1}^{n} f(x_i), (f(\frac{1}{n}\sum_{i=1}^{n} x_i) \ge \frac{1}{n}\sum_{i=1}^{n} f(x_i)).$$

A real-valued function $f(x)$ is continuous on interval [a, b] and satisfying $f(a)f(b) < 0$, then there exists a zero point of $f(x)$ in the interval (a, b) (Strang, 1991).

On the increasing order of function, we have: $\ln\ln n < \ln n < n^c < a^n$ ($a > 1$, $c > 0$), and for any $\varepsilon > 0$, we have:

$$\ln \ln n < \ln^\varepsilon n, \ln n < (n^c)^\varepsilon, n^c < (a^n)^\varepsilon.$$

5.2 Basic Assumptions

For an n-dimensional resource space $RS(X_1, X_2, \ldots, X_n)$, we assume that the n axes are stored in the order $(X_1, X_2, \ldots, X_n)$, but they are not sorted in alphabet. For every axis $X_i = (C_{i1}, C_{i2}, \ldots, C_{ij})$, the coordinates on the axis are also stored in the order $(C_{i1}, C_{i2}, \ldots, C_{ij})$ and are not sorted in alphabet. Here the comparison between coordinate and the query name is regarded as the basic operation.

Suppose N is the number of all of the points in the resource space $RS(X_1, X_2, \ldots, X_n)$, $|X_i|$ is the number of coordinates on axis X_i, $1 \le i \le n$, then

$\prod_{i=1}^{n}|X_i|=N$. We fix N and then study the relationship between the searching complexity and the dimension n as well as the relationship between searching complexity and the distribution of coordinates on every axis. Assume that points are as basic search units, axes are unsorted set, and the order of axes is unknown, then we have the following theorem.

Theorem 5.1. Given a resource space $RS(X_1, X_2, ..., X_n)$, where every X_i and its coordinates are unsorted in alphabet, $1 \leq i \leq n$. Suppose the number of coordinates on axis X_i is $|X_i|$, then any comparison-based algorithm to find the answer to $Q(X_1=q_1, ..., X_n=q_n)$ in $RS(X_1, X_2, ..., X_n)$ must do at least $\dfrac{n(n+1)}{2} + \sum_{i=1}^{n}|X_i|$ times of comparison in the worst case.

Proof. To get a point $Q(X_1=q_1, ..., X_n=q_n)$ in the space $RS(X_1, X_2, ..., X_n)$, search needs to check every q_i on axis X_j, $1 \leq i \leq n$. Suppose T_i is the number of comparisons needed to find q_i, then, the times of comparison needed to find point $Q(X_1=q_1, ..., X_n=q_n)$ is $T = \sum_{i=1}^{n}T_i$. To find q_1, we need to determine the axis X_i it belongs to first, then search q_1 on X_i. Since there are in all n axes which are not sorted in alphabet, so it takes at least n times of comparisons to find a specific axis X_i in the worst case. There are $|X_j|$ coordinates not sorted in alphabet on axis X_i, so searching for q_1 among them needs at least $|X_j|$ times of comparison in the worst case. So finding q_1 needs at least $n+|X_j|$ times of comparison in the worst case. We can use the same procedure to find q_2, the only difference is we only need to search the remaining $n-1$ axes. Then, finding q_2 needs at least $n-1+|X_j|$ times of comparisons in the worst case. So in the worst case, finding point $Q(X_1=q_1, ...,$ $X_n=q_n)$ needs at least $n+(n-1)+\cdots+1+\sum_{i=1}^{n}|X_i|=\dfrac{n(n+1)}{2}+\sum_{i=1}^{n}|X_i|$ times of comparison. $\square$

Theorem 5.1 shows that the searching complexity is related to the dimension and the distribution of coordinates on axes. Then, what is the relationship between the searching complexity and the changing of the dimension? And what is the relationship between the searching complexity and the distribution of coordinates on every axis? The following two parts answer these questions.

Corollary 5.1. To find the answer to $Q(X_1=q_1, ..., X_k=q_k)$ in $RS(X_1, X_2, ...,$ $X_n)$ must do at least $\dfrac{n(n+1)}{2} - \dfrac{(n-k)(n-k+1)}{2} + \sum_{i=1}^{k} |X_i|$ times of comparison in the worst case $(k \le n)$.

5.3 Distribution of Coordinates on Axes

Because the number of points N in resource space is fixed, the distribution of coordinates on axes indicates the possible case of the number of coordinates on every axis when N is given. For example, if the number of points N is 8 and the dimension of space is 3, according to $\prod_{i=1}^{n} |X_i| = N$, then all the possible distributions of coordinates on axes are: (1, 2, 4), (1, 1, 8) and (2, 2, 2). We can see that the distribution (1, 1, 8) is the most uneven, almost all of coordinates locate on only one axis. The distribution (2, 2, 2) is the most even, the number of coordinates on every axis is equal. Then from the perspective of searching complexity, which case of distribution is better? The following will answer this question.

5.3.1 Best Distribution of Coordinates

First we give the following theorem:

Theorem 5.2. Given a class of resource spaces $RS(X_1, X_2, ..., X_n)$, where every X_i and its coordinates are unsorted in alphabet, $1 \le i \le n$. Let N be the number of points in the space and $|X_i|$ be the number of coordinates on axis X_i, n be fixed dimension and every $|X_i|$ be variable. Assume that the number of comparisons for any comparison-based algorithm for searching $Q(X_1=q_1, ..., X_n=q_n)$ in the resource space must do at least in the worst case is $W(n)$. Then, $Min\ W(n)= \dfrac{n(n+1)}{2} + nN^{\frac{1}{n}}$, and only when $|X_1| = |X_2| = ...= |X_n|$, this minimum can be reached.

Proof. Given any class of resource spaces $RS(X_1, X_2, ..., X_n)$, according to theorem 5.1, $W(n)= \dfrac{n(n+1)}{2} + \sum_{i=1}^{n} |X_i|$. Because the space dimension n is fixed, we only need to find the minimum of $\sum_{i=1}^{n} |X_i|$ under the constraint:

$\prod_{i=1}^{n} |X_i| = N$. According to the Mean Inequalities [R. P. Agarwal, *Differ-ence Equations and Inequalities*, 2nd edition, CRC, 2000]: $\sqrt[n]{x_1 x_2 \cdots x_n} \leq \dfrac{x_1 + x_2 + \cdots + x_n}{n}$, $x_i \geq 0$, $1 \leq i \leq n$, (and the equality holds only when $x_1 = x_2 = \ldots = x_n$), so we have: $\sum_{i=1}^{n} x_i \geq n(\prod_{i=1}^{n} x_i)^{\frac{1}{n}}$. Replace every x_i with $|X_i|$, we can get: $\sum_{i=1}^{n} |X_i| \geq n(\prod_{i=1}^{n} |X_i|)^{\frac{1}{n}} = nN^{\frac{1}{n}}$, which can con-clude that *Min W(n)*$= \dfrac{n(n+1)}{2} + nN^{\frac{1}{n}}$, and only when $|X_1| = |X_2| = \ldots = |X_n|$, the minimum can be reached. $\square$

Theorem 5.2 shows that if the space dimension keep fixed, then when the distribution of coordinates on every axis is the most even, the searching complexity in the worst case is the least, i.e., in the above example the dis-tribution (2, 2, 2) is the best. It is worth to note that for some N and space dimension n, the lower bound $\dfrac{n(n+1)}{2} + nN^{\frac{1}{n}}$ can never be reached. For example, given $N=8$ and $n=4$, the best distribution (2, 2, 2) cannot be reached. And for $N=12$ and space dimension $n=3$, no matter what the dis-tribution of coordinates is, the minimum in the theorem cannot be reached. This means that only when the given N and n satisfy some conditions, the theorem would hold. The following corollary gives the conditions that N and n should satisfy.

Corollary 5.2. Given a class of resource spaces $RS(X_1, X_2, \ldots, X_n)$, where every X_i and its coordinates are unsorted in alphabet, $1 \leq i \leq n$. Let N be the number of points in the space and $|X_i|$ be the number of coordinates on axis X_i, n be fixed dimension and every $|X_i|$ be variable. Assume that the num-ber of comparisons for any comparison-based algorithm to find a point $Q(X_1=q_1, \ldots, X_n=q_n)$ in the resource space must do at least in the worst case is $W(n)$. Then *Min* $W(n) = \dfrac{n(n+1)}{2} + nN^{\frac{1}{n}}$, and this minimum can be reached if and only if $n \le \lg N$ and $\log_n^N$ is an integer.

Proof. (1) Suppose $n \le \lg N$ and $\log_n^N$ is an integer. Let $\log_n^N = S$, according to $n \le \lg N$, we get $\log_n^N \ge 2$, i.e., $S \ge 2$. Now we only need to let $|X_1| = |X_2| = \ldots = |X_n| = S$, then the lower bound in theorem 5.2 can be reached.

(2) Suppose the lower bound can be reached, then according to theorem 5.2, $|X_1| = |X_2| = \ldots = |X_n|$, let the value be S, from $\prod\limits_{i=1}^{n} |X_i| = N$ we get $N = S^n$, then $\log_n^N = S$ is an integer. Because $N > 1$, S cannot be 1, then $S \ge 2$, $N \ge 2^n$, we can get $n \le \lg N$. So now both $n \le \lg N$ and $\log_n^N$ is an integer hold. $\square$

5.3.2 The Worst Distribution of Coordinates

First we give the following theorem:

Theorem 5.3. Given a class of resource spaces $RS(X_1, X_2, \ldots, X_n)$, where every X_i and its coordinates are unsorted in alphabet, $1 \le i \le n$. Suppose N is the number of all the points in space and $|X_i|$ is the number of coordinates on axis X_i, the space dimension n is fixed and every $|X_i|$ is variable. Let the times of comparisons for any comparison-based algorithm to find an answer to query $Q(X_1 = q_1, \ldots, X_n = q_n)$ in the resource space must do at least is $W(n)$ in the worst case. Then *Max* $W(n) = N + \dfrac{n^2}{2} + \dfrac{3n}{2} - 1$, and only when some $|X_i| = N$, this maximum can be reached.

Proof. Given any $RS(X_1, X_2, \ldots, X_n)$ in the class of resource spaces, according to theorem 5.1, $W(n) = \dfrac{n(n+1)}{2} + \sum\limits_{i=1}^{n} |X_i|$. Because the space dimension n is fixed, we only need to find the maximum of $\sum\limits_{i=1}^{n} |X_i|$ under the constraint: $\prod\limits_{i=1}^{n} |X_i| = N$. Theorem 5.2 has shown that in the case of the distribution of coordinates on every axis is the most even ($|X_1| = |X_2| = \ldots =$

$|X_n|$), the minimum can be reached, so we can guess that when the distribution of coordinates on every axis is the most uneven, we can get the maximum of $\sum_{i=1}^{n} |X_i|$. As $\prod_{i=1}^{n} |X_i| = N$, we guess the most uneven case is: for some i, $|X_i|=N$ and $|X_j|=1$ for any $j \neq i$. In this case, $\sum_{i=1}^{n} |X_i| = N + n-1$, so we only need to show that for any distribution of $|X_i|$, $1 \leq i \leq n$, we have: $\sum_{i=1}^{n} |X_i| \leq N + n-1$. In the following we will prove this, first we have:

$$\sum_{i=1}^{n} |X_i| = \sum_{|X_j|=1} |X_j| + \sum_{|X_k|>1} |X_k| \ , \tag{5.1}$$

As $\prod_{i=1}^{n} |X_i| = N$, then $|X_i|$ cannot all be 1. On the right side of (5.1) we have: $\sum_{|X_j|=1} |X_j| \leq n-1$. As every $|X_j|$ is 1, so $\prod_{|X_k|>1} |X_k| = N$. Then we only need to show that $\sum_{|X_k|>1} |X_k| \leq N$, i.e., $\sum_{|X_k|>1} |X_k| \leq \prod_{|X_k|>1} |X_k|$. We use mathematical induction to prove this.

We only need to show that for any natural number m, $|X_k|>1$, $1 \leq k \leq m$, $\sum_{k=1}^{m} |X_k| \leq \prod_{k=1}^{m} |X_k|$ holds. When $m=1$, it is obvious.

Suppose $m=p$, $\sum_{k=1}^{p} |X_k| \leq \prod_{k=1}^{p} |X_k|$ holds. When $m=p+1$, we have:

$$\prod_{k=1}^{p+1} |X_k| = |X_{p+1}| \times \prod_{k=1}^{p} |X_k| = \prod_{k=1}^{p} |X_k| + (|X_{p+1}| - 1) \prod_{k=1}^{p} |X_k| .$$

Because $\prod\limits_{k=1}^{p}|X_k|\ge 2$ and $|X_{p+1}|\ge 2$, we have:

$(|X_{p+1}|-1)\prod\limits_{k=1}^{p}|X_k|\ge 2(|X_{p+1}|-1)\ge|X_{p+1}|$, which concludes:

$$\prod_{k=1}^{p+1}|X_k|=\prod_{k=1}^{p}|X_k|+(|X_{p+1}|-1)\prod_{k=1}^{p}|X_k|\ge\sum_{k=1}^{p}|X_k|+|X_{p+1}|=\sum_{k=1}^{p+1}|X_k|.$$

When $m=p+1$, the conclusion also holds. According to the proof process, we can see that the conditions of the equality holds are: $m=1$, or $m=2$ and $|X_1| = |X_2|=2$. The first condition corresponds to the case that some $|X_i|=N$ and $|X_j|=1$ for any $j\ne i$. And when $m=2$, $\sum\limits_{|X_j|=1}|X_j|= n-2 < n-1$, now

$\sum\limits_{i=1}^{n}|X_i|< N + n-1$. So the condition that some $|X_i|=N$ and $|X_j|=1$ for any

$j\ne i$ is the only case satisfying $\sum\limits_{i=1}^{n}|X_i|=N+n-1$.

Combining the above results, we have: $\sum\limits_{i=1}^{n}|X_i|\le N + n-1$, so Max

$W(n)=\dfrac{n(n+1)}{2}+N+n-1 = N+\dfrac{n^2}{2}+\dfrac{3n}{2}-1$, and only when some $|X_i|=N$ (in this case $|X_j|=1,j\ne i$), this maximum can be reached. □

Theorem 5.3 shows that if the space dimension is fixed, when the distribution of coordinates on every axis is the most uneven, the searching complexity in the worst case is the highest. Then in the above example, distribution (1, 1, 8) is the worst distribution. It is worth to note that for any given N and space dimension n, the upper bound $N+\dfrac{n^2}{2}+\dfrac{3n}{2}-1$ can always be reached. According to theorem 5.3, we only need to let some $|X_i|=N$ and all the other $|X_j|=1$. For example, for $N=12$ and space dimension $n=3$, let $|X_1|=12$ and $|X_2|=|X_3|=1$, then we can get the worst distribution (12, 1, 1).

We have studied the searching complexity in the worst case when the space dimension is fixed, got the best case (theorem 5.2, the most even distribution) and the worst case (theorem 5.3, the most uneven distribution), these are two extreme cases. Intuitively, in the case that the distribution of coordinates is the most uneven, all information is on one axis, so the searching is more difficult. This shows that to design a resource space, we should keep the distribution of coordinates on every axis as even as possible (in the sense of search efficiency).

Then, we can guess whether the following conclusion holds: the distribution of coordinates more uneven, the searching complexity the higher? How to evaluate the unevenness? First, we can think of the variation in the probability and statistics. According to the above proof process, we can guess whether the following conclusion holds: given natural numbers N and n, if two sequences of natural numbers $M=(m_1, m_2, \ldots, m_n)$ and $Y=(y_1, y_2, \ldots, y_n)$ satisfying $\prod_{i=1}^{n} m_i = \prod_{i=1}^{n} y_i = N$ and $Var(M) < Var(Y)$, then whether

we have $\sum_{i=1}^{n} m_i < \sum_{i=1}^{n} y_i$, i.e., $E(M) < E(Y)$?

Intuitively, the above conclusion should hold, in fact when $n=2$, we have the following corollary:

Corollary 5.3. Given natural number N, if two sequences of natural numbers $M=(m_1, m_2, \ldots, m_n)$ and $Y=(y_1, y_2, \ldots, y_n)$ satisfying $\prod_{i=1}^{2} m_i = \prod_{i=1}^{2} y_i = N$ and $Var(M) < Var(Y)$, then $E(M) < E(Y)$ holds.

Proof. According to the definition of expectation and variation, we have

$E(M)=(m_1+m_2)/2$, $Var(M)=E((M-E(M))^2)=E(M^2)-(E(M))^2$. Then,

$$Var(M) < Var(Y) \Rightarrow E(M^2)-(E(M))^2 < E(Y^2)-(E(Y))^2.$$

Replace $E(M)$ with $(m_1+m_2)/2$, we can get

$$\frac{1}{2}(m_1^2 + m_2^2) - \frac{1}{4}(m_1 + m_2)^2 < \frac{1}{2}(y_1^2 + y_2^2) - \frac{1}{4}(y_1 + y_2)^2 .$$

Which can be simplified is $(m_1^2 + m_2^2 - 2m_1m_2) < (y_1^2 + y_2^2 - 2y_1y_2)$.

According to $m_1m_2=y_1y_2=N$, adding $4m_1m_2$ to the left side of the above inequality, adding $4y_1y_2$ to the right side, we can get: $(m_1^2 + m_2^2 + 2m_1m_2) < (y_1^2 + y_2^2 + 2y_1y_2)$. i.e.,

$(m_1 + m_2)^2 < (y_1 + y_2)^2 \Rightarrow (m_1 + m_2) < (y_1 + y_2) \Rightarrow E(M) < E(Y)$ holds.

□

Above corollary shows that when $n=2$, the conclusion holds. Then whether the conclusion still holds when $n \geq 3$? We have the following counterexample: given $N=1944$ and $n=3$, sequences $M=(6, 18, 18)$ and $Y=(9, 9, 24)$ satisfying $\prod_{i=1}^{n} m_i = \prod_{i=1}^{n} y_i = N$, and $Var(M)=32$, $Var(Y)=50$, also satisfying $Var(M) < Var(Y)$. But $E(M) = E(Y)=14$ does not satisfy $E(M) < E(Y)$. This shows that the conclusion does not hold when $n=3$. According to this counterexample, we can construct counterexamples for any given n $(n>3)$, so our guess does not hold when $n \geq 3$.

5.4 The Changing of Space Dimension

We have studied the relationship between the searching complexity and the distribution of coordinates on every axis when the dimension of resource space is fixed. When changing dimension, what is the relationship between the searching complexity and the change of dimension? In the perspective of searching complexity, the dimension of resource space is the higher the better, or the lower the better? This section answers these questions.

5.4.1 Relationship between Dimension and Searching Complexity

Theorem 5.4. Given a class of resource spaces $RS(X_1, X_2, ..., X_n)$, where every X_i and its coordinates are unsorted in alphabet, $1 \leq i \leq n$. Suppose N is the number of points in space and $|X_i|$ is the number of coordinates on axis X_i, and the space dimension n and every $|X_i|$ are all variable. Let $f(n)$ be the Min $W(n)$ in theorem 5.2, then there exists a unique critical dimension n_0 $(1< n_0 < \lg N)$, such that if $n < n_0$, $f(n)$ decreases according to the increase of n; if $n > n_0$, $f(n)$ increases according to the increase of n.

Proof. When the space dimension n is fixed, according to theorem 5.2,

$$f(n) = Min\ W(n) = \frac{n(n+1)}{2} + nN^{\frac{1}{n}}.$$ Then we study the properties of $f(n)$ ac-

cording to the changing of dimension n. Let $f(x) = \dfrac{x(x+1)}{2} + xN^{\frac{1}{x}}$, x is real

and $1 \le x \le \lg N$, then we only need to study the properties of $f(x)$, then discuss its values on integers. The differential of $f(x)$ is:

$$f'(x) = x + N^{\frac{1}{x}}(1 - \frac{\ln N}{x}) + \frac{1}{2}.$$

Then $f'(1) = 1.5 + N(1 - \ln N) < 0$ and $f'(\lg N) = \lg N + 2(1 - \dfrac{\ln N}{\lg N}) + \dfrac{1}{2} > 0$. It

is obvious that $f'(x)$ is continuous, so according to the median theorem of continuous functions [G. Strang, Calculus, Wellesley-Cambridge, 1991], there exits a zero point of $f'(x)$ between 1 and $\lg N$. Then we can get the differential of $f'(x)$ again:

$$f''(x) = 1 + N^{\frac{1}{x}}\frac{\ln N}{x^2} + N^{\frac{1}{x}}\ln N\frac{-1}{x^2}(1 - \frac{\ln N}{x}) = 1 + N^{\frac{1}{x}}\frac{\ln^2 N}{x^3}.$$

It is obvious that $f''(x) > 0$, then $f(x)$ is a concave function and $f'(x)$ is strictly increasing, so the zero point of $f'(x)$ between 1 and $\lg N$ is unique. Let the zero point be Z, since $f(x)$ is concave, we can get that $f(Z)$ is the minimum of $f(x)$ between 1 and $\lg N$, and when $x < Z$, $f(x)$ is strictly decreasing, when $x > Z$, $f(x)$ is strictly increasing. If Z is an integer, let $n_0 = Z$. If Z is not an integer and $f(\lfloor Z \rfloor) < f(\lceil Z \rceil)$, let $n_0 = \lfloor Z \rfloor$, else let $n_0 = \lceil Z \rceil$. Then we have that n_0 is the unique minimum point of $f(n)$, and if $n < n_0$, $f(n)$ decreases with the increasing of n; if $n > n_0$, $f(n)$ increases with the increasing of n. □

Theorem 5.4 shows that from the perspective of searching complexity, the space dimension is not the higher the better, and is not the lower the better either. There is a unique critical dimension, at first the searching complexity in the worst case decreases according to the increasing of space dimension, when space dimension reaches the critical dimension, the searching complexity in the worst case increases according to the increasing of space dimension, i.e., the searching complexity in the worst case is the least when the space dimension is the critical dimension.

In the case of the most uneven distribution of coordinates on every axis, we have the following corollary:

Corollary 5.4. Given a class of resource spaces $RS(X_1, X_2, \ldots, X_n)$, where every X_i and its coordinates are unsorted in alphabet, $1 \le i \le n$. Suppose N is the number of points in space and $|X_i|$ is the number of coordinates at axis X_i, and the space dimension n and every $|X_i|$ are all variable. Let $F(n)$ be the *Max W(n)* in theorem 5.3, then $F(n)$ increases according to the increasing of n.

5.4.2 Value of Critical Dimension

Theorem 5.4 only gives the existence of critical dimension, but what is the value of critical dimension? The following theorem will answer this question.

Theorem 5.5. Given a class of resource spaces $RS(X_1, X_2, ..., X_n)$, where every X_i and its coordinates are unsorted in alphabet, $1 \le i \le n$. Suppose N is the number of points in the space and $|X_i|$ is the number of coordinates on axis X_i, and the space dimension n and every $|X_i|$ are all variable. Let n_0 be the critical dimension in theorem 5.4, then for any $\varepsilon > 0$, there exists N_0, such that if $N > N_0$, then we have $\ln^{1-\varepsilon} N < n_0 < \ln N$.

Proof. According to the proof of theorem 5.4, we only need to estimate the value of Z. As Z is the unique zero point of $f'(x)$ between 1 and lg$N$, we have:

$$f'(Z) = Z + N^{\frac{1}{Z}}(1 - \frac{\ln N}{Z}) + \frac{1}{2} = 0.$$

This is a transcendental equation, it is impossible to solve the value of Z accurately, so we will estimate the value of Z in the next. We will prove that for any $\varepsilon > 0$, if N is big enough, then we have $\ln^{1-\varepsilon} N < Z < \ln N$. Because $f'(x)$ is strictly increasing, we only need to show that when N is big enough, $f'(\ln^{1-\varepsilon} N) < 0$ and $f'(\ln N) > 0$. It is clear that $f'(\ln N)$ $= 0.5 + \ln N > 0$. When $\varepsilon \ge 1$, $f'(\ln^{1-\varepsilon} N) < 0$ is obvious. When $\varepsilon < 1$, $f'(\ln^{1-\varepsilon} N) < 0$ is equivalent to $\ln^{1-\varepsilon} N + \frac{1}{2} < N^{\frac{1}{\ln^{1-\varepsilon} N}}(\ln^\varepsilon N - 1)$, and because $\lim\limits_{N \to \infty} \ln^{1-\varepsilon} N = \infty$ and $\lim\limits_{N \to \infty} \ln^\varepsilon N = \infty$, there exists $N_1 > 0$, if $N > N_1$, then $\ln^{1-\varepsilon} N > \frac{1}{2}$ and $\ln^\varepsilon N > 2$, which means that $\ln^{1-\varepsilon} N + \frac{1}{2} < 2\ln^{1-\varepsilon} N$ and $(\ln^\varepsilon N - 1) > \frac{1}{2}\ln^\varepsilon N$. Now we have:

$$\ln^{1-\varepsilon} N + \frac{1}{2} < 2\ln^{1-\varepsilon} N < N^{\frac{1}{\ln^{1-\varepsilon} N}} \frac{1}{2}\ln^{\varepsilon} N < N^{\frac{1}{\ln^{1-\varepsilon} N}} (\ln^{\varepsilon} N - 1).$$

So we only need to let $2\ln^{1-\varepsilon} N < N^{\frac{1}{\ln^{1-\varepsilon} N}} \frac{1}{2}\ln^{\varepsilon} N$, which is equivalent to

$4\ln^{1-2\varepsilon} N < N^{\frac{1}{\ln^{1-\varepsilon} N}}$, get the natural logarithm for both sides, we have:

$$\ln 4 + (1-2\varepsilon)\ln\ln N < \frac{\ln N}{\ln^{1-\varepsilon} N} = \ln^{\varepsilon} N.$$

Because $\lim_{N\to\infty} \ln \frac{\ln^{\varepsilon} N}{\ln\ln N} = \lim_{N\to\infty} (\varepsilon \ln\ln N - \ln\ln\ln N) = \infty$, we have

$\lim_{N\to\infty} (\ln^{\varepsilon} N - \ln\ln N) = \infty$, then $\lim_{N\to\infty} (\ln^{\varepsilon} N - (1-2\varepsilon)\ln\ln N) = \infty$. So

there exists N_2, if $N > N_2$, then $\ln^{\varepsilon} N - (1-2\varepsilon)\ln\ln N > \ln 4$, i.e.,

$\ln 4 + (1-2\varepsilon)\ln\ln N < \ln^{\varepsilon} N$ holds. If we let $N_0=\text{Max}\{N_1, N_2\}$, then if

$N > N_0$, we have $2\ln^{1-\varepsilon} N + N^{\frac{1}{\ln^{1-\varepsilon} N}} (1 - \frac{\ln N}{\ln^{1-\varepsilon} N}) < 0$, i.e.,

$f'(\ln^{1-\varepsilon} N) < 0$.

Combining above results, we can get that for any $\varepsilon>0$, there exists N_0 such that if $N>N_0$, then $\ln^{1-\varepsilon} N < n_0 < \ln N$. □

Theorem 5.5 shows that when N is big enough, the critical dimension n_0 can approach $\ln N$ to any extent. The minimum of $f(n)$ is about:

$$f(\ln N) = \ln^2 N + \ln N \times N^{\frac{1}{\ln N}} = \ln^2 N + e\ln N = O(\ln^2 N).$$

5.5 Summary

This chapter discusses the complexity of searching a point in the resource space based on comparisons. We have studied the relationship between the searching complexity and the distribution of coordinates on every axis and reach that: *from the perspective of searching complexity, the distribution of coordinates on every axis is the evener the better*. We also discuss the relationship between the searching complexity and changing the dimension of resource space, and conclude that *the space dimension is neither the higher the better, nor the lower the better. There is a unique critical dimension which is optimal from the perspective of searching, and the value of the critical dimension is about* ln$N$ (N is the number of points in the resource space). These results are very helpful to design and analyze resource spaces.

Chapter 6 Resource Space Model Storage

The characteristics of the Resource Space Model require a special storage mechanism for efficient resource storage and retrieval. A novel multidimensional indexing structure is proposed to realize semantic-based resource re-organization and efficient retrieval.

6.1 Current Approaches to Storing Resource Space

Relational tables, XML files and spatial indexing structures could be used to store resource space, but it is hard to realize semantic integrity and storage efficiency.

The following are two ways of storing resource space in a single relational table:

1. Let each axis correspond to an attribute of the table, and each coordinate of the corresponding axis corresponds to the attribute value. In this way, it is hard to represent hierarchical coordinates and to support efficient multi-attribute search.
2. Let each coordinate correspond to an attribute of the table. The attribute value is of boolean type. This will result in low utilization ratio of storage space due to the magnitude of attribute number as well as the loss of hierarchical semantics.

Fig. 6.1 depicts the transformation from a two-dimensional resource space into a table with attributes X and Y, and the transformation from a resource space into a table with attributes C_1, C_{11}, C_{12}, C_2, C_3, C_{31}, C_{32} and C_4, by the above two kinds of representation respectively.

It is feasible to represent all the resources in a single XML file. Each axis or coordinate in resource space corresponds to a tag of XML file. Hierarchical relationships between tags reflect the same semantics as hierarchical coordinates. The value of a tag is the list of all the resources belonging to the classification of that tag. Fig. 6.2 is an XML file representing the resource space described in Fig. 6.1. Tag $<C_{31}>$ is a sphere node whose value is indicated by the retangle node $\{r_1, r_2\}$, which means both resource r_1 and r_2 are in the classification of C_{31}. This storage manner is isimilar to inverted list. Each resource has the same number of copies in XML tree as the dimensionality of resource space. Such a redundancy requires an additional cost of integrity maintenace.

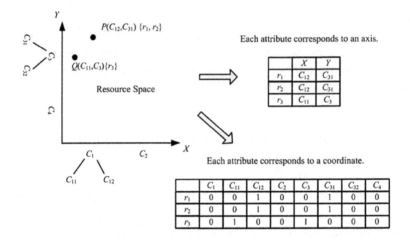

Each attribute corresponds to an axis.

	X	Y
r_1	C_{12}	C_{31}
r_2	C_{12}	C_{31}
r_3	C_{11}	C_3

Each attribute corresponds to a coordinate.

	C_1	C_{11}	C_{12}	C_2	C_3	C_{31}	C_{32}	C_4
r_1	0	0	1	0	0	1	0	0
r_2	0	0	1	0	0	1	0	0
r_3	0	1	0	0	1	0	0	0

Fig.6.1. Two ways of storing resource space by relational table.

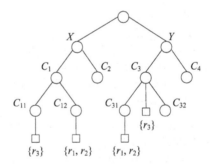

Fig. 6.2. An example of using XML file to store resource space.

Most spatial indexing structures are dedicated to such a space that each dimension has a linear ordering of its coordinates (Gaede and Gnther, 1998). Coordinates in resource space model, however, represent conceptual classification along their axes. They are discrete and usually have hierarchical semantic relationships rather than linear order. Datacube in

OLAP resembles RSM, but it is mainly for online data analysis and statistics.

6.2 Problem Definition

In this chapter, we devise a specific multidimensional access method named C-tree for resource space storage. It organizes resources by classification semantics and stores semantic-close resources in adjoining place of storage space. Moreover, it preserves hierarchy semantics between concepts.

We state the problem formally as follows:

How to make the underlying index structures represent hierarchy semantics between concepts so as to implement effective and efficient resource insertion, deletion, exact query and range query on resource space.

Hierarchy semantics is prevailing in concept classification. It reflects two important relationships between concepts. One is concept combination. For example, a car is composed of wheel, engine and fuel. The other is concept refinement. For example, book is one kind of publication. In fact, we recognize objects in the real world by such hierarchy semantics in many situations. If it is preserved in the process of index creation, we can utilize it to organize resources much better.

The underlying index structures should satisfy the following two goals.

1. **The semantic Goal** — the preservation of hierarchical semantics between concepts. Hierarchy semantics between concepts should be kept in the underlying structure. Concepts and their hierarchy relationships are designed by system managers according to classification semantics. The design process of RSM already refines resource organization to a certain extent. The normal forms of RSM guarantee the quality of resource classification at the logical level. Meanwhile, it matches people's thinking way of resource organization.
2. **The operation Goal** — efficient resource operations including insertion, deletion, exact query and range query. The reason of preserving the hierarchical semantics of resource space is that the underlying indexing structure should be guided by such semantics in the process of resource insertion, deletion and query.

6.3 System Architecture

An overview of system architecture is depicted in Fig. 6.3. It includes four major components: *RSM Schema Definition Module, Resource Operation Input Module, RSM Schema Tree Module,* and *Physical Storage Space Module.*

RSM Schema Definition Module is responsible for the input of RSM schema in the format of $RS(X_0(C_{00}, C_{01}, ..., C_{0p}), X_1(C_{10}, C_{11}, ..., C_{1q}), ..., X_{n-1}(C_{n-1\ 0}, C_{n-1\ 1}, ..., C_{n-1\ r}))$. We use $C(C_0, ..., C_t)$ to represent the hierarchy relationships between parent concept C and its child concepts C_0 to C_t.

Fig. 6.4 depicts an example of $RS(X(C_1(C_{11}, C_{12}, C_{13}), C_2(C_{21}, C_{22}))$, $Y(C_3(C_{31}, C_{32}), C_4(C_{41}, C_{42}))$, where $C_2(C_{21}, C_{22})$ means concept C_2 is the super-concept of C_{21} and C_{22}. Point P contains resource r_1 and r_2 both of which belong to the classification "$X=C_{21}, Y=C_{41}$".

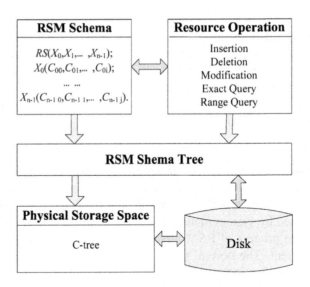

Fig. 6.3. System architecture.

Resource Operation Input Module is responsible for the input of re-source operation from users. Five major kinds of resource operations are considered here: *insertion, deletion, modification, exact query* and *range query*. They are expressed by users who only know RSM schema but not the underlying storage format. In this sense, the resource query "$X=C_1$, $Y=C_2$" is equivalent to the query "$Y=C_2$, $X=C_1$".

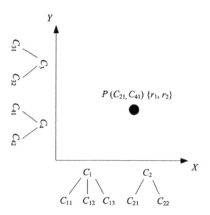

Fig. 6.4. A point and its resources in a resource space.

RSM Schema Tree Module encodes the input RSM schema into bit strings which preserve all hierarchy semantics between concepts. In this way, a one-to--one mapping is set up between RSM concepts and bit strings, and stored in a single disk file. If the file is small, load it into internal memory before doing resource operations. Otherwise, build up an index in the head of the file which will be loaded into internal memory instead of the whole file. The index should well support the search for bit string given concept as well as the search for concept given bit string. *RSM Schema Tree Module* also sends related RSM schema information to *Physical Storage Space Module* to help the initialization of the underlying indexing structure C-tree. It transforms the resource operations input from *Resource Operation Input Module* into the format of the underlying storage.

Physical Storage Space Module is responsible for the creation and maintenance of C-tree. C-tree is stored in a single disk file. Each node corresponds to a page in the file. In default, the first page stores the root node of C-tree. Leaf node keeps a certain number of classification points in RSM space. Each classification point corresponds to another page which keeps resource locations like file path and URI (Uniform Resource Identifier). C-tree extends R-tree to index the underlying multidimensional bit string space where there is no linear order but hierarchy relationships between coordinates.

6.4 RSM Storage Mechanism

To achieve the semantic goal, we devise a RSM schema tree to encode all hierarchy semantics of a given RSM in a single binary tree. It provides three basic functions as follows:

1. **void** *createStorageSpace*(**RS** rs)—it accepts a RSM schema as input and creates an underlying physical storage space, a multidimensional bit string space.
2. **BitString** *normalize*(**Concept** c) —it accepts a concept as input, and returns its path in the schema tree as a bit string. RSM schema tree plays the role of mapping RSM and resource operations at the logical level into those at the physical level.
3. **BitString** *normalize*(**Axis** a) —it accepts an axis as input, and returns its path in the schema tree as a bit string.

To achieve the operation goal, we devise C-tree to index the underlying multidimensional bit string space. It provides the following four basic functions:

1. **ResourceSet** *exactQuery*(**Classification** c) — it finds out all the re-sources belonging to the input conceptual classification. Each concep-tual classification is a point in the multidimensional bit string space.
2. **Boolean** *insert*(**Resource** r) —it inserts the given resource in C-tree. The input resource contains its conceptual classification as well as lo-cation.
3. **Boolean** *delete*(**Resource** r) —it deletes the given resource from C-tree.
4. **ResourceSet** *rangeQuery*(**ClassificationRange** range) —it returns all the resources whose conceptual classifications are inside the given conceptual classification range.

C-tree puts nearby classification points together in external memory so as to achieve an amortized cost of $O(\log N + T)$ where N is the number of resources and T is the number of retrieved resources.

6.5 RSM Schema Tree

Each axis of RSM corresponds to a concept tree as depicted in Fig.6.6. For an RSM of dimensionality d, its schema consists of d concept trees. By forest-to-tree transformation, we can construct a binary tree of the given RSM. By labeling each left edge with bit 0 and each right edge with bit 1, we encode all axes and concepts into bit strings by combining all the bits in their root-to-node paths. Fig. 6.5 demonstrates the generation of an RSM schema tree from the resource space in Fig. 6.4.

Theorem 6.1.   Let s_1 be the bit string of axis X and s_2 be the bit string of concept C. C is a concept in X if and only if $s_1 0$ is the prefix of s_2.

Proof. The proof consists of the following two parts:

(=>) In the construction process of RSM schema tree, if C is a concept in X, C's corresponding node in RSM schema tree is in the left subtree of X's corresponding node. Therefore, $s_1 0$ is the prefix of s_2.
(<=) If $s_1 0$ is the prefix of s_2, C's corresponding node in RSM schema tree is in the left subtree of X's corresponding node. Hence C is a concept in X.
□

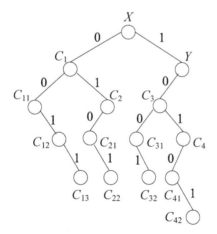

Fig. 6.5. RSM schema tree.

Theorem 6.2.   Let s_1 be the bit string of concept C_1 and s_2 be the bit string of concept C_2. C_2 is a sibling concept of C_1 if and only if $s_1 = s_2(1^+)$ or $s_2 = s_1(1^+)$, where 1^+ is a regular expression representing a sequence of one or more 1.

Proof. The proof consists of the following two parts:

(=>) Since C_2 is a sibling concept of C_1, there are only sibling concepts between them. In terms of their bit strings, $s_1=s_2(1^+)$ or $s_2=s_1(1^+)$.
(<=) Without loss of generality, we just examine the case $s_1=s_2(1^+)$. Since bit 1 represents one sibling concept is passed over and bit 0 represents one time of concept refinement, C_2 is a sibling concept of C_1. □

Theorem 6.3.   Let s_1 be the bit string of concept C_1 and s_2 be the bit string of concept C_2. C_2 is the parent concept of C_1 if and only if s_1 equals $s_2 0(1^*)$, where 1^* is a regular expression representing a sequence of zero or more 1.

Proof. The proof consists of the following two parts:

(=>) Suppose C_2 is the parent of C_1. If C_1 is the first child (or 0th) of C_2, then s_1 equals $s_2 0$ which can be easily inferred from the construction process of RSM schema tree. If C_1 is the ith child of C_2, then s_1 equals $s_2 0(1^+)$ where the number of 1 is i. Therefore, s_1 equals $s_2 0(1^*)$.
(<=) From the construction process of RSM schema tree, we know 0 represents one time of concept refinement and 1 represents one sibling concept is passed over. Therefore, if s_1 equals $s_2 0(1^*)$, only one time of concept refinement occurs. So C_2 is the parent of C_1. □

Theorem 6.4.   Let s_1 be the bit string of concept C_1 and s_2 be the bit string of concept C_2. C_2 is the ancestor concept of C_1 if and only if $s_2 0$ is the prefix of s_1.

Proof. The proof consists of the following two parts:

(=>) If C_2 is the parent concept of C_1, then s_1 equals $s_2 0$ or $s_2 0(1^+)$ by Theorem 6.2. Therefore, $s_2 0$ is the prefix of s_1 in this case. Otherwise, one child C_3 of C_2 is the ancestor concept of C_1. Let s_3 be the bit string of C_3. From the construction process of RSM schema tree, we know that $s_2 0$ is the prefix of s_3 and that s_3 is the prefix of s_1. Therefore, $s_2 0$ is the prefix of s_1.
(<=) If $s_2 0$ is the prefix of s_1, C_1 must be at least one time of concept refinement of C_2. Hence C_2 is the ancestor concept of C_1. □

Since the shortest path between two concepts in the concept tree reflects the distance between the two concepts and their common ancestor, we define the semantic distance as follows.

Definition 6.1. Semantic distance $dist(C_1, C_2)$ between two concepts C_1 and C_2 in the same axis X is the length of the shortest path between them in the multi-way concept tree of X.

Fig. 6.6 depicts the multi-way concept tree of axis $X(C_1(C_{11}, C_{12}, C_{13}), C_2(C_{21}, C_{22}))$. $dist(\cdot, \cdot)$ defines the semantic closeness between concepts in the same tree. For example, $dist(C_{12}, C_{21})$ is 4 since the shortest path from C_{12} to C_{21} is $C_{12} \rightarrow C_1 \rightarrow X \rightarrow C_2 \rightarrow C_{21}$.

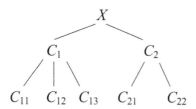

Fig. 6.6. Concept tree of axis X.

Theorem 6.5. $dist(\cdot, \cdot)$ is a metric function.

Proof. For any three concepts C_1, C_2, C_3 in axis X, $dist(\cdot, \cdot)$ satisfies the following properties:

1. $dist(C_1, C_2) \geq 0$, since the path length is always a non-negative integer.
2. $dist(C_1, C_2) = 0$ if and only if $C_1 = C_2$, since the length of the shortest path is 0 if and only if two concepts actually are the same.
3. $dist(C_1, C_2) = dist(C_2, C_1)$, since the path between two concepts has no direction.
4. $dist(C_1, C_2) + dist(C_2, C_3) \geq dist(C_1, C_3)$. Given C_1 and C_3, $C_1 \rightarrow C_2 \rightarrow C_3$ is a path from C_1 to C_3. It must be no shorter than the shortest path from C_1 to C_3. Therefore, $dist(\cdot, \cdot)$ satisfies the triangle inequality. $\square$

There are two most commonly used bit string operators, notated as follows.

1. $lcp(s_0, s_1, ..., s_{k-1})$ is the longest common prefix of the input bit strings s_0, $s_1, ...,$ and s_{k-1}.
2. $s.cutTail(s')$ represents cutting the bit string s' from the tail of bit string s. s' can also be in format of a regular expression.

Theorem 6.6. Let C be the nearest common ancestor of concepts C_0, C_1, C_2, ..., and C_{k-1}. s is the bit string of C. s_i is the bit string of C_i. Then $s=lcp(s_0, s_1,..., s_{k-1}).cutTail(01*)$ holds.

Proof. We first confine k to be 2. Without loss of generality, we consider the case in Fig. 6.7. C is the nearest common ancestor of C_0 and C_1. C_0 precedes C_1 in the preorder traverse of RSM schema tree. C' is the child of C and the ancestor of C_0. Let s' be the bit string of C'. Therefore, s' is the longest common prefix of s_0 and s_1, and $s'=s0(1*)$. So $s=s'.cutTail(01*)$ holds, where $01*$ is a regular expression representing zero or more 1. So $s=lcp(s_0, s_1).cutTail(01*)$ holds.

In case of $k > 2$, let C' be the child of C and the ancestor of the concept C_i. C_i is the first concept among C_0, C_1, C_2, ..., and C_{k-1} in the pre-order traverse of the RSM schema tree. By the same reasoning, we can conclude $s=lcp(s_0, s_1,..., s_{k-1}).cutTail(01*)$. □

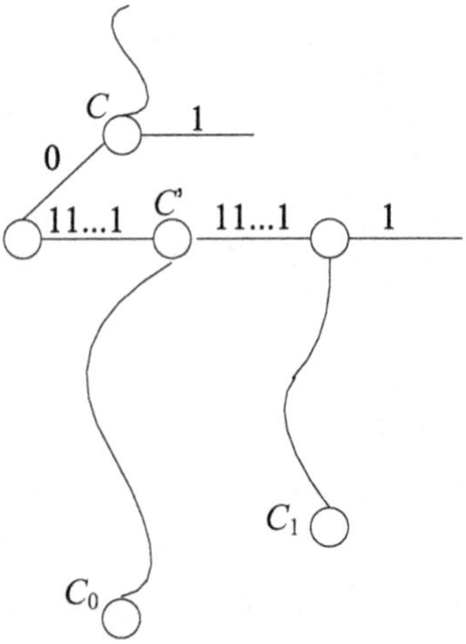

Fig.6.7. C is the nearest common ancestor of C_0 and C_1. C' is the child of C as well as the ancestor of C_0.

Theorem 6.7.   Suppose concept C_1 and C_2 are in the same axis X. s_1 is the bit string of C_1. s_2 is the bit string of C_2. C is their nearest common ancestor in the concept tree of X. s is the bit string of C. Then $dist(C_1, C_2) = zeroCount(s_1') + zeroCount(s_2')$, where $s=lcp(s_1, s_2)$, $s_1=ss_1'$, $s_2=ss_2'$, and $zeroCount(str)$ is the number of 0 in the bit string str.

Proof. Since bit 0 represents one time of concept refinement, the number of 0 in s_1' is equal to the shortest path between C_1 and C, and the number of 0 in s_2' is equal to the shortest path between C_2 and C. Since the shortest path from C_1 to C_2 is the concatenation of the shortest path from C_1 to C and the shortest path from C to C_2, $dist(C_1, C_2) = zeroCount(s_1') + zeroCount(s_2')$. $\Box$

By Theorem 6.7, we can calculate the semantic distance between any two concepts given their bit strings. Theorem 6.5 shows that the semantic distance function is a metric function.

According to Theorem 6.1 to 6.4, all hierarchy semantics can be determined just according to concepts' bit strings, which include ancestor-descendant relationship, parent-child relationship, sibling relationship, and concept-in-axis relationship. Therefore, it is enough to only store the bit strings of axes and concepts rather than the schema tree. File *file_schema* depicted in Fig. 6.8 is on this purpose.

Using RSM schema tree, all hierarchy semantics between concepts are encoded into bit strings. By certain rules of computation on given concepts' bit strings, their semantics can be exposed. The RSM schema tree plays the role of interface between the above logical resource space and the underlying physical storage space which is a multidimensional bit string space.

file_shema

Coord in Pre-order	Path
X	#
C_1	0 #
C_{11}	0 0 #
C_{12}	0 0 1 #
C_{13}	0 0 1 1 #
C_2	0 1 #
C_{21}	0 1 0 #
C_{22}	0 1 0 1 #
Y	1 #
C_3	1 0 #
C_{31}	1 0 0 #
C_{32}	1 0 0 1 #
C_4	1 0 1 #
C_{41}	1 0 1 0 #
C_{42}	1 0 1 0 1 #

Fig.6.8. The One-One mapping between concepts and bit strings is stored in File *file_schema*.

One remaining problem in RSM schema tree is that a bit string may be extremely long even up to a linear order of the number of axis concepts. It is mainly caused by the magnitude of the number of sibling nodes. As known to us, the number of concept refinements is rather small in applications, say, less than 32 levels, which is confined by people's recognition ability. Hence the depth of concept hierarchy tree is limited in applications. However, the number of a concept's children can be quite large. For example, there are 193 countries in the world. In RSM schema tree, it requires 192 consecutive "1" bits appended to the bit string of concept *world* to represent the last country.

We propose a compressed encoding method to set an upper bound for the length of concepts' bit strings. It works as follows. Given a bit string, retrieve the first 7 bits. If it contains at least one 0, pack it with a byte by setting the first bit as 1. Otherwise, read more bits until 0 appears or the number of 1 bit adds up to 120. In either case, pack the number of counted 1 bits with a byte by setting the first bit as 0. Proceed with the above process until the residual bit number is no more than seven. Some packing bits are necessary when the residual bit number is less than seven.

```
Algorithm compressCode(s) // in Java language
    ByteList bl = ∅; // byte sequence
    byte count = -1;
    while(s.length > 7)
            if(count == -1)
            byte tmp = cut 7 bits from s head;
        if(tmp == (01111111)₂)
        count = 7;
    else
        tmp = tmp.setFirstBit(1)
        bl.append(tmp);
    else
            cut all successive 1 at most 120
        from the head of s;
        count += the number of 1 cut off;
            bl.append(count);
            count = -1;
    count = s.length;
    bl.append(pack(s)); // pack s with all 0 at the end
    bl.append(count);
```

Take the bit string 1101011 - 1111111 - 1111111 - 1110111 - 0101 in format of 7-bit segments as an example. The first 7-bit segment is packed in byte 11101011. Since the next 7-bit segment comprises seven 1, more bits are consumed until 0 appears. The counted number of 1 bit is 17 whose binary value is 00010001 which is treated as the second packing byte. The next 7-bit segment is 0111010. It is packed in byte 10111010. Now the residual bits are a single 1. We append successive 000000 to align its length with seven. Then we set the first bit of its packing byte as 1. So we get the third packing byte 11000000. At last, we append one more byte which records the length of the residual bits at the previous step. Its first bit is set as 0. Therefore, the final byte sequence is 11101011 - 00010001 - 10111010 - 11000000 - 00000001. More 1 bits does the original bit string have, more efficiency is our compressed encoding approach. Algorithm **compressCode** describes the above approach in detail.

The following theorem gives an estimation of the byte number after compression.

Theorem 6.8.   Assume the depth of concept hierarchy is at most D and the maximal number of any concept's children is at most $127c$, where c is a constant. Then, the number of bytes after compression is at most $D(1+c)$.

Proof. One time of concept refinement incurs one 0 bit, so one byte needs to preserve this information during bit string compression. Since the maximal number of child of any concept is $127c$ at most, c bytes are enough to represent all 1 bits incurred by sibling concepts of the same parent concept. Therefore, $1+c$ bytes are enough to go down one level in the axis's concept tree. Because the concept hierarchy depth is D at most, the byte number after compression is $D(1+c)$ at most. □

It is easy to decode a compressed bit string to the original. Each time decode one byte. Examine the first bit of the byte. If it is 1, the left seven bits belongs to the original bit string. If it is 0, recover a number of 1 bits which is equal to the value of the byte. The above process is carried out until only two bytes are left. The value of the second one is the number of packing bits in the first byte. So it is also convenient to recover the original information. In fact, we do not need to fully recover all the information since most of the time we just compare or do partial calculation upon their bit strings.

6.6 C-tree

Utilizing RSM schema tree, resource space is converted to multidimensional bit string space where each coordinate is a bit string. Hierarchy semantics exist between bit string coordinates, but there is no total ordering between them.

Current multidimensional access methods can do little in this setting. From their perspective, the underlying storage device is abstracted as a linear array, which supports fast sequential access but time-consuming random access. In contrast, there is no total ordering among points in a multidimensional space. Accordingly, current multidimensional access methods concentrate on devising efficient ways of putting nearby points into adjoining pages.

In multidimensional bit string space, the proximity of points is more complex than conventional multidimensional space. The shortcoming is that bit string coordinates do not have a linear ordering. Fortunately, they have a metric semantic distance as defined in Definition 6.1. Therefore, semantic distance between concepts (bit strings) can help construct more effective and efficient indexing structures.

We propose C-tree to get this work done, where C means *Concept* and *Classification*. It inherits the basic ideas of classic R-tree and its variants (Guttman, 1984). Moreover, the hierarchy semantics encoded in bit strings is extremely useful for resource insertion and query. It has not only spatial-close but also semantic-close resources stored in adjoining storage space.

6.6.1 Resource Operations

R-tree can be seen as the multidimensional version of B-tree. Points nearby in the space are grouped together in the same leaf node. Hence each leaf node corresponds to a *Minimum Bounding Rectangle* (MBR) of the points inside it. Leaf nodes with nearby MBRs are grouped together again to form the next upper level. This procedure continues until only one node is remaining which is made as the root node. Fig. 6.9 depicts an example of R-tree.

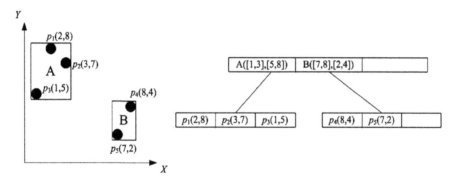

Fig. 6.9. An example of R-tree.

Nowadays, R-tree has already become a design rationale of spatial index structures, far more than just a specific indexing tree. It has three basic components: MBR format, **INSERT_POLICY**, and **SPLIT_POLICY**. MBR format is usually a hyper-rectangle or hyper-sphere in conventional multidimensional access methods. It should have certain transitivity property, say, spatial containment relationship. The two policies follow the *good* standards like the minimization of blank space, overlap area and area margin. Usually, distinct definitions of these four components lead to different spatial index trees, such as R^+-tree, R^*-tree, etc.

Procedures for resource operations are generally as follows.

```
// find point p inside node n.
Algorithm exactQuery(p, n)
     if(n is leaf)
               foreach(point c inside n)
                     if(p = = c)
                               output c;
          else
               foreach(branch nᵢ of n)
                     if(p is inside nᵢ's MBR)
                               exactQuery (p, nᵢ);
```

```
// find points inside given range and node n.
Algorithm rangeQuery(range, n)
    if(n is leaf)
            foreach(point c inside n)
                    if(c is inside range)
                            output c;
    else
            foreach(branch nᵢ of n)
                    if(range intersects with nᵢ's MBR)
                            rangeQuery(range, nᵢ);
```

```
// insert point p
Algorithm insert(p)
        node n = root;
        while(n is non-leaf)
                nᵢ is the best branch of n by
INSERT_POLICY;
                n = nᵢ;
        add p into n;
        if(n overflows)
                split(n);
        else if(n needs adjust)
```

```
// delete point p
Algorithm delete(p)
        // n is the leaf node containing point p
        node n = find(p, ROOT);
        if(n not exist)
                return;
        delete p from n;
        if(n underflows)
                condense(n);
        else if(n needs adjust)
                adjust(n);
```

```
// node n need to adjust its MBR as a result
// of child change
Algorithm adjust(n)
        do
                if(n is root)
                        adjust ROOT;
                        return;
                node n' = n.pp; // n' is the parent of n.
                adjust entry n in n';
                n = n';
        while(n needs adjust);
```

```
// node n need to split as a result of overflow
Algorithm split(n)
        do
                split n to new nodes p and q by
SPLIT_POLICY;
                if(n is root)
                        generate a new ROOT with
                        entry p and q;
                        return;
                node n' = the parent of n;
                remove entry n from n' and
                add p and q into n';
                n = n';
```

```
// node n need to condense as a result of underflow
Algorithm condense(n)
    Queue Q = ∅; // FIFO queue
    while(n is not root && n underflows)
        // add into queue's tail
        Q.addTail(all the entries of n);
        node n' = the parent of n;
        remove entry n from n';
        n = n';
    adjust(n);
    // get head node in Q and reinsert it
    while(n = Q.getHead())
        reinsert(n);
```

```
// reinsert n at its original level
Algorithm reinsert(n)
    node n' = root;
    // n.lev is the level of node n.
    // Leaf node's level is 0.
    while(n'.lev > n.lev + 1)
        n_i is the best branch of n' by
INSERT_POLICY;
        n' = n_i;
    add n into n';
    if(n' overflows)
```

6.6.2 Minimum Bounding Rectangle

In multidimensional bit string space, MBR is not easy to perceive and visualize. The impediment lies on no linear ordering between bit string co-ordinates. So no two coordinates can be found enough to set the range of several given coordinates. If we simply list them all, too many coordinates must be stored in the upper-level nodes of the index tree. It seems inevitable to predefine an order between concepts. However, such an order should preserve hierarchy semantics between concepts as much as possible. Meanwhile, resource operations should follow the hierarchy semantics.

In our implementation, we define the order as the pre-order traverse of RSM schema tree. Fig. 6.10 depicts an example. $[C_s, C_e]$ is the range of the concepts in shape of dark nodes. $[C_s, C_e]$ covers all dark nodes and shadow nodes. Therefore, an MBR is in format of $([s_0, e_0], [s_1, e_1], ..., [s_{n-1}, e_{n-1}])$ where s_i is the bit string of C_{is}, e_i is the bit string of C_{ie}, $[C_{is}, C_{ie}]$ is the concept range on the ith dimension, and n is the dimensionality of the multidimensional bit string space.

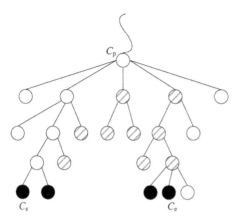

Fig. 6.10. Concept range $[s, e]$ in the concept tree.

Theorem 6.9. The containment relationship between C-tree's MBRs satisfies the transitivity property.

Proof. MBR's projection in each dimension satisfies containment transitivity property, so MBR satisfies containment transitivity property. □

Definition 6.2. Bit string s is the *proper prefix* of s' if and only if s is the prefix of s' but not equal to s'.

Theorem 6.10. Let s be the bit string of concept C_s, e be the bit string of concept C_e, and t be the bit string of concept C. C is in range of $[C_s, C_e]$ in the concept tree if and only if $s \leq_\alpha t \leq_\alpha e$ where $\leq_\alpha$ is the alphabetical order between bit strings assuming 0 is in front of 1 in the alphabetic.

Proof. Since the preorder traverse of concept tree is the same as the pre-order traverse of transformed binary tree, C is in range of $[C_s, C_e]$ if and only if t is in range of $[s, e]$, that is, $s \leq \alpha t \leq \alpha e$.□

MBR may need update after point insertion. Assume the point is $p(p_0, p_1,..., p_{n-1})$ and the MBR is $mbr([s_0, e_0], [s_1, e_1],..., [s_{n-1}, e_{n-1}])$. If p_i is contained by the range of $[s_i, e_i]$, $[s_i, e_i]$ remains no change. If p_i precedes s_i, then $[s_i, e_i]$ is changed to $[p_i, e_i]$. If e_i precedes p_i, then $[s_i, e_i]$ is changed to $[s_i, p_i]$.

One characteristic of multidimensional bit string space is that coordinates can be inserted or deleted. It is useful in real applications, since concept hierarchy semantics evolutes with time. New concept refinement represents a deeper understanding of the application's semantics.

6.6.3 On INSERT_POLICY

Insert policy decides which MBR among several sibling MBRs is the *best* to incorporate the given point. In conventional multidimensional space, *good* means least area enlargement, least overlap area enlargement, least perimeter, etc. The basic idea is making MBR more compact so that blank space is as small as possible. In this way, less space needs accessed in the query process.

In multidimensional bit string space, however, such three *good* measurements are hard to compute since we do not know exactly how many coordinates are inside a given concept range. What we are able to know is the following two:

1. whether the containment relationship satisfies between concept and concept range, and
2. the semantic distance between concept and the start/end concepts of the concept range.

We will show how to define the semantic distance between a concept and a concept range, which contributes to more compact MBRs as well as better grouping according to semantic clustering.

Definition 6.3. Given a point $p(p_0, p_1,..., p_{n-1})$ and an MBR $mbr([s_0, e_0], [s_1, e_1],..., [s_{n-1}, e_{n-1}])$, the semantic distance between p and mbr is measured by $distPM(p, mbr) = \Sigma_{i=0..n-1} \min\{dist(p_i, s_i), dist(p_i, e_i)\}$.

The smaller is *distPM*, the better is the insertion of *p* into *mbr*. Two cases needs to be taken into account when deciding the *best* sibling MBR to insert point *p* into.

When *p* is inside one or more MBRs, resolve tie by selecting the MBR which has the smallest semantic distance to *p* according to Definition 6.3. This aims at promoting the compactness of MBR.

When *p* is outside each MBR, three measurements are considered in decreasing priority.

1. *least overlap*. Let *overlapNum(mbr, i)* be the number of sibling MBRs whose projections on *i*th dimension intersect with MBR *mbr*'s projection on *i*th dimension. Let *mbr'* be the MBR after inserting point *p* into *mbr*. Then *overlapNum(mbr', i)-overlapNum(mbr, i)* measures the increased projection overlap number on *i*th dimension for inserting point *p* into *mbr*. *least overlap* is the MBR with the smallest $\Sigma_{i=0..n-1}$ (*overlapNum(mbr', i)-overlapNum(mbr, i)*).
2. *least semantic distance*. Select the MBR which has the smallest semantic distance to *p* as defined in Definition 6.3.
3. *least perimeter enlargement*. Suppose *mbr'* ([s_0', e_0'], [s_1', e_1'],..., [s_{n-1}', e_{n-1}']) is the resulting MBR of inserting point $p(p_0, p_1,..., p_{n-1})$ into MBR *mbr* ([s_0, e_0], [s_1, e_1],..., [s_{n-1}, e_{n-1}]). The perimeter enlargement is $\Sigma_{i=0..n-1}$ ([s_i', e_i']−[s_i, e_i]), where [s_i', e_i'] − [s_i, e_i] is equal to *dist* (s_i', s_i)+*dist* (e_i', e_i).

6.6.4 On SPLIT_POLICY

When a node in the tree index overflows, it needs split since the allocated storage space for it is limited. The *goodness* standards for node split are much the same as that of insert policy. Blank space should be minimized to improve query efficiency. The difficulty of achieving this goal in C-tree is the same as that of insertion.

Our approach consists of two steps. At the first step, pick up two children of current node as seeds. They should be the *farthest* pair of child nodes. Suppose mbr_1=([s_{10}, e_{10}], [s_{11}, e_{11}],..., [$s_{1\,n-1}$, $e_{1\,n-1}$]) and mbr_2=([s_{20}, e_{20}], [s_{21}, e_{21}],..., [$s_{2\,n-1}$, $e_{2\,n-1}$]). Their *pre-order distance distPre(mbr$_1$, mbr$_2$)* is defined to be $\Sigma_{i=0..n-1}f$([s_{1i}, e_{1i}], [s_{2i}, e_{2i}]) where

f([s_{1i}, e_{1i}], [s_{2i}, e_{2i}])

$$= \begin{cases} 0 & s_{2i} \in [s_{1i}, e_{1i}] \vee s_{1i} \in [s_{2i}, e_{2i}] \\ \min\{dist(s_{1i}, e_{2i}), dist(s_{2i}, e_{1i})\} & \text{otherwise} \end{cases}$$

distPre(mbr₁, mbr₂) computes the distance in the pre-order traverse of RSM shema tree. It measures the *farness* of a pair of child nodes by the sum of the semantic distances of their projections on each dimension. It measures an overall semantic closeness from the perspective of multidimensional classification.

The second step is assigning each left child nodes of current node to the nearer one of the two seeds. For example, *mbr'* will be assigned to *mbr₁* if *distPre(mbr₁, mbr')* is smaller than *distPre(mbr₂, mbr')*. This process will group together similar classification zones in the space.

6.6.5 Disk management

Fig. 6.11 depicts an example of C-tree. Three classification points p_1, p_2 and p_3 are grouped together in node A. The other two are grouped in node B. A and B are the children of the root node.

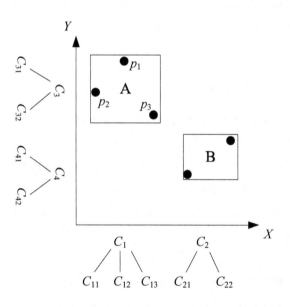

Fig. 6.11. An example of C-tree. Three points $p_1(C_{12},C_{31})$ {*fp₁, fp₂, fp₃*}, $p_2(C_{11},C_3)$ {*fp₆*} and $p_3(C_{13},C_{32})$ {*fp₄, fp₅*} are grouped together in rectangle A.

Fig. 6.12 describes the corresponding external memory storage using a single file *file_ctree*. It is divided into pages each of which corresponds to a certain size of consecutive storage space. The size of the page would better match disk's block size to enable efficient page read and write. The first page is allocated for root node of C-tree in default. Each of the other tree nodes is also stored in one page which is randomly allocated. The pointer to the child node in C-tree is transformed to page shift of the child node's page in *file_ctree*. Each point inside a leaf node represents some kind of conceptual classification. It is accompanied by the shift number of the page storing its resources, for example, a list of file paths if the resources are local files, or URI (Uniform Resource Identifier) in the network setting.

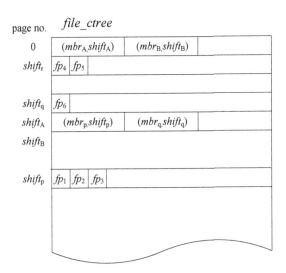

Fig. 6.12. *file_ctree* stores C-tree in external memory.

6.7 Summary

The Resource Space Model uses hierarchical classification semantics to reflect semantics in the real world, document world, machine world and mental world. Relational tables are not effective in supporting hierarchical classification semantics. XML files bring into resource redundancy. Moreover, their performance in multi-attribute search is not good. Multidimensional access methods depend on linear order between coordinates of axis, while there is no linear order on coordinates in Resource Space Model.

The proposed RSM storage mechanism transforms a resource space into a multidimensional bit string space by encoding coordinates into bit strings, and then uses C-tree to index the multidimensional bit string space. Hierarchy semantics is embodied in the bit strings and used by C-tree in resource insertion and deletion to group semantic-close resources in disk. C-tree is not only a novel multidimensional indexing structure but also a semantic-based resource re-organization mechanism for efficient search.

Chapter 7 Structured Peer-to-Peer Resource Space

The Resource Space Model represents normalization while Peer-to-Peer systems represent autonomy. Integrating resource space with the structured Peer-to-Peer network can construct a structured Peer-to-Peer resource space to realize the synergy between normalization and autonomy.

7.1 Basic Idea

7.1.1 The Problem

Peer-to-Peer (P2P) networks can be largely classified into two types: unstructured and structured.

In unstructured P2P networks like Freenet (Clarke et al., 2000), Gnutella (http://www.gnutella.com) and Napster (http://www.napster.com), each peer manages its own data, and there is no particular assumption about the assignment of data onto peers.

In structured P2P networks, data items (or indexes of data items) are assigned onto peers according to some rules. One popular type of structured P2P networks is the Distributed Hash Table (DHT) based networks like CAN (Ratnasamy et al., 2001), Pastry (Rowstron and Druschel, 2001), Chord (Stoica et al., 2001) and Tapestry (Zhao et al., 2001). They mainly aim at finding efficient ways to locate resources.

The Resource Space Model uses normalized classification semantics to uniformly specify and manage various resources. Integrating the resource space with P2P networks offers a chance for P2P networks to manage complex resources by content.

It is also a chance for the Resource Space Model to support decentralized applications by cooperating with P2P networks. Previous works on

Resource Space Model mainly focused on the model itself and the central-ized storage mechanism. If we want to use the Resource Space Model to manage a Web community or an office network, the following issues are critical:

1. How to implement the Resource Space Model in a decentralized envi-ronment?
2. How to find a decentralized data structure to represent the Resource Space Model and appropriate algorithms to efficiently implement its operations?

   This chapter presents an approach to construct a resource space overlay to form a structured P2P Resource Space Model. The basic idea is similar to the space partition idea of CAN (Ratnasamy et al. 2001).

7.1.2 A Brief Introduction to CAN

Like other DHT-based P2P networks, CAN provides applications with an interface that maps *key* of a resource into the *peer* storing this resource. It organizes an *n*-dimensional Cartesian space. This Cartesian space is parti-tioned into zones, with one or more peers serving as owner(s) of the zone. An example of 2-dimensional CAN is shown in Fig. 7.1. Each *key* in the system is mapped into a point in the space using the distributed hash table. The peer that owns the zone containing the point owns the corresponding *key*, and is responsible for returning the resources it holds.

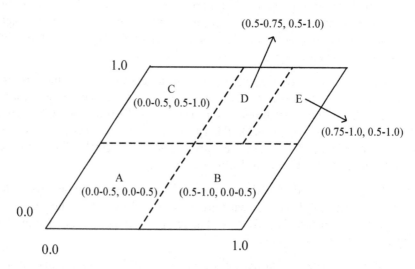

Fig. 7.1. A 2-dimensional Cartesian space of CAN with 5 peers.

The issue of routing from a source peer to a destination peer in CAN turns into the issue of routing from one zone to another in the Cartesian space. This routing will follow the path through the Cartesian space from the source point to the destination point.

A peer joins the CAN by picking a *random* point in the Cartesian space, routing to the zone that contains the point, splitting the zone into two, and occupying one by itself. A peer departs from the CAN by asking one of its neighbors to take over its zone.

7.1.3 Basic Approach

The following is the basic approach to deploy a resource space on structured P2P networks (structured P2P RSM).

It divides the topological space of the resource space into many independent zones. Each node in the P2P network takes charge of one zone. Each node maintains the information of its neighbor nodes for routing. The approach naturally reserves the topological space view of the resource space and supports the basic operations of the Resource Space Model.

The following are challenges of partitioning the resource space:

1. The resource space is not a Cartesian Space like CAN's partition space. It is a discrete classification space. Moreover, its coordinates could be in tree structure. Therefore, the partition of resource space needs some preprocessings and constraints.
2. There is no guarantee that the indices (i.e. the coordinates of resources) of resources are evenly distributed in the resource space, since resources are likely to center around the hot points (a point in resource space represents a topic). Load balancing becomes a major issue of the system.

7.2 The System Design

7.2.1 The Basis

The resource space is a special n-dimensional topological space. For efficient routing, our approach assumes that the coordinates at every axis are ordered. The order specified by the designer takes the highest priority. If the designer does not specify the order, the coordinates are ordered according to some simple semantics such as the lexicographical order, numerical order, and time order. This is reasonable once the resource space has been designed and used to stably support applications. After ordering, the distance between two coordinates is defined as the number of coordinates between them.

The structured P2P RSM only concerns resource locating operation — the most basic operation of the Resource Space Model. All the nodes share the same resource space schema in the structured P2P RSM. The entire resource space is dynamically partitioned among all the nodes in the system such that every node owns its individual and distinct zone in the overall resource space. Each zone owns a continuous range of coordinates along each dimension.

Fig. 7.2 shows a 2-dimensional resource space partitioned by 6 nodes.

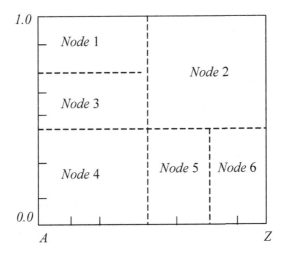

Fig. 7.2. Example of 2-dimensional space with 6 nodes.

The resources in resource space are stored as follows:

Each resource in the resource space can be represented by a point whose coordinate will be taken as the index of this resource. Then, the (*key, value*) pair is stored at the node that owns the zone within which the corresponding point lies. Here, *key* is the coordinate values of the point in the resource space, and *value* is either the resource itself or the pointer to the resource, like IP address of the node possessing this resource.

To retrieve a resource, the requesting node must route the query message in the structured P2P RSM overlay to the target node storing the resource. Effective routing is therefore a crucial aspect of the design of the structured P2P RSM.

Nodes in the structured P2P RSM self-organize into an overlay that represents the resource space. No super node is needed in this overlay. Each node maintains a small piece of information such as IP addresses of its neighbors and coordinate information of the corresponding zones. This information will serve as the routing table that enables routing between two arbitrary nodes in the structured P2P RSM overlay.

7.2.2 Node State

Each node maintains a routing table that holds the IP addresses and the virtual coordinate zones of its neighbors in the resource space. In an *n*-

dimensional resource space, two nodes are neighbors if their coordinate zones overlap at $n-1$ dimensions and adjoin at one dimension. In Fig. 7.2, node 3 is a neighbor of node 1 because its coordinate zone overlaps with the node 1's at the X-axis and adjoins at the Y-axis. Node 6 is not a neighbor of node 1 because their coordinate zones do not adjoin at both the X and Y axes.

The zone of each node is an n-dimensional rectangle and can be denoted by R.

$$R = (R^0, R^1, \ldots, R^{n-1}) \tag{7.1}$$

Here, n is the number of dimensions and R^k is a closed interval $[a, b]$ describing the scope of the zone along dimension k.

The size of the routing table is very small, i.e. $O(n)$ for a n-dimensional resource space. No special effort is needed to well design the structure of the routing table. The speed of searching the routing table is fast.

7.2.3 Routing

The local neighbor states are sufficient to route between two arbitrary points in the space. All structured P2P RSM messages include destination coordinates. The node uses a greedy method to forward the message to the destination.

The routing procedure is executed whenever a message destined for coordinate D is arrived at a node P. It is shown in pseudo code as follows.

Notations:

1. Z: the zone occupied by P.
2. N_i: one neighbor of node P, suppose P has m neighbors, $0 \leq i < m$.
3. R_i: the zone occupied by neighbor N_i.
4. R_i^k: the closed interval describing the scope of the zone R_i along dimension k.
5. $D = (D^0, D^1, \ldots, D^n)$: D^k is the value describing the coordinate position of D along dimension k.
6. $Dist(D, R)$: the distance between coordinate D and zone R.

The routing procedure:

(1) if $(D \text{ in } Z)\{$
(2)   // D is within the range of zone Z

(3)   *P* is the targeting node;
(4) } else {
(5)   forward to N_j, satisfying $Dist(D, R_j) = Min_{0 \leq i < m}(Dist(D, R_i))$;
(6) }

The *Dist* function can be defined in many ways according to the applications. A good definition could highly reduce the number of routing hops, while a poor definition may make the routing procedure run into an endless loop. The poor definition is not obvious, for example, one may define $Dist(D, R)$ as the point distance between D and the centroid of R. This is meaningful in geometry and likely applicable. But actually it causes endless loop with high probability, especially when D is close to an edge of its targeting zone. Therefore, giving a guideline for the definition of *Dist* function is helpful.

We have defined R^k as a closed interval $[a, b]$ describing the scope of the zone R at dimension k. So, before discussing the guidelines of $Dist(D, R)$, we firstly define the distance between a coordinate value and a coordinate interval as follows:

$$Dist'(D^k, R^k) = \begin{cases} Dist''(a, D^k) & if & D^k < a \\ 0 & if & a \leq D^k \leq b \\ Dist''(D^k, b) & if & b < D^k \end{cases} \qquad (7.2)$$

The *Dist''* here is the distance between two coordinates in an axis. Then the guideline can be described as follows.

Guideline. Suppose R_i and R_j are zones of two neighbors which adjoin at a certain dimension k. If $Dist'(D^k, R_i^k) < Dist'(D^k, R_j^k)$, then the definition of *Dist* function should satisfy $Dist(D, R_i) < Dist(D, R_j)$.

The guideline can ensure that the routing correctly terminates at the targeting node.

It is intuitively correct since the routing procedure always steps close to the target along a dimension if the guideline is satisfied. The following is the detailed proof.

Proof. Suppose R_i and R_j are zones of two nodes, and the *Dist* definition satisfies the guideline. We firstly have the following lemma:

If $\forall k \in [1,n]$, $Dist'(D^k, R_i^k) \leq Dist'(D^k, R_j^k)$ and $\exists l \in [1,n]$, $Dist'(D^l, R_i^l) < Dist'(D^l, R_j^l)$, then $Dist(D, R_i) < Dist(D, R_j)$ holds.

From the lemma, we can deduce that the zone of the target node has the globally lowest *Dist* value with *D*. At the same time, any non-target node has at least one neighbor whose *Dist* value is lower. This is straightforward since there are neighbors at two sides of one node along each dimension. So at each step, the routing process reaches a node with lower *Dist* value. As the routing leads to a direction of lower *Dist* value, it will eventually terminate at the valley bottom, i.e. the targeting node. □

The following gives one sample of the *Dist* definition:

$$Dist(D, R_i) = \sqrt{Dist'^2(D^0, R_i^0) + Dist'^2(D^1, R_i^1) + \ldots + Dist'^2(D^n, R_i^n)} \quad (7.3)$$

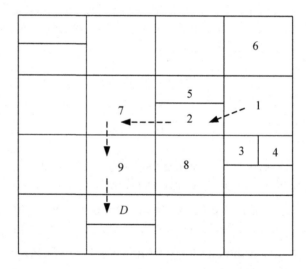

Fig. 7.3. Sample routing path from node 1 to coordinate *D*.

Fig. 7.3 shows a sample routing path using equation 7.3 as the definition of *Dist*. We can also see that there are many routing ways to the destination. A simple node failure in the routing path cannot detain the routing process. The routing of the structured P2P RSM is robust to node failures.

For a *n*-dimensional resource space partitioned into *m* equal zones, the average routing path length is $(n/4)(m^{1/n})$ and each individual node maintains $2n$ neighbors' information. These scaling results mean that for a n-dimensional space, we can increase the number of nodes (and hence zones) without increasing per node state while the path length grows as $O(m^{1/n})$.

7.2.4 Node Join

Here we discuss how the structured P2P RSM deals with node join which allows the structured P2P RSM to grow incrementally. As described above, the entire resource space is partitioned amongst the nodes currently in the structured P2P RSM. Thus when a new node joins the system, one new zone of the coordinate space must be allocated for it. Also, the new node needs to initiates its node state, and then informs other nodes of its presence.

The strategy for new zone allocation is that an existing node splits its zone into two parts, retains one part and gives the other part to the new node.

In order to join the structured P2P RSM system, the new node must first find a node, called introducer, currently in the system and its IP address. Many techniques can help to find the introducer. One example of such techniques is introduced in (Eugene and Zhang, 2001). This technique assumes that the system has an associated DNS domain name, and that this DNS name can resolve to the IP address of one or more bootstrap nodes. A bootstrap node maintains a partial list of structured P2P RSM nodes it believes are currently in the system. To join a structured P2P RSM, a new node looks up the domain name in DNS to retrieve a bootstrap node's IP address. The bootstrap node then supplies the IP addresses of several randomly chosen nodes currently in the system.

Then, the new node must select a coordinate D that is suitable for itself so as to allow the system to allocate one zone for it. One method is that the coordinate D is randomly selected in the resource space. The advantage of this method is that the entire resource space can be divided evenly amongst the nodes currently in the structured P2P RSM system. If the resource indices are also distributed evenly in the resource space, then this method can achieve the load balance simply and naturally. However, this assumption is not tenable in the real resource space. And, the random selection may lead to an imbalance in the distribution of resource indices across the nodes.

To cope with this uneven distribution of resource indices, a content-aware coordinate D selection method is proposed to force the distribution of nodes to follow the distribution of resources indices. When a node joins, the coordinate D is selected as the center of the coordinates of resources which will be published by the new node. Apparently, if D is selected in this way, more nodes will be located in the area where more resource indices exist. Thus, a more balanced index distribution across nodes is achieved. Moreover, this method makes the structured P2P RSM have the locality property. As the nodes occupy the zones covering the indices of their resources, some redirections from indices nodes to resource nodes are saved. And, assuming the resources published by a node can reflect its interests, most of the queries initiated by a node would be answered within a small range of neighbors in the structured P2P RSM system.

Fig. 7.4 evaluates this load balancing technique by distributing 5×10^4 papers onto 1000 nodes using the structured P2P RSM. The X-axis gives the number of indices per node, while the Y-axis gives the percentage of nodes containing the coioresponding number of indices. The *CAN* series evaluates the original CAN solution. It serves as the baseline for comparison. The *structured P2P RSM-random* series uses the random selection of coordinate D. The *structured P2P RSM-Content* series uses the content-aware coordinate D selection. Note that the load for *structured P2P RSM-random* is poor as the number of indices per node varies largely across nodes. Using content-aware coordinate D selection, most nodes contain less than 70 indices, which is close to the average number 50. The load becomes more balanced as expected.

After the coordinate D is selected, the new node sends a join request destined for the coordinate D. This message is sent into the structured P2P RSM system via the introducer described above. Each structured P2P RSM node then uses the structured P2P RSM routing mechanism to forward the message until it reaches the node whose zone contains D. This current occupant node then splits its zone into two parts and assigns one part to the new node. The resource indices located in the part to be handed over are also transfered to the new node.

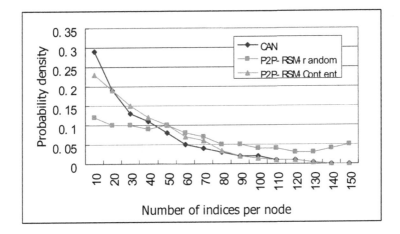

Fig. 7.4. The effect of content-aware coordinate D selection.

The splitting method can also be implemented in several strategies, like splitting on the halves. But in order to enhance the balance in the distribution of resource indices across the nodes, we take the strategy that splits the zone into two parts having the same number of resource indices. This strategy enhances the load balance by evenly dividing the whole resource space into zones possessing nearly the same number of resource indices.

Finally, the neighbors of the split zone must be notified so that routing can include the new node. After obtaining its zone from the previous occupant, the new node learns its neighbor set and the IP addresses of them, since this set is obviously a subset of the previous occupant's neighbors, plus the occupant itself. The new node uses these information to initiate its node state. And at the same time, the previous occupant updates its neighbor set to eliminate those nodes that are no longer neighbors. Both the new and old nodes' neighbors must be informed of the node join and reallocation of space, and update their node states to the current of the times. Fig. 7.3 and Fig. 7.5 show an example of a new node (node 10) joining a 2-dimensional structured P2P RSM.

The cost of node join is reasonably small. Only the neighbors in a very small range of resource space are involved in the state update process. And the number of neighbors of a node depends only on the dimensionality of the coordinate space. Thus, *node join affects only O(number of dimensions) existing nodes*. This performance is important for structured P2P RSM systems with huge number of nodes.

Besides, in order to ensure that all node states are up-to-date and the involved neighbors in node join quickly learn about the change and update their own neighbor sets accordingly, every node in the system should periodically send its currrent node state with its currently assigned zone to all its neighbors. This heart-beat style refreshment is suitable for such distributed environments.

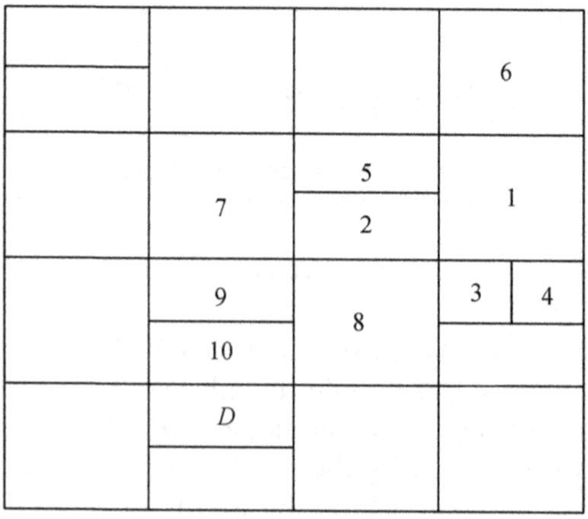

Fig. 7.5. Example of 2-dimensional structured P2P RSM after node 10 joins.

7.2.5 Node Departure

The idea for the normal node departure is quite simple. When a node leaves the structured P2P RSM, it explicitly hands over its zone and the associated (*key*, *value*) list to one of its neighbors. The important thing is how to select this neighbor. The structured P2P RSM has an implicit restriction on the zone that it must be an *n*-dimensional rectangle. Thus, if the zone of one neighbor can be merged with the departing node's zone to produce a valid zone, then this is done. The selected neighbor takes over the (*key*, *value*) list, and also gets the neighbor state of the departing node to produce its own neighbor state. If such neighbors do not exist, for example, the node 11 in Fig. 7.6 cannot produce any valid single zone with its neighbors, the zone is handed to the neighbor who has the smallest number of resource indices. However, this neighbor does not merge the two zones, but just temporarily handle both zones, much like this neighbor acts as two virtual nodes. Afterwards, the two zones will be reoccupied by two joining nodes along with node join or merged with other zones into a valid single zone along with node departure. In both cases, the neighbors must be informed of this reallocation of space. The previously mentioned heart-beat style refreshment will be used here to ensure all node states are up-to-date.

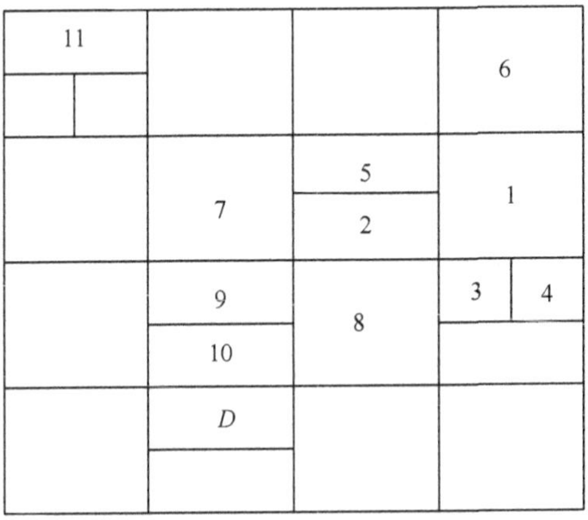

Fig. 7.6. Node 11 cannot produce any valid single zone with its neighbors.

7.3 Improvement

The basic structured P2P RSM algorithm described in the previous sections provides a fundamental knowledge about how the Resource Space Model is used in a P2P network. This section improves the basic structured P2P RSM model in the following two aspects:

(1) Improve the efficiency of the routing algorithm and the stability facing node failure.
(2) Extend the structured P2P RSM to support the important feature of the Resource Space Model: coordinates in tree structure.

7.3.1 Routing Performance

In the previously given routing algorithm, the neighbor selection for the next hop is based on the distance defined in the resource space. This routing algorithm can be improved by considering the underlying network IP topology. Each node measures the network level Round-Trip-Time (*RTT*) to its neighbors. Then, for a given destination, the neighbor selection is based on both the distance in resource space and *RTT*.

The following is the procedure of routing.

(1) if (*D* in *Z*){
(2)   // *D* is within the range of zone *Z*
(3)   *P* is the targeting node;
(4) } else{
(5)   // considering *RTT*
(6)   forward to N_j,   satisfying $Dist(D, R_j) < Dist(D, Z)$ AND $Dist(D,$
(7) $R_j)+RTT(P, N_j) = Min_{0 \leq i < m}(Dist(D, R_i) +RTT(P, N_i))$;
(8) }

Besides considering the underlying network, the structured P2P RSM routing performance can also be improved by adding augment information to each node. The basic structured P2P RSM only stores neighbor information, thus one step can only advance one zone in such a context. If we add some long links from a distant span onto nodes, the routing performance can be improved greatly. This improvement is illustrated in Fig. 7.7.

Using long links can dramatically reduce the total number of routing hops, especially when the whole resource space is divided into many small zones. In Fig. 7.7, we can see the routing path from zone 1 to *D* using long link is shorter than the original one.

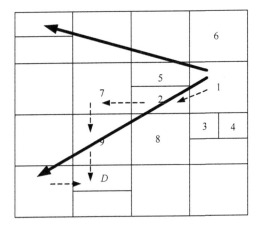

Fig. 7.7. Example of long links (denoted by thick arcs).

The following are two methods to construct the long links:

1. Constructing long links while system growing (Xu and Zhang, 2002).
2. Constructing long links while routing.

The idea behind the constructing while growing algorithm is quite simple. At regular intervals of system growth, like the zone of one node shrinks to a ratio threshold, snapshots are taken. A snapshot is simply a "frozen" copy of a current routing table of one node. That means the copy of the following things should be recorded at the node: the set of neighboring zones, and the set of corresponding addresses of the neighbors. This frozen routing table will be used as long links in the future routing process.

The routing algorithm will firstly consider the snapshots in the current node. If there are zones in snapshots containing the destination coordinate, the routing process will take the smallest one and send the request message to the corresponding node. Otherwise if no zone contains the destination coordinate, the routing process fallbacks to the original routing strategy.

The process is as follows.

(1) if (D in Z){
(2)   // D is within the range of zone Z
(3)   //P is the targeting node;

(4) } else {
(5)   if (D in snapshots){
(6)   forward to N, satisfying $R_N = Min(R : D$ within $R)$;
(7)   } else {
(8)   // considering RTT
(9)   forward to N_j, satisfying $Dist(D, R_j) < Dist(D, Z)$ AND
(10) $Dist(D, R_j) + RTT(P, N_j) = Min_{0 \le i < m}(Dist(D, R_i) + RTT(P, N_i))$;
(11)   }
(12) }

When using constructing while routing method, each node allocates a buffer to store long links. The long link is detected while the node routes a search request, and is added to the buffer. The buffer can simply take FIFO replacement strategy. The routing algorithm selects the node of next hop by considering both neighbors' information and long link buffer.

The process is as follows.

(1) if (D in Z){
(2)   // D is within the range of zone Z
(3)   // P is the targeting node;
(4) } else {
(5)   // long links, L represents the long link buffer
(6) L_k, satisfying $Dist(D, R_k) < Dist(D, Z)$ AND $Dist(D, R_k) + RTT(P,$
(7) $L_k) = Min_{0 \le i < buffersize}(Dist(D, L_i) + RTT(P, L_i))$;
(8)   // neighbors
(9) N_j, satisfying $Dist(D, R_j) < Dist(D, Z)$ AND $Dist(D, R_j) + RTT(P,$
(10) $N_j) = Min_{0 \le i < m}(Dist(D, R_i) + RTT(P, N_i))$;
(11)   if ($Dist(D, R_k) + RTT(P, L_k) < Dist(D, R_j) + RTT(P, N_j)$)
(12)   forward to L_k
(13)   else
(14)   forward to N_j

(15) }

7.3.2 Node Failure Recovery

A node in the structured P2P RSM may fail or depart without warning. We need to ensure that the zones they occupied are taken over by the remaining nodes such that the structured P2P RSM is robust to node failures. As mentioned, under normal conditions a node sends periodic update messages, which contains its zone coordinates and a list of its neighbors and their zone coordinates, to each of its neighbors. Node failure can be detected when an update message from a neighbor is prolonged. We have explained that such an event of node failure does not detain the routing process, since the routing message can be forwarded to another node. However, the zone of the failed node should be taken over by an existing node to preserve the integrity of the structured P2P RSM.

To complete the zone takeover, one of the failed node's neighbors should be selected to run an immediate takeover algorithm, which is similar to the takeover algorithm of normal node departure. However in this case the resource indices held by the departing node would be lost until the state is refreshed by the holders of the resources.

The selection of this neighbor is based on a timer-based protocol. Once a node has detected that its neighbor has died, it initiates the takeover mechanism and starts a takeover timer running. Each neighbor of the failed node will do this independently, with the timer initialized in proportion to the number of resource indices occupied by the node. When the timer expires, a node sends a takeover message with its own zone information to all of the failed node's neighbors. When receiving a takeover message, a node cancels its own timer if the zone in the message is more suitable than its own zone to produce a valid single zone, or it replies with its own takeover message. In this way, a neighbor, which is still alive, is efficiently chosen to complete the zone takeover.

7.3.3 Coordinates in Tree Structure

The resource space described above is a standard n-dimensional topological space where each dimension has a flat coordinate space. However, a resource space may have coordinates in tree structure. Here discusses the implementation of these extensions for coordinates in tree structure. An example of the coordinates in tree structure is shown in Fig. 7.8. Such coordinates enable the resource space to represent rich semantics.

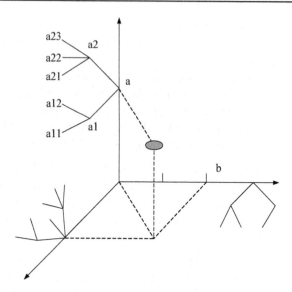

Fig. 7.8. Example of coordinates in tree structure.

When involving coordinates in tree structure, the design of the structured P2P RSM may face two main problems. The first is how to compute the distance between coordinates in such a resource space. The second is how to locate a coordinate in tree structure.

In order to use distance computing method in the flat coordinate view, we map the coordinates in tree structure into a flat one. Each leaf in a tree corresponds to a path from the root. And we use this path to name the leaf. Then, we replace the coordinates in tree structure with the leaf path's names. An example of the flattened coordinates for Fig. 7.8 is shown in Fig. 7.9. The path name is composed of names of passing nodes which are separated with a slash.

From the figures, we can see that one coordinate a in the tree structure should be represented by five coordinates in flat structure. Thus, to compute the distance between a and any other coordinates becomes to compute the distance between the span $(a/a1/a11 - a/a2/a23)$ and these coordinates. Essentially the original algorithm is designed to settle the single key search problem, but the coordinate locating in the coordinate tree turns into a range search. Thus, the original coordinate locating algorithm should be adjusted to reflect this difference.

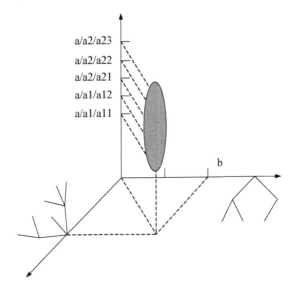

Fig. 7.9. The coordinates after flattening.

As the coordinates in the resource space are discrete, one possible solution is to decompose a into $a/a1/a11$, $a/a1/a12$, $a/a2/a21$, $a/a2/a22$, $a/a2/a23$, and set up searches for these five coordinates, and finally compose the search result. But this solution may introduce a search request flood, and produce unnecessary network overhead.

To eliminate the unnecessary search requests, we change the request for a to request for its lower bound $a/a1/a11$, and on the node responsible for $a/a1/a11$, we initiate a range search for ($a/a1/a11$, $a/a2/a23$) which will return the correct results.

The process for the range search is as follows.

```
// suppose P is the node responsible for lower bound of tree structured
// coordinates. This span search will be initiated on P.
(1) if ( D in Z) {
(2)     // D is within the range of zone Z
(3)     P is the targeting node;
(4)
(5)     // span search
(6)     for each dimension i
(7)         forward to N, if N and P adjoin along dimension i;
(8) }
```

7.4 Summary

The idea of deploying the resource space onto P2P systems is to divide the whole resource space into many small zones. Each node manages one zone of the resource space.

The structured P2P RSM is efficient and stable in distributed environment. For a n-dimensional space partitioned into m equal zones, the average routing path length is $(n/4)(m^{1/n})$ and individual nodes maintain $2n$ neighbors' information. These scaling results mean that, for a n-dimensional space, the increase of the number of nodes (i.e., the increase of the number of zones) does not lead to the increase of per node state, while the path length grows with $O(m^{1/n})$.

The routing performance is further improved by considering the underlying network IP topology and adding long links. Thus for time-sensitive applications, they can gain lower time cost by sacrificing some spaces. A timer-based failure recovery mechanism is proposed for stability. The improved mechanism can also deal with the coordinate tree.

The structured P2P RSM provides a decentralized, efficient and stable storage infrastructure for the Resource Space Model.

Chapter 8 Unstructured Peer-to-Peer Resource Space

Integrating the classification semantics of the resource space with unstructured Peer-to-Peer networks can construct an unstructured Peer-to-Peer resource space to realize the synergy between normalization and autonomy.

8.1 Unstructured Peer-to-Peer

Unstructured Peer-to-Peer networks allow resources to be randomly placed in self-organized peers. Connections between peers are optionally established. Any peer can join the network by an introducer. A peer can query its neighbors, and each neighbor forwards the query to their neighbors. The process stops when a predefined number of hops (Time-To-Live) is reached. During this process, any peer with the answer to the query can contact the query initiator directly and finish the file transmission. The topology and protocol are simple and can sustain the extremely dynamic environment.

The success of the unstructured Peer-to-Peer networks depends on its simplicity and usability. Such networks have low maintenance cost and are robust against accidental failures.

Routing in unstructured Peer-to-Peer networks often adopts one of the following three mechanisms: *flooding*, *random walk* and *gossip*.

In the flooding mechanism, each peer forwards the query to all of its neighbors except the one it receives the query from. Gnutella (http://rfc-gnutella.sourceforge.net) is a popular unstructured Peer-to-Peer application adopting the flooding mechanism.

In the random walk mechanism, a walker randomly chooses its next hop following certain probabilistic preference for each neighbor (Gkantsidis et al., 2004). The random walk requires little index and state maintenance.

This chapter focuses on the gossip mechanism.

Simulating the propagation of contagious diseases, gossip mechanisms have attractive scalability, reliability and degradation properties in realizing information dissemination in large networks (Bailey, 1975). Every peer that receives a message randomly selects a certain number of peers from its neighbors to multicast the message. They scale well since the load of peers grows logarithmically compared with the number of peers in the network.

The inherent scalability of the gossip-based mechanisms makes them suitable for disseminating information in large-scale networks. Meanwhile, they are resilient to changes in the underlying network topology and participants' failures (Briman et al., 1999; Demers et al., 1987; Eugster and Guerraoui, 2002; Eugster et al., 2001; Iamnitchi et al., 2002; Lin and Marzullo, 1999; Renesse et al., 2003).

Moreover, the gossip-based mechanisms are easy to implement and inexpensive to run, and they impose constant loads on participants. The throughput is stable over a relatively long period, and overheads are flat, predictable, and can be balanced with information about network topology (Vogels et al., 2003).

The performance of the gossip mechanisms can be improved by designing appropriate mapping from the network to a semantic space (Zhuge and Li, 2007a).

8.2 Incorporating Resource Space with Unstructured Peer-to-Peer

8.2.1 Peer-to-Peer in e-Science

Peer-to-Peer systems are playing more and more important role in resource sharing fields. Take scientific research for example, researchers are usually specialized in one area during a period of time and may concern other relevant areas. When there exists a Peer-to-Peer e-science system supporting researchers in different areas to share resources, intuitively a researcher will communicate with those sharing the same interests more frequently, because he/she could get the satisfied answers with high probability and save time by avoiding communication with irrelevant peers. But peers should not be constraint to the community of their fields as they need to communicate with peers in other fields, although not frequently. So classification of peers plays an important role in improving the performance of a Peer-to-Peer system.

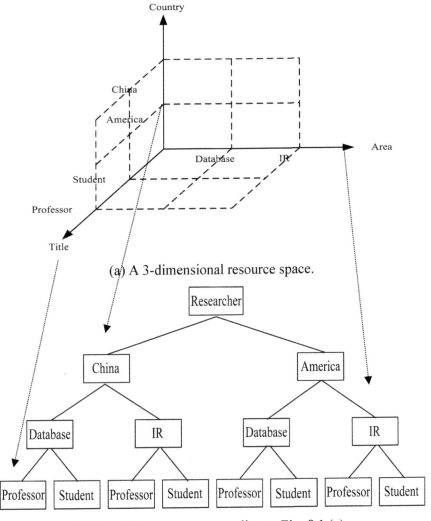

(a) A 3-dimensional resource space.

(b) A partition tree corresponding to Fig. 8.1 (a).

Fig. 8.1. Mapping a 3-dimensional resource space into a partition tree.

An n-dimensional resource space represents n kinds of partition on a set of resources. A resource space can be mapped into a partition tree (e.g., Fig. 8.1(a) can be mapped into Fig. 8.1(b)).

The classification semantics of the partition tree can be used to improve the performance of a Peer-to-Peer system because a peer could get the satisfied answers with high probability by interacting more frequently with the peers of the same community sharing common interests. Peers also need to communicate with peers of other communities.

We can make each leaf correspond to the peers in the same category. The communities in the leaves of the partition could change with peers' joining and departing behaviors.

The ACM Computing Classification System (CCS) is a classification hierarchy, which can help scientific activities such as submitting, reviewing, publishing and searching papers. It is based on the following philosophy:

1. The core of the CCS is a classification tree to present a hierarchical structure of disciplines and research areas.
2. The classification tree is restricted to three levels to accurately reflect the essential structure of the disciplines.
3. The uncoded fourth level of the classification tree, subject descriptors, provides sufficient detail to cope with new developments in the field (http://www.acm.org/class/1998/ccs98.html). Taking "Information systems → Database management → Languages → Query languages" for example, the first three levels correspond to the classification hierarchy, and "Query languages" is a subject descriptor.

The CCS is actually a 1-dimensional classification space. The Resource Space Model supports multi-dimensional classification semantics. Such classification knowledge can be used to improve the query efficiency if we implement a Peer-to-Peer e-science system. Actually, ontology has been used to improve structured Peer-to-Peer systems (Schlosser et al., 2002).

Incorporating resource space with gossip mechanisms is a way to improve the performance of this type of Peer-to-Peer networks and enables the Resource Space Model to support decentralized applications.

8.2.2 Integrating Resource Space with Gossip

As shown in Fig. 8.2, peers can be classified into communities belonging to the leaves of the partition tree. Each peer maintains neighbors with a hierarchical structure, where the number of levels a peer maintains depends on the depth that the peer lies in the partition tree.

Taking a peer p in the bottom left-hand community of the partition tree for example, it should maintain its neighbors at four layers, denoted as View(i) where $0 \leq i \leq 3$. View(i) is a set/list containing the neighbors' information (IP address etc.) that shares the nearest common ancestor at ith level with p. Therefore p's View(3) maintains the information of some peers within the same community, while p's View(2) maintains the information of its neighbors sharing the nearest common ancestor at level 2, and so on. The dashed lines show the mapping from the partition tree into the real Peer-to-Peer network.

When a peer sends a query, it will make a decision which level(s) in its view should be selected to forward the query (categories of that level are relevant to the query). Then, neighbor(s) at that level will be selected to forward the query. When a query reaches a community, a gossip-based mechanism will be adopted to disseminate the message. The peer that receives and could answer the query sends back the resources.

In the partition tree, the universe resource is *Level*0. The universe space is divided into the categories (e.g., *China* and *America* in Fig. 9.1(b)) constituting *Level*1. The categories of *Level*1 are further partitioned into finer categories constituting *Level*2, and so forth.

The Resource Space Model provides multi-dimensional classifications for accurately locating queries of multiple facets according to the content of query.

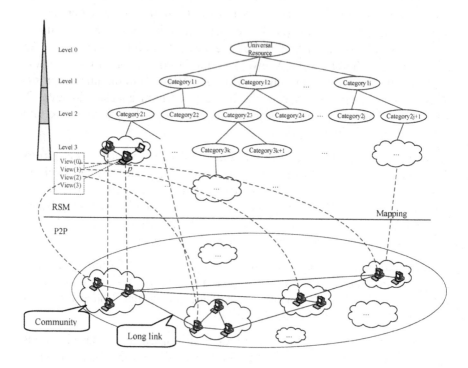

Fig. 8.2. Incorporating the resource space with the Peer-to-Peer network. A peer p has views of four levels: View(3), View(2), View(1) and View(0). View(3) maintains its neighbors of the same community. View(2), View(1) and View(0) maintain long links pointing to the neighbors of the other communities that shares the nearest common ancestor at ith (i.e., 2, 1, 0) level with p.

8.3 The Construction Mechanism

It is easy for a newly joined peer to know the partition hierarchy by contacting an introducer. So we assume that all peers share a consistent knowledge of partition.

The approach to determine the category of a new peer varies with applications. For example in an e-science environment, every peer can use a set of keywords to describe the papers it manages. Let A and B be term vectors of a new peer and a category respectively, the similarity between the new peer and the category can be measured by $\cos\theta = A \cdot B/(\|A\| \cdot \|B\|)$, (Berry et al., 1999). The category with the maximum similarity value can be chosen as the candidate category that the new peer belongs to. The final classification decision can be made by considering the application requirement, for example, classification by journal name or publisher.

Other techniques that can be used to help classification include Decision Tree (Quinlan, 1993), Bayes Classification (Duda and Hart, 1973), Neural Network (Ripley, 1996), Genetic Algorithms (Mitchell, 1996), k-nearest Classification (James, 1985) and Rough sets (Pawlak, 1991).

The static partition of the resource space can bring benefits to the Peer-to-Peer system. When a new peer joins, it just needs to contact one peer which will feed back the partition information. Using the partition information, the peer determines which category it belongs to. If some resource indices included in the peer belong to the other categories, the indices are reissued to other peers in charge of those resource categories. Using the information the introducer provides, the peer contacts the peers in the categories it belongs to and updates its neighbors' information.

Along with peers' joining, the leaf categories produced in the aforementioned mechanism can be further partitioned dynamically into two parts. The dynamic partition of leaves can be realized through a group size limit gl. When the size exceeds the limit, the group is partitioned into two parts of size $\lfloor gl/2 \rfloor$ and $\lceil gl/2 \rceil$ respectively.

The dynamic partition of the space works well with the skewed data distribution like the power-law distribution in many circumstances. Meanwhile, the static characteristics of the resource space partition improve the scalability of Peer-to-Peer system that peers join and depart autonomously and frequently, and reduce the cost of update when peers join or depart.

The disseminated message contains the content and some assistant information:

1. the type of the message, which could be *join*, *leave*, *issuing*, or *query*;

2. time to live (*TTL*) of the message, which is used in the *join*, *issuing* and *query* messages;

3. a list of identifiers of the peers that have received the message; and,

4. the IP address of the message initiator.

The following are notations for easier discussion:

1.   *fanout* — the number of neighbors one peer selects to disseminate when it receives a message;
2.   *TTL* (Time To Live) — the iterative rounds for a message to disseminate;
3.   *outView(i)* — the neighbors that peer *i* can send messages to; and,
4.   *inView(i)* — the neighbors that peer *i* can receive messages from.

8.3.1 Resource Index Issuing Process

When a resource index is issued by one peer, the peer *r* first decides the category the resource belongs to by utilizing the partition information of the resource space. A limit *l* restricting the whole process should be set. Along with each hop the message has transferred, *l* will be reduced by one. Then the peer forms an *issuing* message including the resource index, and sends the message to one of the peers in that category through its level views. When a peer receives the message, it first decides whether to add the index to its maintaining repository in consideration of its capacity. If the capacity exceeds its upper limit, then it randomly selects one neighbor from its proper level view and disseminates the *issuing* message. The issuing process will proceed until the resource index is accepted or *l* reaches zero. When *l* is zero, peer *r* also joins the community to which the index belongs to manage the resources.

8.3.2 Peer Join Process

When one peer joins the system, it first connects to one of the introducers. With the information fed back from the introducer, the newly joined peer decides its category with reference to the categories of its major resources. If there is more than one community in the category, the introducer randomly chooses a community. Then, the introducer forms a *join* message including the joining peer's information, and forwards the message to one of the peers in that community utilizing its level views.

During the process, a limit *sl* restricting the whole steps of dissemination should be set. Along with each hop the message transferred, *sl* will be reduced by one. When a peer in the community receives the message, it first decides whether to add the joining peer to its view with reference to its view size. If this causes the overflow of the view size, it forwards the *join* message to one randomly selected neighbor in the community until the joining peer is accepted or *sl* is zero. If the joining peer is still not accepted by any peer when *sl* reaches zero, the community is regarded as full and a new community should be created in the same resource space position as the full community. The joining peer forms its level views by exchanging information with the peers in the same category.

The newly joined peer maintains the index information of its major resources and issues the resource indices not belonging to its resource space position to the system adopting the aforementioned resource issuing mechanism.

With continuously peer joining, some communities become so large that decreases the effect of query routing. The following mechanism is adopted to split a large community into two parts of approximately equal size: Every peer initiates a random interaction with its neighbors when it has not decided to join which part. If the contacted peer is undecided also, both the initiating peer and the contacted peer choose different communities; otherwise, the initiating peer joins the part different from the contacted peer. Fig. 8.3 depicts the peer join process.

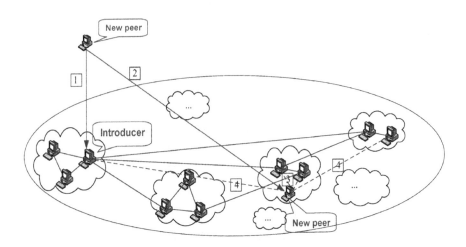

Fig. 8.3. Peer join process. Step 1: A new peer contacts the Introducer; Step 2: The new peer finds the community it belongs to; Step 3: The new peer contacts one peer in that community; Step 4: the new peer establishes its views. The dashed lines denote the links to the new peer's neighbors by establishing its views.

8.3.3 Peer Departure Process

When a peer r wants to depart the system, the following method keeps the peers in r's *inView* and those in its *outView* connected.

For each peer (take peer s for example) in its *outView*, peer r selects one peer ID (q for example) from its *inView* randomly, then forms a *failure* message including q and forwards it to s. When s receives the message, it substitutes r's ID(r) with q in its *inView*, then forwards a message with r and q. When q receives the message, it updates r with s in its *outView*. So in this way, the withdrawal behavior of a pivot peer does not lead to the partition of the whole network.

When a peer crashes without notifying other peers, the peers detect this situation by interchanging their states periodically. If no response within a certain period elapsed is returned from one of its neighbors, the peer regards it as being crashed and removes it from the corresponding view (Renesse et al, 1998).

Peer departure reduces the size of a community. It is necessary to merge communities in the same parent category if an existing community is small. The following is the approach to merge communities:

If the size of community p becomes small, it needs to coalesce with another community, and it should find its siblings in the partition tree first. If the siblings of the community p are also leaves of the partition tree and the number of its siblings is one (q, for example), then coalesce p and q, make their direct parent a leaf, and assign the coalesced community to that leaf. If the number of its siblings is larger than one, then select one leaf that has the least load and coalesce with the selected community.

If the siblings of the community p are not the leaves of the partition tree, perform the depth-first search in the sub-tree of the partition tree rooted at one of its siblings (e.g., q) until the leaves (e.g., r) of the sub-tree are reached, and then merge the two communities r and p into one.

Fig. 8.4 depicts the peer departure process.

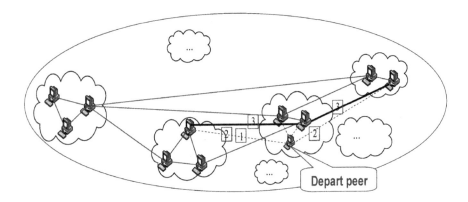

Fig. 8.4. Peer departure process. Step 1: The depart peer informs its neighbors; Step 2: The peer leaves the Peer-to-Peer network; Step 3: Neighbors establish new links. The dashed lines denote the links that will be removed since the depart peer leaves the network, and the darker lines denote the new links established by the depart peer's neighbors.

8.3.4 Query Processing Process

Before sending a query, the peer needs to compare the query with its index on resources, and then adopts different mechanisms to gossip queries by making use of the neighbor lists at different levels. In most applications, the resources a peer possesses reflect its interests, and the queries from the peer would be similar to its interests with high probability. In this situation, the query could be answered in the community the query-initiator belongs to, and only the neighbor list at the lowest level is needed for the query processing. While the query fits the other level, it is routed to that appropriate category, and a gossip process initiates there. When the query corresponds to more than one level, several gossip processes take place in parallel in the corresponding categories. The top-k correlative categories are selected to make trade-off between the whole network cost and the acceptable results.

Hamming distance $dist(\alpha_1, \alpha_2)$ between vectors α_1 and α_2 in a discrete data space is the number of dimensions on which the corresponding components of α_1 and α_2 are different (Qian et al., 2006). The distance between a vector $\alpha=(a_1, a_2, ..., a_d)$ and a discrete rectangle $S=S_1 \times S_2 \times ... \times S_d$ can be defined as:

$$dist(a, S) = \sum_{i=1}^{d} f(a_i, S_i), \text{ where } f(a_i, S_i) = \begin{cases} 0 & a_i \in S_i \\ 1 & otherwise \end{cases}.$$

The distance measures how many components of vector a are not contained in the corresponding component sets of rectangle S. In Resource Space Model, S_i corresponds to a specified coordinate set of the ith axis.

Haming distance is suitable for measuring distance in multidimensional non-ordered discrete data space, which is regarded as the correlative metric between query and the categories.

8.4 Performance Analysis

8.4.1 Reliability

The following analysis shows that the proposed mechanisms are reliable. Suppose the number of peers in the system is n, and the resource space partitions the peers into m categories. For simplicity, group members are assumed to be evenly distributed, that is, the sizes of categories are equal to n/m approximately. The following notations are used in the following discussion.

1. s—the source peer of one message;

2. ε—the probability of message loss during the gossip process.

3. τ—the probability of a peer crash during the gossip process.

4. A—the event that there is a directed path from s to all peers in the category s belongs to.

5. B—the event that there is at least one link directed from s to other categories.

6. $P(C)$—the probability that the event C happens.

Gossip style protocols are reliable in a probabilistic sense. According to the analysis in (Kermarrec et al, 2003), the probability of a given peer receiving the disseminated message is $1-(1/n^{fanout})(1 + o(1))$. And if the message loss is considered, the probability is $1-(1/n^{(1-\varepsilon)fanout})(1+o(1))$.

Messages can be disseminated in three different mechanisms:

1. Using the partition tree, the query initiator selects one level in its views. Thereafter it randomly selects one peer in its view at this level, and a gossip process is initiated with the selected peer being the source of the gossip. In this precondition: P(every peer in the selected category receives the message) $= P(A) \cdot P(B) = (1 - (1/(n/m)^{(1-\varepsilon)fanout})$ $(1 + o(1))) \cdot (1-\varepsilon) \cdot (1-\tau)$. Applications could make the messages communicate reliably through protocols like TCP, and in this way, ε would approach zero. The large number of peers n makes the protocol reliable.

2. The query initiator randomly selects one peer from each of its views at different levels, and disseminates the message to them, (the number of levels is m at most). The selected peers launch the gossip process in its community in parallel. And under the condition: P(every peer in the system receives the message)$= P^m(A) \cdot P(B)= (1-(1/(n/m)^{(1-\varepsilon)fan-out})(1+o(1)))^m \cdot (1-\varepsilon) \cdot (1-\tau)$. In the selection process, if sending message to the selected peer is failed, another peer could be selected randomly in the view at the same level. In this way, the negative influence of m in the previous equation is further reduced to guarantee the reliability of the mechanism.

3. The query initiator selects peers in views of different levels with different probabilities. And then the selected peers receive the message and disseminate it in their communities. Therefore, P(every peer in the selected communities receives the message) $= P^l(A) \cdot P(B)$, where l is the number of communities being selected and $1 \leq l \leq m$. Consequently, $P^m(A) \cdot P(B) \leq P^l(A) \cdot P(B) \leq P(A) \cdot P(B)$, and the gossip process adopting the proposed mechanism is reliable.

8.4.2 Hop Count Expectation

With reference to the work introduced in (Pittel, 1987), the total rounds $TTL(n, fanout)$ in the gossip-style system, which is necessary to infect an entire group of size n obeys:

$$TTL(n, fanout) = \log n \cdot (1/fanout + 1/\log(fanout)) + c + o(1),$$

where c is a constant.

A tradeoff exists between *fanout* and *TTL* in the network of n peers. Therefore in our systems, all peers are partitioned into different categories by one resource space. Assume the size of categories is equal approximately, i.e., n / m, the round of message dissemination in the sub-partitions is: $TTL(n \,/\, m, fanout)$. Considering the category selecting process, the hop count of message dissemination $TTL_1(n, fanout)$ in the whole system is as follows:

$$TTL_1(n, fanout)$$

$$= 1 + TTL(n \,/\, m, fanout)$$

$$= \log(n/m) \cdot (1/fanout + 1/\log(fanout)) + c_1 + o(1), \text{ where } c_1 \text{ is a constant.}$$

8.5 Experimental Evaluation

To compare the flat gossip mechanism and the RSM-based gossip mechanisms, experiments are carried out on two kinds of directed networks of 1000 peers: random networks and random power-law networks. Each experiment with different parameters (*fanout* and *TTL*) is repeated 100 times on each network we generated, and the initial peer is randomly selected at each time. The average value of these 100 results is used to illustrate the result.

Considering the graph of n nodes where the edge between each pair of nodes exists with probability $[\log(n) + c + o(1)] \,/\, n$. In the prerequisite, the probability that the graph is connected goes to $exp(- exp(- c))$, where c is a constant. And the target is reached by defining the appropriate *View* sizes of nodes. The gossip systems with size n have promising effect when the *fanout* value is set to be around $\log(n)$.

The following are two metrics to compare the performance of the two mechanisms:

1. Average network load, and

2. The number of peers that do not receive the message.

8.5.1 Experiments in Random Networks

An epidemic algorithm must make a tradeoff between scalability and reliability: larger views reduce the probability that nodes are isolated or that the network is partitioned, while smaller views help the network obtain better scalability.

For the random networks, the number of neighbors of each peer at the lowest level is 10 on average in our experiments. And the view size of other levels is rather smaller. It is 2 in this simulation. The community size is 100 in the experiments.

8.5.2 Experiments in Random Power-law Networks

Many large networks like the hyperlink network follow the power-law distribution of node degrees (Leland et al., 1994). The degree distribution is $p_k = Ak^{-\tau}$, where $A^{-1} = \sum_{k=2}^{k_{max}} k^{-\tau}$, k is the degree, k_{max} is the maximum degree, and $\tau > 0$ is the exponent of the distribution (Sarshar et al., 2004). Researches have shown that only when the virus accumulates to certain critical threshold, it will be prevalent. And, the critical threshold does not exist when the virus on the networks follows the power-law distributions. The virus does not need to accumulate to certain threshold to propagate quickly through hubs of the network.

The reason of considering power-law networks is that some unstructured Peer-to-Peer networks are characterized by random power-law and heavy tailed degree distributions. To keep the peers connected, we adjust degree from 15 to 100 following the aforementioned distribution with $\tau = 2.0$ in constructing random power-law networks. For each link, the start peer and the end peer are selected randomly, and as a result, the random power-law graph is constructed with average 14 neighbors at the lowest level in the experiment. The view size of other levels is 2, a rather small size. The community size is 100.

The simulation results from gossip networks without considering semantic partitions are denoted as *FlatGossip*, while the results making use of semantic partitions are denoted as *RSMGossip*. In the RSM-based gossip mechanisms, different number of gossip levels is chosen according to the comparison between the query and the category of the initiator. If the query strictly belongs to one category, then routing the query to other categories will not bring any benefit. And in this situation, the results are denoted by *RSMGossip1*.

When the query corresponds to several categories, it should be routed to all the categories that are potential to have the answers. For example, the query could be answered in 3 or 5 categories, and the results are denoted by *RSMGossip3* and *RSMGossip5*.

Both the random networks and the random power-law networks have the same network loads, if the networks have the equal size and the gossip mechanisms have the same parameters (*fanout* and *TTL*). Fig. 8.5 shows the average network load according to different parameters. The horizontal axis denotes the parameter *TTL*, and the vertical axis denotes the average network load during 100 times operations.

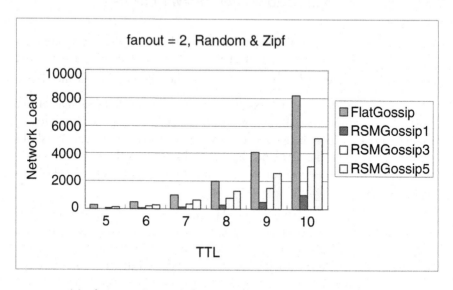

(a) *fanout* = 2 on random and power-law networks.

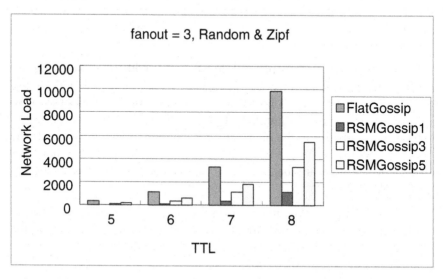

(b) *fanout* = 3 on random and power-law networks.

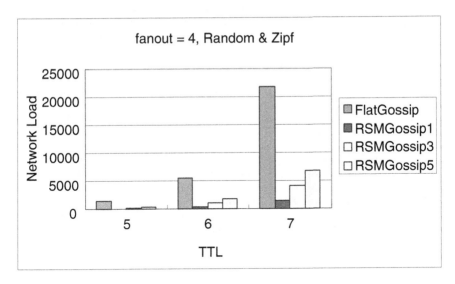

Fig. 8.5. Comparisons of the network load of different mechanisms on the networks of 1000 peers.

As Fig. 8.5(a) presents, we set the *fanout* value as 2 uniformly and range *TTL* from 5 to 10. Fig. 8.5(b) and Fig. 8.5(c) are obtained in the similar way by using different parameter values. We can see from the figures that the network loads are reduced sharply when adopting the partition-based gossip mechanisms. Taking *fanout* = 3 for example, when *TTL* approaches 8, about 88.9%, 66.7% and 44.5% network load is reduced by *RSMGossip1*, *RSMGossip3* and *RSMGossip5* respectively compared with the flat gossip mechanism. This justifies our approach.

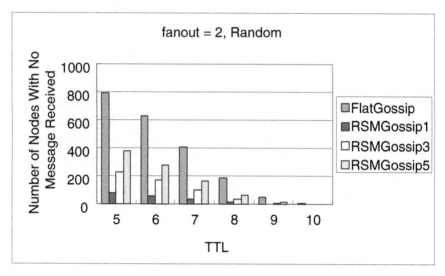

(a) *fanout* = 2 on random networks.

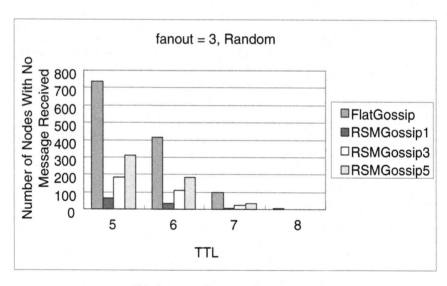

(b) *fanout* = 3 on random networks.

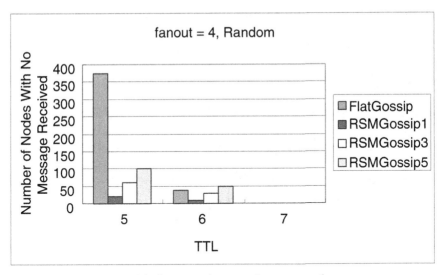

(c) *fanout* = 4 on random networks.

Fig. 8.6. Comparisons of the number of peers that do not receive messages on the 1000-peer randomly connected networks.

During message dissemination, the number of peers that do not receive the disseminated messages is an important metric. Compared with previous algorithms, the number of peers that do not receive messages decreases evidently after adopting the proposed mechanisms as presented in Fig. 8.6. Taking *fanout* = 3 for example, when *TTL* approaches 6, about 36.44, 109.32 and 182.2 number of peers, which should receive the disseminated message, have not received it when using *RSMGossip1*, *RSMGossip3* and *RSMGossip5* mechanisms separately. Meanwhile it is 416.57 for the flat gossip mechanism. The performance is improved considerably though it is partially because the range is decreased for the RSM-based mechanism. This justifies the rationale of the RSM-based mechanism.

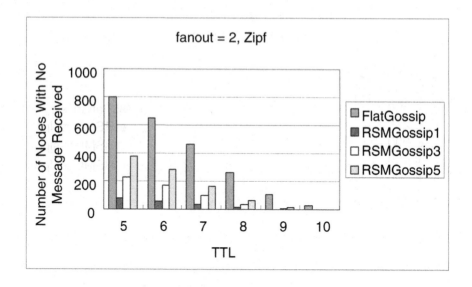

(a) *fanout* = 2 on power-law networks.

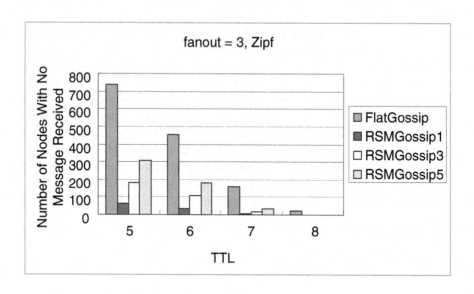

(b) *fanout* = 3 on power-law networks.

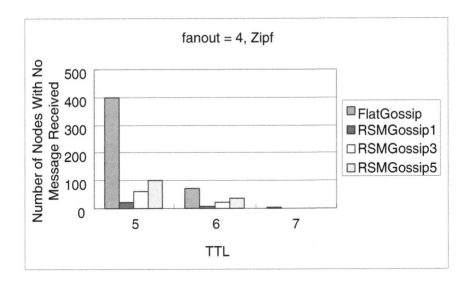

(c) *fanout* = 4 on power-law networks.

Fig. 8.7. Comparisons of the number of peers that do not receive messages on the 1000-peer random power-law networks.

For the random power-law networks, the results about the number of peers that do not receive messages are shown in Fig. 8.7. We can see the similar phenomena as those on the random networks: the number of peers that do not receive messages is also reduced sharply compared with the partition-based gossip mechanisms with the flat gossip. Taking *fanout* = 3 for example, when *TTL* approaches 6, about 35.77, 107.31 and 178.85 number of peers on average do not receive the disseminated message when making use of *RSMGossip1*, *RSMGossip3* and *RSMGossip5* mechanisms respectively. Meanwhile for the flat gossip mechanism it is 455.13. The results are better than those on the random networks for the RSM-based mechanisms, while the flat gossip mechanism performs worse on the random power-law networks than those on the random networks. This also declares the necessary of our approaches.

8.6 Architecture of a RSM-based Gossip Network

The architecture of the Peer-to-Peer network adopting the proposed hierarchical gossip mechanism is depicted in Fig. 8.8.

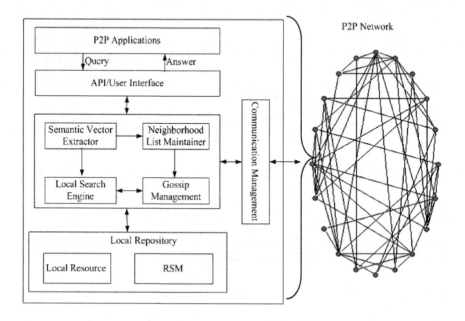

Fig. 8.8. Peer architecture in the RSM-based gossip network.

The framework includes the following modules:
1. The *API/User Interface* facilitates users' operations such as joining in and departing from the network, issuing some resources and generating queries.
2. The *Semantic Vector Extractor* makes use of some technologies in information retrieval area (Vector Space Model and Latent Semantic Index, etc.) to extract term vectors of resources and queries. The term vectors can be used to help decide the category of the newly joined peer belongs to.
3. The *Neighborhood List Maintainer* maintains the list of different levels of the neighbors in the network.
4. The *Local Search Engine* is in charge of searching in the local repository when some queries are reached.

5. The *Gossip Management module* executes the proposed gossip mechanisms, such as selecting the appropriate levels and choosing some peers in that level view to disseminate corresponding messages.
6. In the *Local Repository* and the *RSM* (Resource Space Model) manage the resources (papers in e-science application) stored in the peer and the global resource space partition structure respectively.
7. The *Communication management* module is responsible for the communication with the peers in the Peer-to-Peer network.

8.7 Summary

Classification is a kind of basic semantics that people often use to manage the contents of versatile resources in daily life. The Resource Space Model is a semantic model for sharing and managing various resources using normalized classification semantics. Gossip-based Peer-to-Peer techniques are reliable and scalable protocols for information dissemination. Incorporating the Resource Space Model with the gossip-based techniques can construct a new decentralized resource sharing mechanism (Zhuge and Li, 2007b). The unstructured Peer-to-Peer Resource Space owns the advantages of both the Resource Space Model and the unstructured Peer-to-Peer network, and can synergy the normalization and autonomy in decentralized resource management. The Resource Space Model's normalization theory, integrity theory and operation language can support semantic-rich applications over Peer-to-Peer networks. Theoretical analysis and experiments presented in this chapter validate the feasibility of the mechanism.

It is an interesting issue to apply the operations of the Resource Space Model like *join* and *split* to the Peer-to-Peer resource space system to realize a scalable RSM. To realize this, we need to investigate the effect of the operations on the Peer-to-Peer network.

Chapter 9 Probabilistic Resource Space Model

Incorporating probability with the Resource Space Model can deal with the uncertainty in resource classification and resource operation.

9.1 Basic Concepts

The probabilistic event in the Probabilistic Resource Space Model is that a resource belongs to a certain class. $Prob(r \in T)$ denotes the membership probability of resource r belonging to class T. T may represent a class of resources of a resource space, an axis, a coordinate, a point or any of their combination by set operations.

The following are two strategies on how to specify the probabilistic distribution of a given resource r belonging to a resource space RS.

1. For any resource r, specify its membership probability distribution on every point of RS.
2. For each axis X of RS, specify the membership probability distribution of any resource r on every coordinate of X.

The second strategy is more feasible because of the following reasons:

1. The amount of points in resource space $RS(X_1, X_2, \dots , X_n)$ is $|X_1| \times |X_2| \times \dots \times |X_n|$ and the amount of coordinates is $|X_1|+|X_2|+\dots+|X_n|$, where $|X|$ is the number of coordinates on X. Large number of points makes it difficult to assign the membership probability of every resource to every point.
2. Each axis in a resource space represents a resource classification method. For a point $p(C_{i1}, C_{i2}, \dots, C_{in})$, C_{ij} is at axis X_j ($1 \leq j \leq n$), and $R(p)=R(C_{i1}) \cap R(C_{i2}) \cap \dots \cap R(C_{in})$. Each point is a combination of all axes of RS and involves all classification methods used in resource space. It is more feasible for users and automatic classification algorithms to specify the membership probability distribution of resource r by axis.

Definition 9.1. The resource space $RS(X_1, X_2, \ldots , X_n)$ is a *probabilistic resource space* if for any resource r and any axis X_i of RS, there exists a membership probability function β_{ri} from X_i to the real number interval $[0, 1]$ such that $\beta_{ri}(C_{ij})$ represents the probability of resource r belonging to class $R(C_{ij})$ for any top-level coordinate C_{ij} at X_i.

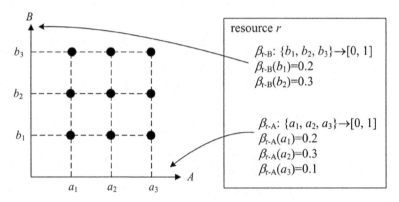

Fig. 9.1. An example of probabilistic resource space.

According to above definition, any resource r in a probabilistic resource space $RS(X_1, X_2, \ldots , X_n)$ has n membership probabilistic functions. Take the probabilistic resource space $RS(A, B)$ in Fig. 9.1 for example, resource r has two membership probabilistic functions, $\beta_{r\text{-}A}$: $A \rightarrow [0, 1]$ and $\beta_{r\text{-}B}$: $B \rightarrow [0, 1]$. $\beta_{r\text{-}B}(b_1)=0.2$ means that the probability of resource r belonging to coordinate b_1 is 0.2 at axis B.

Resource r belongs to resource space $RS(X_1, X_2, \ldots , X_n)$ if and only if there exists at least one axis X_i such that the membership probabilistic function of r on X_i has been explicitly specified.

From the membership probabilities on the coordinates, the membership probabilities on other classes in the classification hierarchy can be evaluated as follows:

1. For axis $X_i = \{C_{i1}, C_{i2}, \ldots, C_{im}\}$, since $R(X_i) = R(C_{i1}) \cup R(C_{i2}) \cup \ldots \cup R(C_{im})$, the probability of r belonging to X_i falls into the interval $[max\{\beta_{ri}(C_{i1}), \ldots, \beta_{ri}(C_{im})\}, min\{1, \beta_{ri}(C_{i1}) + \beta_{ri}(C_{i2}) + \ldots + \beta_{ri}(C_{im})\}]$.
2. For point $p(C_{1j1}, C_{2j2}, \ldots, C_{njn})$, since $R(p) = R(C_{1j1}) \cap R(C_{2j2}) \cap \ldots \cap R(C_{njn})$, the probability of r belonging to p falls into the interval $[0, min\{\beta_{r1}(C_{1j1}), \ldots, \beta_{rn}(C_{njn})\}]$.
3. For a hierarchical coordinate, the probability of r belonging to a coor-

dinate C' in the hierarchy depends on the probability that r belongs to its parent C, i.e., $\beta_{ri}(C') = Prob(r \in R(C') \mid r \in R(C))$. Since C' is a child coordinate of C, $Prob(r \in R(C')) = Prob(r \in R(C') \wedge r \in R(C))$ holds. According to $Prob(r \in R(C') \wedge r \in R(C)) = Prob(r \in R(C)) \times Prob(r \in R(C') \mid r \in R(C))$, we have $Prob(r \in R(C')) = \beta_{ri}(C) \times \beta_{ri}(C')$. So the probability of r belonging to $R(C')$ is $\beta_{ri}(C) \times \beta_{ri}(C')$.

Take Fig. 9.1 for example, the probability of resource r belonging to axis A is $Prob(r \in R(A)) \in [max\{\beta_{r-A}(a_1), \beta_{r-A}(a_2), \beta_{r-A}(a_3)\}, min\{1, \beta_{r-A}(a_1)+\beta_{r-A}(a_2)+\beta_{r-A}(a_3)\}]=[0.3, 0.6]$. The probability of resource r belonging to point $p(a_2, b_2)$ is $Prob(r \in R(p(a_2, b_2))) \in [0, min\{\beta_{r-A}(a_2), \beta_{r-B}(b_2)\}] = [0, 0.3]$.

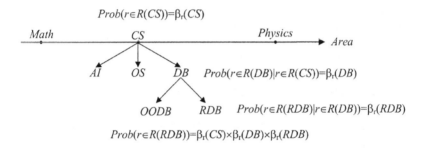

Fig. 9.2. Conditional probabilities in coordinate hierarchy.

In Fig. 9.2, the axis $Area$ is used to classify scientific publications according to their area. In the classification hierarchy of coordinate CS (Computer Science) on axis $Area$, DB (DataBase) is a sub-class of CS and RDB (Relational DataBase) is a sub-class of DB. For resource r and its membership probability function β_r, $\beta_r(RDB)$ represents the conditional probability of r belonging to RDB given r belonging to DB has occurred, i.e. $\beta_r(RDB)=Prob(r \in R(RDB) \mid r \in R(DB))$. Similarly, $\beta_r(DB)= Prob(r \in R(DB) \mid r \in R(CS))$. Since DB is a sub-class of CS, the probability of r belonging to DB is $Prob(r \in R(DB)) = Prob(r \in R(DB) \wedge r \in R(CS)) = Prob(r \in R(CS)) \times Prob(r \in R(DB) \mid r \in R(CS)) = \beta_r(CS) \times \beta_r(DB)$. In fact, the probability of r belonging to a sub-coordinate is the multiplication of all the conditional probabilities along the path from the top-level coordinate to this sub-coordinate. So the probability of r belonging to RDB is $\beta_{\ell}(CS) \times \beta_{\ell}(DB) \times \beta_{\ell}(RDB)$.

9.2 Normal Forms of Probabilistic Resource Space

9.2.1 The First Normal Form and Second Normal Form

The first normal form of the Resource Space Model is used to eliminate the redundancy caused by name duplication between coordinates. It also applies to the probabilistic Resource Space Model. The second normal form of the Resource Space Model is to eliminate the redundancy caused by coordinate dependency. Any second normal form resource space is also a first normal form resource space.

Definition 9.2. A probabilistic resource space $RS(X_1, X_2, \ldots, X_n)$ is a 2NF resource space if for any resource r and any two coordinates C and C' on X_i ($1 \leq i \leq n$), $Prob(r \in R(C) \land r \in R(C')) = 0$ holds.

Above definition is actually an explanation of the 2NF of Resource Space Model from probability point of view.

Theorem 9.1. For axis X, if any two coordinates on X are independent of each other, then for any resource r, $Prob(r \in R(X)) = \sum_{C \in X} Prob(r \in R(C)) \leq 1$ holds.

Proof. For axis $X = \{C_1, C_2, \ldots, C_m\}$, $R(X) = R(C_1) \cup R(C_2) \cup \ldots \cup R(C_m)$ holds. Because any two coordinates C_i and C_j ($1 \leq i \neq j \leq m$) on X are independent of each other, $Prob(r \in R(C_i) \land r \in R(C_j)) = 0$ holds. So the probability of resource r belonging to $R(C_i) \cup R(C_j)$ is the sum of the probability of r belonging to $R(C_i)$ and the probability of r belonging to $R(C_j)$, i.e. $Prob(r \in R(C_i) \lor r \in R(C_j)) = Prob(r \in R(C_i)) + Prob(r \in R(C_j))$. So the probability of r belonging to X is the sum of the probability of r belonging to each coordinate on X, i.e. $Prob(r \in R(X)) = \sum_{C \in X} Prob(r \in R(C))$ holds. □

In theorem 9.1, $\sum_{C \in X} Prob(r \in R(C)) < 1$ means that there is a probability of r not belonging to axis X. For a resource space RS satisfying 2NF,
the probability of r belonging to any axis can be evaluated from the membership probability function of r on this axis.

9.2.2 The Third Normal Form

A more general definition of fine classification in the probabilistic Resource Space Model is given as follows:

Definition 9.3. Let $X=\{C_1, C_2, ..., C_n\}$ be an axis and C' be a coordinate at
another axis X', we say that X *finely classifies* C' (denoted as C'/X) if and
only if for any resource r:

1. $Prob(r \in (R(C') \cap R(C_i)) \wedge r \in (R(C') \cap R(C_j)) = 0$ for $1 \le i \ne j \le n$; and,
2. $Prob(r \in R(C')) = \sum_{C \in X} Prob(r \in R(C')|r \in R(C)) \times Prob(r \in R(C))$

hold.

According to definition 9.3 and the total probability theorem, coordinate
C' can be finely classified by axis X if and only if the probability of resource r belonging to $R(C')$ can be partitioned into the probabilities of r
belonging to $R(C') \cap R(C_1)$, $R(C') \cap R(C_2)$, ... and $R(C') \cap R(C_n)$ respectively.

For two axes $X=\{C_1, C_2, ..., C_n\}$ and $X'=\{C_1', C_2', ..., C_m'\}$, X finely
classifies X' (i.e., X'/X) if and only if X finely classifies C_1', C_2', ..., and
C_m'. Two axes X and X' are called orthogonal with each other (i.e., $X \perp X$')
if both X'/X and X/X' hold.

Definition 9.4. A probabilistic resource space $RS(X_1, X_2, ... , X_n)$ satisfies
the third normal form of the Resource Space Model if for any two axes X_i
and X_j $(1 \le i \ne j \le n)$ in RS, $X_i \perp X_j$ holds.

In the Probabilistic Resource Space Model, for any given 3NF resource
space $RS(X_1, X_2, ... , X_n)$, the following constraints should be satisfied:

Theorem 9.2. Let $RS(X_1, X_2, ... , X_n)$ be a probabilistic resource space satisfying 3NF. For any two axes X_i and X_j $(1 \le i, j \le n)$ and resource r in RS,

$$\sum_{C \in X_i} Prob(r \in R(C)) = \sum_{C' \in X_j} Prob(r \in R(C')) \text{ holds.}$$

Proof. Since RS satisfies 3NF, coordinate C at axis X_i can be finely classified by axis X_j. So $Prob(r \in R(C)) =$

$$\sum_{C' \in X_j} (Prob(r \in R(C) \wedge r \in R(C'))) \quad \text{holds.} \quad \text{Thus}$$

$$\sum_{C \in X_i} Prob(r \in R(C)) = \sum_{C \in X_i} \sum_{C' \in X_j} (Prob(r \in R(C) \wedge r \in R(C'))) \text{ holds. On}$$

the other hand, coordinate C' at axis X_j can be finely classified by axis X_i,

$$Prob(r \in R(C')) = \sum_{C \in X_i} (Prob(r \in R(C') \wedge r \in R(C))) \quad \text{holds.} \quad \text{Thus}$$

$$\sum_{C \in X_j} Prob(r \in R(C')) = \sum_{C' \in X_j} \sum_{C \in X_i} (Prob(r \in R(C') \wedge r \in R(C))) \quad \text{holds.}$$

Therefore $\sum_{C \in X_i} Prob(r \in R(C)) = \sum_{C' \in X_j} Prob(r \in R(C'))$ holds. □

Theorem 9.2 indicates that for any two axes X_i and X_j of a resource space satisfying 3NF, the probability of resource r belonging to X_i is equal to the probability of r belonging to X_j.

Theorem 9.3. Let $RS(X_1, X_2, \ldots, X_n)$ be a 3NF probabilistic resource space. For any axis X_i ($1 \leq i \leq n$) and any coordinate C at X_i, $Prob(r \in R(C)) =$

$$\sum_{p[Xi]=C} Prob(r \in R(p)) \text{ holds, where } p \text{ represents a point in } RS \text{ and } p[X_i] \text{ is}$$

the projection of p at axis X_i.

Proof. Let T be the union of all points whose projections on X_i are C. So $R(T) = R(C) \cap \bigcap_{1 \leq j \neq i \leq n} \bigcup_{Cj \in Xj} R(C_j)$. Since resource space RS satisfies 3NF,

any two points in RS are independent of each other. So we have $Prob(r \in R(T)) = \sum_{p[Xi]=C} Prob(r \in R(p))$. On the other hand,

$$Prob(r \in R(T)) = Prob(r \in (R(C) \cap \bigcap_{1 \leq j \neq i \leq n} \bigcup_{Cj \in Xj} R(C_j))) = Prob(r \in (R(C) \cap$$

$\bigcap_{1 \leq j \neq i \leq n} R(X_j)))$ holds. Since coordinate C can be finely classified by axis X_j

($1 \leq j \neq i \leq n$), $R(C)$ is a subclass of $R(X_j)$. So $Prob(r \in R(T)) =$

$$Prob(r \in (R(C) \cap \bigcap_{1 \le j \ne i \le n} R(X_j))) = Prob(r \in R(C)) \text{ holds. Therefore}$$

$$Prob(r \in R(C)) = \sum_{p[X_i]=C} Prob(r \in R(p)) \text{ holds. } \square$$

9.3 Operations of Probabilistic Resource Space

9.3.1 Point Query

The result of a point query is a set of points, each of which contains a set of resources with membership probability. For a resource space RS, the point query operation is used to select the desirable points according to a given restriction. This type of query can be denoted as $\sigma_p(RS) = \{p \mid p \in RS \land F_p(p)\}$, where F_p is a logic expression. The basic form of F_p is: $p_m[X_i] \theta Y$, where Y may be $p_n[X_j]$ or just a noun phase in domain ontology, p_m and p_n are points and θ represents $=, \ne, <, \le, \ge$ or $>$. F_p is usually a logical combination of basic forms by using $\land$, $\lor$ and $\lnot$.

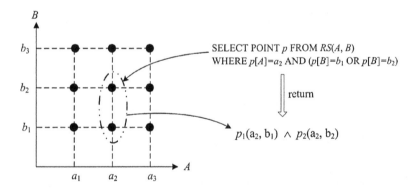

Fig. 9.3. An example for point query.

The probabilistic Resource Space Model uses the following SQL-like ROL statement to support point queries. The *conditional expression* in this statement is the logical combination of restrictions on the projections on axes of points.

> SELECT POINT p FROM $RS(X_1, \ldots X_n)$
> [WHERE <*conditional expression*>]

Take Fig. 9.3 as an example, if the user wants to query all resources in points $p_1(a_2, b_1)$ and $p_2(a_2, b_2)$, the logical expression should be $\sigma_p(RS)=\{p \mid p \in RS \wedge p[A]=a_2 \wedge (p[B]=b_1 \vee p[B]=b_2\}$ and the issued point query statement should be:

> SELECT POINT p FROM $RS(A, B)$
> WHERE $p[A]=a_2$ AND ($p[B]=b_1$ OR $p[B]=b_2$)

Thus, the points $p_1(a_2, b_1)$ and $p_2(a_2, b_2)$ will be returned with resources and their membership probabilities belonging to these two points.

9.3.2 Resource Query

The query result of a resource query is a set of resources, each of which satisfies the specified restrictions on membership probabilities. This type of query can be represented as $\sigma_r(RS) = \{r \mid r \in RS \wedge T=\sigma_p(RS) \wedge F_r(r, T)\}$, where F_r is a logic expression and $\sigma_p(RS)$ is a point query result. The basic form of F_r is $Prob(r \in T) \theta Y$, where Y may be a real number or a real number interval. If Y is a real number, θ is $=, \neq, <, \leq, \geq$, or $>$. If Y is a real number interval, θ is $\in$ or $\notin$.

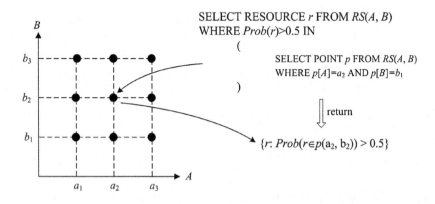

Fig. 9.4. An example for resource query.

The probabilistic Resource Space Model uses the following statement to support resource queries.

SELECT RESOURCE *r* FROM $RS(X_1, \ldots X_n)$

[WHERE *<conditional expression>*]

The *<conditional expression>* in this statement is a logical expression combination of restrictions on membership probabilities. The *<conditional expression>* takes the following form: $Prob(r)\theta Y$ IN *point-query-sub-expression*, where $Prob(r)\theta Y$ has the same meanings as mentioned above and *point-query-sub-expression* is a point query statement returning a set of points. So $Prob(r)\theta Y$ IN *point-query-sub-expression* represents a logical expression that *Y* and the probability of resource *r* belonging to *point-query-sub-expression* satisfies the relation θ.

For example in Fig. 9.4, if the user wants to query all resources which belong to point $p(a_2, b_2)$ with the probability greater than 0.5, the corresponding logical expression is $\sigma_F(RS)=\{r \mid r \in RS \land T=\{p \mid p \in RS \land p[A]=a_2 \land p[B]=b_2\} \land Prob(r \in T)>0.5\}$ and the issued resource query statement should be:

SELECT RESOURCE *r* FROM $RS(A, B)$
WHERE $Prob(r)>0.5$ IN
   (
        SELECT POINT *p* FROM $RS(A, B)$
        WHERE $p[A]=a_2$ AND $p[B]=b_1$
)

Thus, all resources belonging to point $p(a_2, b_2)$ with the probability greater than 0.5 will be returned to users.

9.3.3 Resource Modification

In the classical Resource Space Model, before a resource *r* can be inserted into a resource space *RS*, we have to identify the coordinates which *r* belongs to on each axis in *RS*.

Take Fig. 9.5 as an example. The resource space *RS(Classes, Courses)* is used to manage students according to their classes and selected courses. Once the resource *r* has been identified that it belongs to coordinate *Database* on axis *Courses* and to coordinate C_2 on axis *Classes*, it can be inserted into the point *(Database, C_2)*.

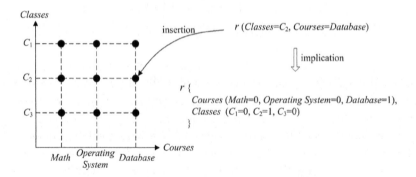

Fig. 9.5. Insert a resource into a resource space.

From the perspective of probability, $r(Courses=Database, Classes=C_2)$ implies the fact that the membership probability functions of resource r on axes *Courses* and *Classes* are $\beta_{r\text{-Courses}}$ and $\beta_{r\text{-Classes}}$ respectively such that $\beta_{r\text{-Courses}}(Math)=0$, $\beta_{r\text{-Courses}}(Operating\ System)=0$ and $\beta_{r\text{-Courses}}(Database)=1$ as well as $\beta_{r\text{-Classes}}(C_1)=0$, $\beta_{r\text{-Classes}}(C_2)=1$ and $\beta_{r\text{-Classes}}(C_3)=0$.

The process of inserting a resource into a probabilistic resource space is the same as the classical resource space except that the membership probability functions in the Probabilistic Resource Space Model can take value within the range [0, 1].

The following is the insertion statement used to insert a resource r into a resource space *RS*. β_1, β_2, ..., β_n are the membership probability functions of r on axes $X_1, X_2, ..., X_n$ respectively.

$$\text{INSERT } r<\beta_1, \beta_2, ..., \beta_n> \text{ INTO } RS<X_1, X_2, ..., X_n>$$

The probabilistic Resource Space Model also supports the following delete operation and update operation:

DELETE r FROM *RS*
[WHERE <*conditional expression*>]

UPDATE $r<\beta_i,..., \beta_j>$ INTO $RS<X_i,..., X_j>$
[WHERE <*conditional expression*>]

9.3.4 Operations on Probabilistic Resource Space

The Join, Disjoin, Merge and Split operations on the probabilistic Resource Space Model can be defined by using the membership probability function.

Join. Let $|RS|$ be the number of the dimensions of the RS. If two resource spaces RS_1 and RS_2 store the same type of resources and have k common axes, then they can be *joined* together as one resource space RS such that RS_1 and RS_2 share these k common axes and $|RS|=|RS_1| + |RS_2| - k$. For any resource r, we have:

1. r belongs to RS if and only if r belongs to both RS_1 and RS_2;
2. For any common axis X_i in RS_1 and RS_2 and any coordinate C on X_i, let β_r, β_r' and β_r'' be the membership probability function of r at X_i in RS, RS_1 and RS_2 respectively. Then $\beta_r(C) = \alpha \times \beta_r'(C) + (1-\alpha) \times \beta_r''(C)$, $0 \le \alpha \le 1$;
3. For any non-common axis X_j in RS_1 and any coordinate C' at X_j, let β_r and β_r' be the membership probability function of r at X_j in RS and RS_1 respectively. If there exists a common axis X_i such that $X_j \perp X_i$, then $\beta_r(C')=\beta_r'(C') \times (\sum_{C \in Xi} \beta_{ri}(C) / \sum_{C \in Xi} \beta_{ri}'(C))$, where β_{ri} and β_{ri}' are the membership probability functions of r at X_i in RS and RS_1 respectively. Otherwise, $\beta_r(C')=\beta_r'(C')$.

Disjoin. A resource space RS can be disjoined into two resource spaces RS_1 and RS_2 that store the same type of resources as that of RS such that they have k common axes, and $|RS|=|RS_1| + |RS_2| - k$. For any resource r, we have:

1. r belongs to both RS_1 and RS_2 if and only if r belongs to RS;
2. For any axis X_i in RS_1 and any coordinate C on X_i, let β_r and β_r' be the membership probability functions of r on X_i in RS and RS_1 respectively, then $\beta_r(C)= \beta_r'(C)$.

Merge. If two resource spaces RS_1 and RS_2 store the same type of resources and satisfy: 1) $|RS_1|=|RS_2|=n$; and, 2) they have $n-1$ common axes, and there exist two different axes X' and X'' satisfying the merge condition, then they can be merged into one RS by retaining the $n-1$ common axes and adding a new axis $X^*=X' \cup X''$. RS is called the merge of RS_1 and RS_2, denoted as $RS_1 \cup RS_2 \Rightarrow RS$, and $|RS|= n$. For any resource r, we have:

1. r belongs to RS if and only if r belongs to either RS_1 or RS_2;
2. For any common axis X_i and any coordinate C at X_i, let β_r, β_r' and β_r" be the membership probability functions of r at X_i in RS, RS_1 and RS_2 respectively. If r belongs to both RS_1 and RS_2, then $\beta_r(C) = \alpha \times \beta_r'(C) + (1-\alpha) \times \beta_r"(C)$, $0 \le \alpha \le 1$. Otherwise, $\beta_r(C) = \beta_r'(C)$ if r belongs to RS_1, or $\beta_r(C) = \beta_r"(C)$ if r belongs to RS_2;
3. Let C, C' and C" be any coordinates such that $C \in X' \cap X"$, $C' \in X'-X"$ and $C" \in X"-X'$. And let β_r, β_r' and β_r" be the membership probability functions of r at X^*, X' and $X"$ in RS, RS_1 and RS_2 respectively. If r belongs to both RS_1 and RS_2, then $\beta_r(C) = \alpha \times \beta_r'(C) + (1-\alpha) \times \beta_r"(C)$, $\beta_r(C') = \beta_r'(C')$ and $\beta_r(C") = \beta_r"(C")$. Otherwise, $\beta_r(C) = \beta_r'(C)$, $\beta_r(C') = \beta_r'(C')$ and $\beta_r(C") = 0$ if r belongs to RS_1, or $\beta_r(C) = \beta_r"(C)$, $\beta_r(C') = 0$ and $\beta_r(C") = \beta_r"(C")$ if r belongs to RS_2.

Split. A resource space RS can be *split* into two resource spaces RS_1 and RS_2 that store the same type of resources as RS and have $|RS|-1$ common axes by splitting an axis X into two: X' and $X"$, such that $X = X' \cup X"$. For any resource r, we have:

1. r belongs to both RS_1 and RS_2, if and only if r belongs to RS;
2. For any axis X_i ($1 \le i \le n$) in RS_1 and any coordinate C at X_i, let β_r and β_r' be the membership probability functions of r at X_i in RS and RS_1 respectively, then $\beta_r(C) = \beta_r'(C)$.

9.4 Integrity Constraints under Probability

Integrity constraints play an important role in maintaining consistency of the Resource Space Model. In the probabilistic Resource Space Model, the meaning of some constraint rules is changed and new rules should be taken into consideration.

9.4.1 Key in Probabilistic Resource Space Model

As a coordinate system, the Resource Space Model supports accurate resource location by giving coordinates. However, it is sometimes unnecessary and even arduous to specify all the coordinates to identify a point, especially for high-dimensional resource spaces. The key of the Resource Space Model is to efficiently locate resources.

Definition 9.5 Let CK be a subset of axis set $\{X_1, X_2, ..., X_n\}$, p_1 and p_2 be any two non-null points of resource space $RS(X_1, X_2, ..., X_n)$. CK is called a candidate key of resource space RS if $p_1.X_i=p_2.X_i$, $X_i \in \{X_1, X_2, ..., X_n\}$ is implied by $p_1.X_i=p_2.X_i$, $X_i \in CK$.

Note that there are two concepts in above definition: null point and non-null point. For a given point p, if there exists at least one resource belonging to p, then p is a non-null point, otherwise is a null point. In the Probabilistic Resource Space Model, each resource has a membership probability distribution on all of the points. The null point and non-null point concepts make no sense any more. The key in the probabilistic resource space is defined as follows:

Definition 9.6. Let CK be a subset of axis set $\{X_1, X_2, ..., X_n\}$ and p_1, p_2 be any two points of resource space $RS(X_1, X_2, ..., X_n)$ such that $p_1.X_i=p_2.X_i$, $X_i \in CK$. CK is called a candidate key of resource space RS if CK satisfies: if there exists an axis X_j such that $X_j \in \{X_1, X_2, ..., X_n\}-CK$ and $p_1.X_j \neq p_2.X_j$, then $Prob(r_1 \in R(p_1) \wedge r_2 \in R(p_2))=0$ holds for any two resources r_1 and r_2.

The above definition implies a kind of resource dependency: if the event r_1 belonging to p_1 occurs, the probability of r_2 belonging to p_2 is 0, i.e. $Prob(r_2 \in R(p_2) \mid r_1 \in R(p_1)) = 0$.

Most previous probabilistic relational data models manage entities one by one and seldom concern the relationship between entities. They usually assume that the uncertainty of one entity is independent of another entity. The Probabilistic Resource Space Model should consider some dependency between resources. Theorem 9.4 presents a situation where the probabilistic events of two resources should not be supposed to be independent of each other.

Theorem 9.4. Let CK be a candidate key of 3NF resource space $RS(X_1, X_2, ..., X_n)$ and CK' be a subset of $\{X_1, X_2, ..., X_n\}$ such that $CK \subset CK'$. Let p_1 and p_2 be two points in RS such that $p_1.X_i=p_2.X_i$ ($X_i \in CK$) and $p_1.X_j \neq p_2.X_j$ ($X_j \in CK'-CK$). For any two resources r_1 and r_2, the events $r_1 \in \bigcap_{X \in CK' \wedge p1.X=C} R(C)$ and $r_2 \in \bigcap_{X \in CK' \wedge p2.X=C} R(C)$ are not independent of each other, and $Prob(r_1 \in \bigcap_{X \in CK' \wedge p1.X=C} R(C) \wedge r_2 \in \bigcap_{X \in CK' \wedge p2.X=C} R(C)) =$ 0.

Proof. Suppose that both $Prob(r_1 \in \bigcap\limits_{X \in CK' \wedge p1.X=C} R(C)) \neq 0$ and

$Prob(r_2 \in \bigcap\limits_{X \in CK' \wedge p2.X=C} R(C)) \neq 0$ hold. Since RS satisfies 3NF, both

$\bigcap\limits_{X \in CK' \wedge p1.X=C} R(C) = \bigcup\limits_{X \in CK' \wedge p1.X=p.X} R(p)$ and $\bigcap\limits_{X \in CK' \wedge p2.X=C} R(C) =$

$\bigcup\limits_{X \in CK' \wedge p2.X=p'.X} R(p')$ hold. If $Prob(r_1 \in \bigcap\limits_{X \in CK' \wedge p1.X=C} R(C) \wedge$

$r_2 \in \bigcap\limits_{X \in CK' \wedge p2.X=C} R(C)) \neq 0$, then there must exist at least two points p_3 and

p_4 such that $p_1.X_i=p_3.X_i$ $(X_i \in CK')$, $p_2.X_i=p_4.X_i$ $(X_i \in CK')$ and $Prob(r_1 \in R(p_3)$
$\wedge r_2 \in R(p_4)) \neq 0$ hold. This contradicts to the fact that CK is a candidate
key of RS. So $Prob(r_1 \in \bigcap\limits_{X \in CK' \wedge p1.X=C} R(C) \wedge r_2 \in \bigcap\limits_{X \in CK' \wedge p2.X=C} R(C)) = 0$

holds. □

9.4.2 Integrity Constraints in Probabilistic Resource Space Model

Modification of resources may result in inconsistency in resource spaces.
Entity integrity constraint, membership integrity constraint, reference integrity constraint and user-defined integrity constraint have been proposed
in the classical Resource Space Model. More integrity constraint rules are
needed in the probabilistic Resource Space Model.

Rule 1 For resource space $RS(X_1, X_2, \ldots, X_n)$, let β_{ri} be the membership
probabilistic function of resource r at axis X_i, $(1 \leq i \leq n)$. For any coordinate
C at X_i, $0 \leq \beta_{ri}(C) \leq 1$ must hold. If any two coordinates at X_i are independent of each other, then $\sum\limits_{C' \in Xi} \beta_{ri}(C') \leq 1$ holds.

Since $\beta_{ri}(C)$ represents the probability of resource r belonging to coordi-
nate C, it is natural to require $0 \leq \beta_{ri}(C) \leq 1$. For axis X_i, $R(X_i) = \bigcup\limits_{C' \in X} R(C')$
holds. If any two coordinates at X_i are independent of each other,
$Prob(r \in R(X_i)) = \sum\limits_{C' \in Xi} \beta_{ri}(C')$. So $\sum\limits_{C' \in Xi} \beta_{ri}(C') \leq 1$ must hold. The insertion and modification of resources and merge operations between resource

spaces may violate rule 1.

Rule 2 For resource space $RS(X_1, X_2, ..., X_n)$ and resource r, let β_{ri} and β_{rj} be the membership probabilistic functions of resource r at X_i and X_j ($1 \leq i, j \leq n$) respectively. If X_i can be finely classified by X_j and any two coordinates at X_i are independent of each other, then $\sum_{C \in Xi} \beta_{ri}(C) \leq \sum_{C' \in Xj} \beta_{rj}(C')$ must hold. If X_i is orthogonal with X_j, i.e. $X_i \perp X_j$ holds, then $\sum_{C \in Xi} \beta_{ri}(C)$ $= \sum_{C' \in Xj} \beta_{rj}(C')$ must hold.

The above rule holds because of the following two points:

1. $Prob(r \in R(X_i)) \leq Prob(r \in R(X_j))$ is implied by $R(X_i) \subseteq R(X_j)$, which is implied by X_i / X_j. And both $Prob(r \in R(X_i)) = \sum_{C \in Xi} \beta_{ri}(C)$ and $Prob(r \in R(X_j)) = \sum_{C' \in Xj} \beta_{rj}(C')$ hold since $R(X_i) = \bigcup_{C' \in Xi} R(C')$ and $R(X_j)$ $= \bigcup_{C' \in Xj} R(C')$. Thus $\sum_{C \in Xi} \beta_{ri}(C) \leq \sum_{C' \in Xj} \beta_{rj}(C')$.

2. If $X_i \perp X_j$, both X_i / X_j and X_j / X_i hold, then both $\sum_{C \in Xi} \beta_{ri}(C)$ $\leq \sum_{C' \in Xj} \beta_{rj}(C')$ and $\sum_{C \in Xi} \beta_{ri}(C) \geq \sum_{C' \in Xj} \beta_{rj}(C')$ hold. So $\sum_{C \in Xi} \beta_{ri}(C)$ $= \sum_{C' \in Xj} \beta_{rj}(C')$ holds.

Rule 3 For any 3NF resource space RS and resource r, let β_{ri} be the membership probabilistic function of resource r at X_i of RS. For any coordinate C at X_i and point p in RS, $\sum_{p.Xi=C} Prob(r \in R(p)) = \beta_{ri}(C)$ must hold.

According to theorem 9.3, in any 3NF resource space, the probability of r belonging to coordinate C can be partitioned into all the points having projection C at axis X_i, i.e. $Prob(r \in R(C)) = \sum_{p.Xi=C} Prob(r \in R(p))$ holds. Rule 3 should be checked to make sure the maintenance of theorem 9.3 when inserting or updating resources.

Rule 4 Let RS_1, RS_2 and RS be three resource spaces such that $RS_1 \cdot RS_2 \Rightarrow RS$.

1.   For any resource r in RS and any non-common axis X_i in RS_1, let β_{ri} and β_{ri}' be the membership probabilistic functions of r at X_i in resource spaces RS and RS_1 respectively. If there does not exist any common axis X_j of RS_1 and RS_2 such that $X_j \perp X_i$ holds, then for any coordinate C at X_i, $\beta_{ri}(C) = \beta_{ri}'(C)$ must hold;

2.   For any resource r in RS and any non-common axis X_i in RS_2, let β_{ri} and β_{ri}' be the membership probabilistic functions of r at X_i in resource spaces RS and RS_2 respectively. If there does not exist any common axis X_j of RS_1 and RS_2 such that $X_j \perp X_i$ holds, then for any coordinate C at X_i, $\beta_{ri}(C) = \beta_{ri}'(C)$ must hold;

3.   For any resource r in RS and any common axis X_t of RS_1 and RS_2, let β_{rt}, β_{rt}' and β_{rt}" be the membership probabilistic functions of r at X_t in resource spaces RS, RS_1 and RS_2 respectively. For any coordinate C at X_t, $min\{\beta_{rt}'(C), \beta_{rt}''(C)\} \leq \beta_{rt}(C) \leq max\{\beta_{rt}'(C), \beta_{rt}''(C)\}$ must hold.

Resource space RS results from the join operation on RS_1 and RS_2, and rule 4 maintains the dependency of RS on RS_1 and RS_2. Thus, rule 4 should be checked when insertion, deletion and modification operations are executed.

Rule 5 Let $RS_1(X_1, \ldots, X_{n-1}, X')$, $RS_2(X_1, \ldots, X_{n-1}, X'')$ and $RS(X_1, \ldots, X_{n-1}, X^*)$ be three resource spaces such that $RS_1 \cup RS_2 \Rightarrow RS$ and $X^* = X' \cup X''$.

1.   For any resource r, let β_r, β_r' and β_r" be the membership probabilistic functions of r at X^*, X' and X'' in resource spaces RS, RS_1 and RS_2 respectively. For any coordinate C at X^*, if C is at both RS_1 and RS_2, $min\{\beta_r'(C), \beta_r''(C)\} \leq \beta_r(C) \leq max\{\beta_r'(C), \beta_r''(C)\}$ must hold; otherwise, $\beta_r(C) = \beta_r'(C)$ must hold if C is at RS_1, or $\beta_r(C) = \beta_r''(C)$ must hold if C is at RS_2; and,

2.   For any axis X_i ($1 \leq i \leq n-1$) and resource r, let β_{ri}, β_{ri}' and β_{ri}" be the membership probabilistic functions of r at X_i in resource spaces RS, RS_1 and RS_2 respectively. For any coordinate C at X_i, $min\{\beta_{ri}'(C), \beta_{ri}''(C)\} \leq \beta_{ri}(C) \leq max\{\beta_{ri}'(C), \beta_{ri}''(C)\}$ must hold.

As the result of merge operation on RS_1 and RS_2, RS should satisfy rule 5. Thus, this rule should be checked when insertion, deletion and modification operations are executed.

9.5 Relevant Works

Much attention has been paid to modeling uncertain data in the context of relational model and XML (eXtensible Markup Language).

Researches on modeling relational data fall into two categories depending on whether the resulting models satisfy the first normal form of the classical relational model. Models satisfying 1NF usually assume that the existence of an object is uncertain and associate probabilities with a whole tuple to indicate this type of uncertainty (Cavallo and Pittarelli, 1987; Dey and Sarkar, 1996). Notable works using non-1NF usually assume that the existence of an object is certain, but the attribute values of an object are uncertain (Barbara et al, 1992; Fuhr and Rolleke, 1997). So they associate probabilities with attributes of a tuple. The above two types of probabilistic relational models have limitations. It is very difficult to represent the probabilities of attribute values of an object for probabilistic relational models satisfying 1NF. It can lead to information loss or combinatorial explosion of tuples to specify attribute value probabilities using tuple probabilities. On the other hand, non-1NF probabilistic relational models are often accompanied by complicated algebras and querying mechanisms. ProbView is an attempt to overcome these two types of limitations (Lakshmanan et al, 1997). ProbView firstly transforms non-1NF data to its equivalent annotated 1NF patterns, and then all manipulating and querying operations in ProbView are applied to these equivalent 1NF data.

Other researches on this topic also concern query answering from the view of probability and query evaluation on probabilistic database (Dalvi and Suciu, 2005; Dalvi and Suciu, 2004). A system for managing data, accuracy and lineage in an integral manner is introduced (Widom, 2005).

ProTDB is a XML model to manage probabilistic data in XML, in which stochastic events are the existence of nodes of XML data (Nierman and Jagadish, 2002). A framework is proposed to acquire, maintain and query XML documents with incomplete information, in which order in documents and DTDs is ignored (Abiteboul et al, 2006). A full complexity analysis for managing probabilistic XML data is discussed (Senellart and Abiteboul, 2007). A probabilistic XML approach is proposed to resolve conflicts during data integration, and the order in documents and DTDs plays an important role (Keulen et al, 2005).

9.6 Summary

A Probabilistic Resource Space Model deals with uncertainty in resource operation. It enables membership probability distributions of resources on the classification hierarchies of a resource space to be effectively specified, managed and queried. Operations of the Probabilistic Resource Space Model pay more attention to dealing with membership probability functions of resources in resource spaces. To guarantee the correctness of operations, the normal forms of the Probabilistic Resource Space Model are defined. The integrity constraints concerning membership probability functions are to maintain the consistency of probabilistic resource spaces. The Probabilistic Resource Space Model can be regarded as a more general form of the Resource Space Model.

References

1. Abiteboul, S., Hull, R., and Vianu, V., 1995. Foundations of Data-bases. Addison-Wesley.
2. Abiteboul, S. et al., 2006. Representing and Querying XML with Incomplete Information. ACM Transactions on Database Systems, 31 (1), 208-254.
3. Agrawal, R., Deshpande, P., Gupta, A., Naughton, J., F., Rama-krishnan, R., and Sarawagi, S., 1996. On the Computation of Mul-tidimensional Aggregates. In Proc. VLDB, 506-521.
4. Agarwal, R. P., 2000. Difference Equations and Inequalities (Second Edition). CRC.
5. Aho, A. V., Ullman, J. D. and Hopcroft, J. E., 1983. Data Structures and Algorithms (1st Edition). Addison Wesley.
6. Alashqur, A.M. et al., 1989. OQL: A Query Language for Manipu-lating Object-oriented Databases. In Proc. VLDB, 433-442.
7. Androutsellis-Theotokis, S., Spinellis, D., 2004. A Survey of Peer-to-Peer Content Distribution Technologies. ACM Computing Surveys 36 (4), 335-371.
8. ANSI, 1986. The Database Language SQL. Document ANSI X3.315.
9. Baase, S. and Gelder, A. V., 2000. Computer Algorithms—Introduction to Design and Analysis (3rd Edition). Addison Wesley.
10. Bachman, C., 1974. The Data Structure Set Model. In Proc. VLDB, 43-76.
11. Bailey, N.T.J., 1975. The Mathematical Theory of Infectious Dis-eases and Its Applications. Hafner Press.
12. Barbara, D. et al., 1992. The Management of Probabilistic Data. IEEE Transactions on Knowledge and Data Engineering, 4 (5), 437-502.
13. Berners-Lee, T., Hendler, J., and Lassila, O., 2001. Semantic Web. Scientific American, 284 (5), 34-43.
14. Berry, M.W., et al., 1999. Matrices, Vector Spaces, and Information Retrieval. Society for Industrial and Applied Mathematics Review, 41 (2), 335-362.
15. Boag, S. et al., 2005. XQuery1.0: An XML Query Language.

World Wide Web Consortium, http://www.w3.org/TR/xquery.

16. Bollobás, B., 1998. Modern Graph Theory. Springer-Verlag.
17. Boyce, R. et al., 1975. Specifying Queries as Relational Expressions. Communications of the ACM, 18 (11), 621-628.
18. Bray, T. et al., 1998. Extensible Markup Language (XML) 1.0. W3C Recommendation, www.w3.org/TR/REC-xml/.
19. Briman, K.P., Hayden, M., Ozkasap, O., Xiao, Z., Budiu, M., Minsky, Y., 1999. Bimodal Multicast. ACM Transactions of Computer Systems, 17 (2), 41-88.
20. Cabibbo, L. and Torlone, R., 1997. Querying multidimensional databases. In Sixth Int. Workshop on Database Programming Languages, 253–269.
21. Cavallo, R. and Pittarelli, M., 1987. The Theory of Probabilistic Databases. In Proc. VLDB, 71-81.
22. Chamberlin, D. and Boyce, R., 1976. SEQUEL: A Structured English Query Language. In Proc. VLDB, 249-264.
23. Chamberlin, D. et al., 1976. SEQUEL 2: A Unified Approach to Data Definition, Manipulation and Control. IBM Journal of Research and Development, 20 (6), 560-575.
24. Chen, P., 1976. The Entity-Relationship Model - Toward a Unified View of Data. ACM Transactions on Database Systems, 1 (1), 9-36.
25. Clarke, I., Sandberg, O., Wiley, B., and Hong, T., 2000. Freenet: A Distributed Anonymous Information Storage and Retrieval System. In Proc. the Workshop on Design Issues in Anonymity and Unobservability, 6–66.
26. Codd, E.F., 1970. A Relational Model of Data for Large Shared Data Banks. Communications of the ACM, 13 (6), 377-387.
27. Codd, E.F., 1971a. Normalized Database Structure: A Brief Tutorial. ACM SIGFIDET Workshop on Data Description, Access, and Control, 1-18.
28. Codd, E.F., 1971b. A Data Base Sublanguage Founded on the Relational Calculus. ACM SIGFIDET Workshop on Data Description, Access and Control, 35-61.
29. Codd, E.F., 1972. Relational Completeness of Data Base Sublanguages. Prentice Hall and IBM Research Report RJ 987, Database Systems: 65-98.
30. Codd, E.F. et al., 1996. Providing OLAP (On Line Analytical Processing) to User-Analysts: An IT Mandate. Arbor Software White Paper, 1-12.
31. Cohn, H. and Umans, C., 2003. A Group-theoretic Approach to Fast Matrix Multiplication. In Proc. FOCS, 438-449.

32. Dalvi, N. and Suciu, D., 2004. Efficient Query Evaluation on Probabilistic Databases. In Proc. VLDB, 864-875.

33. Dalvi, N. and Suciu, D., 2005. Answering Queries from Statistics and Probabilistic Views. In Proc. VLDB, 805-816.

34. Date, C.J., 1989. A Note on the Relational Calculus. ACM SIGMOD Record, 18 (4), 12-16.

35. Decker, S. et al., 2000. The Semantic Web: The Roles of XML and RDF. IEEE Internet Computing, 4 (5), 63-74.

36. Demers, A., Greene, D., Hauser, C., Irish, W., Larson, J., 1987. Epidemic Algorithms for Replicated Database Maintenance. In Proc. The 6th ACM Symposium, Principles of Distributed Computing, 1-12.

37. Demuth, H. B., 1956. Electronic Data Sorting. Ph.D. thesis, Stanford University.

38. Dey, D. and Sarkar, S., 1996. A Probabilistic Relational Model and Algebra. ACM Transactions on Database Systems, 21 (3), 339-369.

39. Duda, R. and Hart, P., 1973. Pattern Classification and Scene Analysis. New York: John Wiley & Sons.

40. Eugene, T. S. and Zhang, Ng, H., 2001. Towards Global Network Positioning. In Proc. ACM SIGCOMM Internet Measurement Workshop, 25-29.

41. Eugster, P.T., Guerraoui, R., Handurukande, S., Kermarrec, A.M., Kouznetsov, P., 2001. Lightweight Probabilistic Broadcast. In Proc. International Conference of Dependable Systems and Networks, 443-452.

42. Eugster, P.T., Guerraoui, R., 2002. Probabilistic Multicast. In Proc. International Conference of Dependable Systems and Networks, 313-322.

43. Ford, L. R. and Johnson, S. M., 1959. A Tournament Problem. AMM 66 (5), 387-389.

44. Foster, I., 2000. Internet Computing and the Emerging Grid. http://www-fp.mcs.anl.gov/~foster/.

45. Francis, P., 2000. Yoid: Extending the Internet Multicast Architecture. Available at www.aciri.org/yoid/docs/index.html.

46. Fuhr, N. and Rolleke, T., 1997. A Probabilistic Relational Algebra for the Integration of Information Retrieval and Database Systems. ACM Transactions on Information Systems, 15 (1), 32-66.

47. Gaede, V. and Gnther, O., 1998. Multidimensional Access Methods. ACM Computing Surveys, 30 (2), 170-231.

48. Gkantsidis, C., Mihail, M., and Saberi, A., 2004. Random Walks in Peer-to-Peer Networks. In Proc. the IEEE INFOCOM, 120-130.

49. Graefe, C.J., 1993. Query Evaluation Techniques for Large Data-

bases. ACM Computing Surveys, 25 (2), 73–170.

50. Graham, R. L., Knuth, D. E. and Patashnik, O., 1989. Concrete Mathematics: A Foundation for Computer Science (2nd Edition). Addison Wesley.

51. Gray, J. et al., 1996. Data Cube: A Relational Aggregation Operator Generalizing Group-by, Cross-tab, and Sub-totals. In Proc. IEEE Int. Conference on Data Engineering, 152-159.

52. Guttman, A., 1984. R-Trees: A Dynamic Index Structure for Spatial Searching. In Proc. SIGMOD, 47-57.

53. Gyssens, M. and Lakshmanan, L.V.S., 1997. A Foundation for Multi-Dimensional Databases, In Proc. SIGMOD, 106-115.

54. Gyssens, M., Paredaens, J., Bussche, J., and Gucht, D., 1994. A Graph-Oriented Object Database Model. IEEE Transactions on Knowledge and Data Engineering, 6 (4), 572-586.

55. Han, J. and Kambr, M., 2000. Data Mining: Concepts and Techniques. Morgan Kaufmann Publishers.

56. Heflin, J., and Hendler, J., 2001. A Portrait of the Semantic Web in Action. IEEE Intelligent Systems, 16 (2), 54-59.

57. Hendler, J., 2001. Agents and the Semantic Web. IEEE Intelligent Systems, 16 (2), 30-37.

58. Hoschek, W., Jaen-Martinez, J., Samar, A., Stockinger, H., and Stockinger, K., 2000. Data Management in an International Data Grid Project. In Proc. 1st IEEE/ACM International Workshop on Grid Computing, 77-90.

59. Hull, R., and King, R., 1987. Semantic Database Modeling: Survey, Applications, and Research Issues. ACM Computing Surveys, 19 (3), 201-260.

60. Iamnitchi, A., Ripeanu, M., Foster, I., 2002. Locating Data in (Small-World?) P2P Scientific Collaborations. In Proc. The 1st International Workshop of Peer-to-Peer Systems, 85-93.

61. Ibaraki, T. and Kameda, T., 1984. On the Optimal Nesting Order for Computing N-relational Joins. ACM Transactions on Database Systems, 9 (3), 482-502.

62. Inmon, W. H., 2002. Buding the Data Warehouse. John Wiley & Sons.

63. James, M., 1985. Classification Algorithms. New York: John Wiley & Sons.

64. Kalfoglou, Y. and Schorlemmer, M., 2003. Ontology Mapping: the State of the Art. The Knowledge Engineering Review, 18 (1), 1-31.

65. Kermarrec, A.M., Massoulié, L. and Ganesh, A.J., 2003. Probabilistic Reliable Dissemination in Large-Scale Systems. IEEE Transactions on Parallel and Distributed Systems, 14 (3), 248-258.

66. Keulen, M. et al., 2005. A Probabilistic XML Approach to Data Integration. In Proc. ICDE, 459-470.
67. Kim, W., 1990. Introduction to Object-oriented Databases. MIT Press, Cambridge.
68. Kimball, R., 1996. The Data Warehouse Toolkit. John Wiley & Sons.
69. Klein, M., 2001. XML, RDF, and Relatives. IEEE Internet Computing, 16 (2), 26-28.
70. Klug, A., 1982. Equivalence of Relational Algebra and Relational Calculus Query Languages Having Aggregate Functions. Journal of the ACM, 29 (3), 699-717.
71. Knuth, D. E., 1997a. The Art of Computer Programming, Volume 1: Fundamental Algorithms (Third Edition). Addison-Wesley.
72. Knuth, D. E., 1997b. The Art of Computer Programming, Volume 2: Semi-Numerical Algorithms (Third Edition). Addison-Wesley.
73. Knuth, D. E., 1997c. The Art of Computer Programming, Volume 3: Sorting and Searching (Third Edition). Addison-Wesley.
74. Lakshmanan, L.V.S. et al., 1997. ProbView: A Flexible Probabilistic Database System. ACM Transactions on Database Systems, 22 (3), 419-469.
75. Leland, W.E., et al., 1994. On the Self-Similar Nature of Ethernet Traffic. IEEE/ACM Transactions on Networking, 2 (1), 1-15.
76. Levene, M., and Loizou, G., 1995. A Graph-based Data Model and its Ramifications. IEEE Transactions on Knowledge and Data Engineering, 7 (5), 809-823.
77. Levene, M., and Poulovassilis, A., 1990. The Hypernode Model and its Associated Query Language. In Proc. Jerusalem Conference on Information Technology, 520-530.
78. Levitin, V., 2003. Introduction to the Design & Analysis of Algorithms. Addison Wesley.
79. Lin, M.J. and Marzullo, K., 1999. Directional Gossip: Gossip in a Wide Area Network. In Proc. European Dependable Computing Conference, LNCS 1667, 364-379.
80. Mack, R., Ravin, Y. and Byrd, R. J., 2001. Knowledge Portals and the Emerging Knowledge Workplace. IBM Systems Journal, 40 (4), 925-955.
81. Mairson, H. G., 1977. Some New Upper Bounds on the Generation of Prime Numbers. Communications of the ACM, 20 (9), 664-669.
82. McHraith, S.A., Son, T.C., and Zeng, H., 2001. Semantic Web Services. IEEE Intelligent Systems, 16(2), 46-53.
83. Mitchell, M., 1996. An Introduction to Genetic Algorithms. Cambridge, MA: MIT Press.

84. Mok, W.Y., 2002. A Comparative Study of Various Nested Normal Forms. IEEE Transactions on Knowledge and Data Engineering, 14 (2), 369-385.

85. Nierman, A. and Jagadish, H. V., 2002. ProTDB: Probabilistic Data in XML. In Pro. VLDB, 646-657.

86. Özsu, M.T. and Valduriez, P., 1999. Principles of Distributed Database Systems (2nd edition). Prentice-Hall.

87. Pawlak, Z., 1991. Rough Sets, Theoretical Aspects of Reasoning about Data. Boston: Kluwer Academic Publishers.

88. Pittel, B., 1987. On Spreading a Rumor. SIAM Journal of Applied Mathematics, 47:213-223.

89. Pons, A. P., 2005. Improving the Performance of Client Web Object Retrieval. Journal of Systems and Software, 74(3), 303-311.

90. Pons, A. P., 2006. Object Pre-Fetching using Semantic Links. ACM SIGMIS Database, 37 (1), 97-109.

91. Poulovassilis, A., and Levene, M., 1994. A Nested-Graph Model for the Representation and Manipulation of Complex Objects. ACM Transactions on Information Systems, 12 (1), 35-68.

92. Qian, G. et al., 2006. Dynamic Indexing for Multidimensional Non-Ordered Discrete Data Spaces using a Data-Partitioning Approach. ACM Transactions on Database Systems, 31 (2), 439-484.

93. Quinlan, J.R., 1993. C4.5: Programs for Machine Learning. Morgan Kaufmann.

94. Ratnasamy, S., Francis, P., Handley, M., Karp, R. and Shenker, S., 2001. A Scalable Content-Addressable Network. In Proc. Conference on Applications, Technologies, Architectures, and Protocols for Computer Communications, 161-172.

95. Renesse, R.V., Birman, K.P. and Vogels, W., 2001. Astrolabe: A Robust and Scalable Technology for Distributed Systems Monitoring, Management, and Data Mining. ACM Transactions on Computer Systems, 21 (2), 164-206.

96. Renesse, R.V., Minsky, Y, and Hayden, M., 1998. A Gossip-Style Failure Detection Service. In Proc. IFIP International Conference, Distributed Systems and Platforms and Open Distributed Processing, 55-70.

97. Ripley, B.D., 1996. Pattern Recognition and Neural Networks. Cambridge, UK: Cambridge University Press.

98. Robert, R. S., 1979. Set Theory and Logic. Courier Dover Publications.

99. Robinson, S., 2005. Toward an Optimal Algorithm for Matrix Multiplication. SIAM News, 38 (9), 1-3.

100. Rowstron, A. and Druschel, P., 2001. Pastry: Scalable, Distributed

Object Location and Routing for Large-scale Peer-to-peer Systems. In Proc. ACM/IFIP/USENIX International Middleware Conference, 329-350.

101. Rumbaugh, J., Blaha, M., Premerlani, W., Eddy, F., and Lorensen, W., 1991. Object-Oriented Modeling and Design. Prentice-Hall.

102. Salton, G., 1989. Automatic Text Processing: the Transformation, Analysis, and Retrieval of Information by Computer. Addison-Wesley.

103. Salton, G., 1991. Developments in Automatic Text Retrieval. Science, 253 (8), 974-979.

104. Sarshar, N. et al., 2004. Percolation Search in Power Law Networks: Making Unstructured Peer-to-Peer Networks Scalable. In Proc. 4th International Conference on Peer-to-Peer Computing, 2-9.

105. Schlosser, M. et al., 2002. A Scalable and Ontology-Based P2P Infrastructure for Semantic Web Services. In Proc. 2nd International Conference on Peer-to-Peer Computing, 104-111.

106. Senellart, P. and Abiteboul, S., 2007. On the Complexity of Managing Probabilistic XML Data. In Proc. PODS, 283-292.

107. Shaw, G.M. and Zdonik, S.B., 1990. A Query Algebra for Object-Oriented Databases. In Proc. 6th International Conference on Data Engineering, 154-162.

108. Shipman, D., 1981. The Functional Data Model and the Data Language DAPLEX. ACM Transactions on Database Systems, 6 (1), 140-173.

109. Strang, G., 1991. Calculus. Wellesley-Cambridge.

110. Strassen, V., 1969. Gaussian Elimination is not Optimal. Numerical Mathematics, 14 (13), 354–356.

111. Tam, Y., 1998. Datacube: Its Implementation and Application in OLAP Mining. MSc. Thesis, Simon Fraser University, Canada.

112. Ullman, J. D., 1982. Principles of Database Systems (Second Edition). Computer Science Press.

113. Ullman, J. D., 1988. Principles of Database and Knowledge-Base Systems. Computer Science Press.

114. Vogels, W., Renesse, R.V., Birman, K., 2003. The Power of Epidemics: Robust Communication for Large-Scale Distributed Systems. ACM SIGCOMM Computer Communications Review, 33 (1), 131-135.

115. Widom, J., 2005. Trio: A System for Integrated Management of Data, Accuracy, and Lineage. In Proc. 2nd Biennial Conference on Innovative Data Systems Research, 262-276.

116. William, K., 1983. A Simple Guide to Five Normal Forms in Relational Database Theory. Communications of the ACM, 26 (2), 120-

125.

117. Xu, Z. and Zhang, Z., 2002. Building Low-maintenance Express-ways for P2P Systems. Technical Report HPL-2002-41, HP Laboratories Palo Alto.

118. Zaniolo, C., 1983. The Database Language GEM. In Proc. SIGMOD, 286-295.

119. Zhuge, H., 1998. Inheritance Rules for Flexible Model Retrieval. Decision Support Systems, 22 (4), 383-394.

120. Zhuge, H., 2003. Active e-Document Framework ADF: Model and Platform. Information and Management, 41 (1), 87-97.

121. Zhuge, H., 2004a. Resource Space Grid: Model, Method and Plat-form. Concurrency and Computation: Practice and Experience, 16 (14), 1385-1413.

122. Zhuge, H., 2004b. Resource Space Model, Its Design Method and Applications. Journal of Systems and Software, 72 (1), 71-81.

123. Zhuge, H., 2004c. Fuzzy Resource Space Model and Platform. Journal of Systems and Software, 73 (3), 389-396.

124. Zhuge, H., 2004d. The Knowledge Grid. World Scientific.

125. Zhuge, H. et al., 2004e. Semantic Link Network Builder and Intel-ligent Semantic Browser. Concurrency and Computation: Practice & Experience, 16 (14), 1453-1476.

126. Zhuge, H., 2005a. Semantic Grid: Scientific Issues, Infrastructure, and Methodology. Communications of the ACM, 48 (4), 117-119.

127. Zhuge, H., 2005b. The Future Interconnection Environment. IEEE Computer, 38 (4), 27-33.

128. Zhuge, H. et al, 2005c. Extended Resource Space Model. Future Generation Computer Systems, 21 (1), 189-198.

129. Zhuge, H., Liu, J., Feng, L., Sun, X. and He, C., 2005d. Query Routing in a Peer-to-Peer Semantic Link Network. Computational Intelligence, 21 (2), 197-216.

130. Zhuge, H. and Yao, E., 2006. Completeness of Query Operations on Resource Spaces. Keynote at SKG2006, In Proc. 2nd International Conference on Semantics, Knowledge and Grid, 3-8.

131. Zhuge, H., Shi, P., Xing, P. and He, C., 2006. Transformation from OWL Description to Resource Space Model. In Proc. The 1st Asian Semantic Web Conference 2006, 4-23.

132. Zhuge, H., 2007. Autonomous Semantic Link Networking Model for the Knowledge Grid. Concurrency and Computation: Practice and Experience, 7 (19), 1065-1085.

133. Zhuge, H., Ding, L., and Li, X., 2007. Networking Scientific Re-sources in the Knowledge Grid Environment. Concurrency and Computation: Practice and Experience, 7 (19), 1087-1113.

134. Zhuge, H. and Li, X., 2007a. RSM-Based Gossip on P2P Network. Keynote at ICA3PP, LNCS 4494, 1-12.
135. Zhuge, H. and Li, X., 2007b. Peer-to-Peer in Metric Space and Semantic Space. IEEE Transactions on Knowledge and Data Engineering, 6 (19), 759-771.

Index